BORUTO

-NARU TIONS-

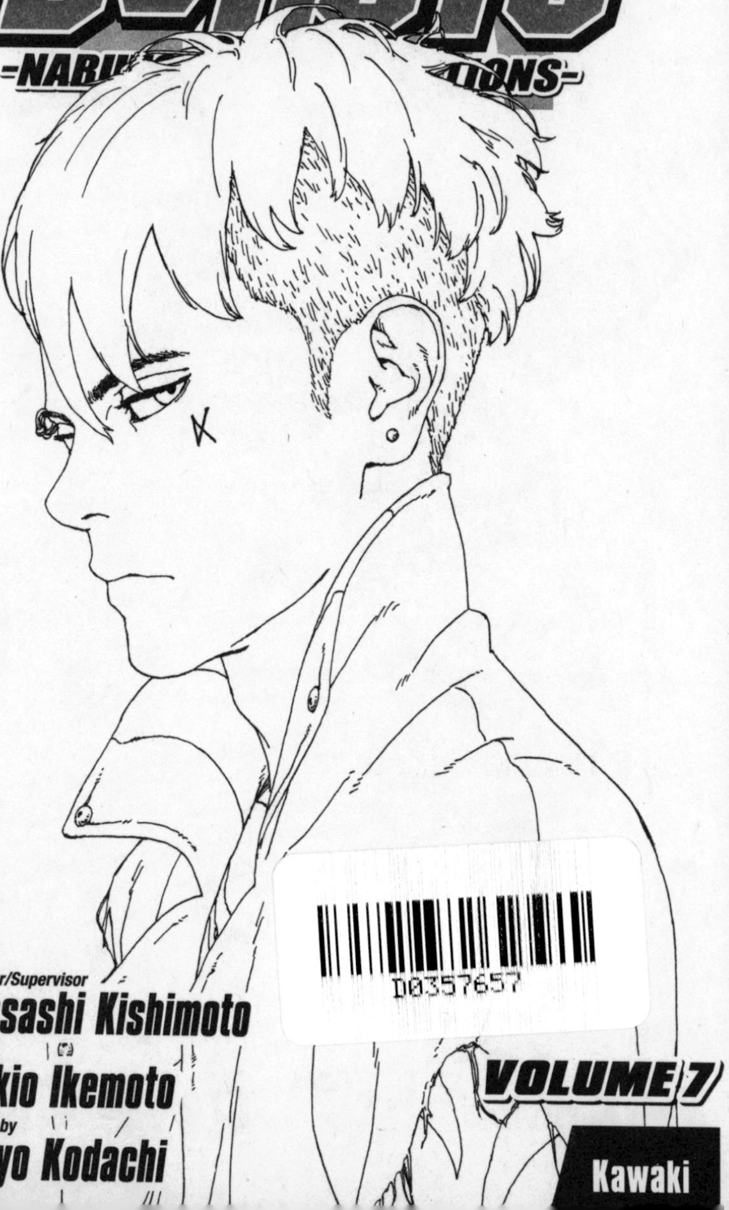

Creator/Supervisor
Masashi Kishimoto

Art by
Mikio Ikemoto

Script by
Ukyo Kodachi

VOLUME 7

Kawaki

BORUTO -NARUTO NEXT GENERATIONS- CHARACTERS

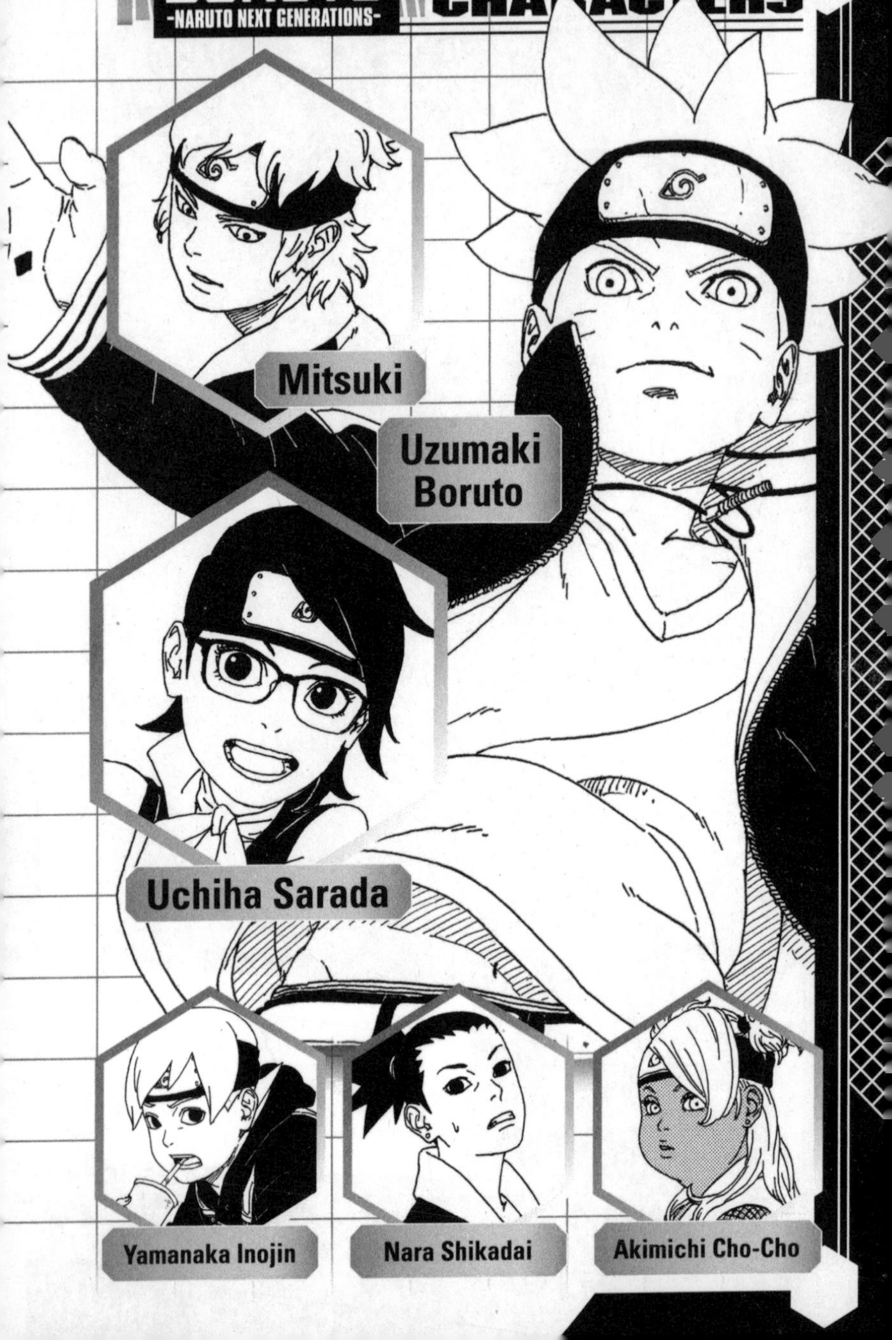
Mitsuki
Uzumaki Boruto
Uchiha Sarada
Yamanaka Inojin
Nara Shikadai
Akimichi Cho-Cho

池本幹雄

I had the good fortune to be invited to an Italian comic book convention, and headed to the Tuscan walled city of Lucca.

The ramparts encircling its four-kilometer perimeter give the city an ambience of *Dragon Quest* or a certain manga about Titans. It was super-fantastic.

And the cosplayers strolling the streets were so dapper and completely fitting in with the setting that I, dressed in ordinary clothes, looked out of place.

The realization that these people all love manga gave me such a happy feeling.

—Mikio Ikemoto, 2019

BARREL ROLL

小太刀右京

I went to Macau on a BARREL ROLL company outing.

One staff member actually hit the jackpot playing slots, surprising all of us. And the Chinese food was delicious and the view was nice. What a blast!

Oh, so how did I do? Well, the house won some, and I lost some, so I think it's fair to say roughly 50-50.

—Ukyo Kodachi, 2019

BORUTO
=NARUTO NEXT GENERATIONS=

VOLUME 7

SHONEN JUMP MANGA EDITION

Creator/Supervisor MASASHI KISHIMOTO
Art by MIKIO IKEMOTO
Script by UKYO KODACHI

Translation: Mari Morimoto
Touch-up Art & Lettering: Snir Aharon
Design: Alice Lewis
Editor: Alexis Kirsch

BORUTO: NARUTO NEXT GENERATIONS © 2016
by Masashi Kishimoto, Mikio Ikemoto, Ukyo Kodachi
All rights reserved.
First published in Japan in 2016 by SHUEISHA Inc., Tokyo.
English translation rights arranged by SHUEISHA Inc.

Printed in the U.S.A.

Published by VIZ Media, LLC
P.O. Box 77010
San Francisco, CA 94107

10 9 8 7 6 5 4 3 2 1
First printing, November 2019

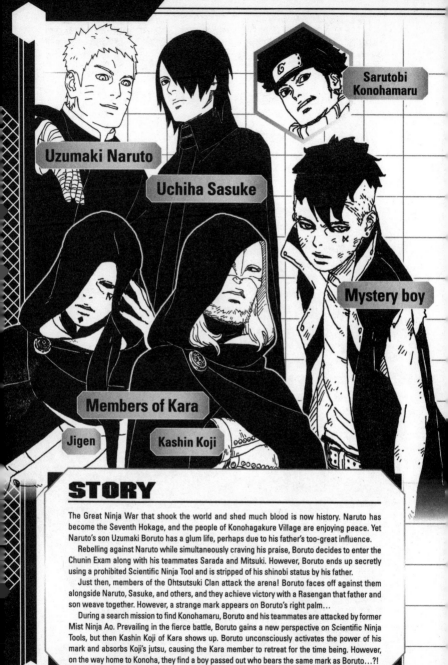

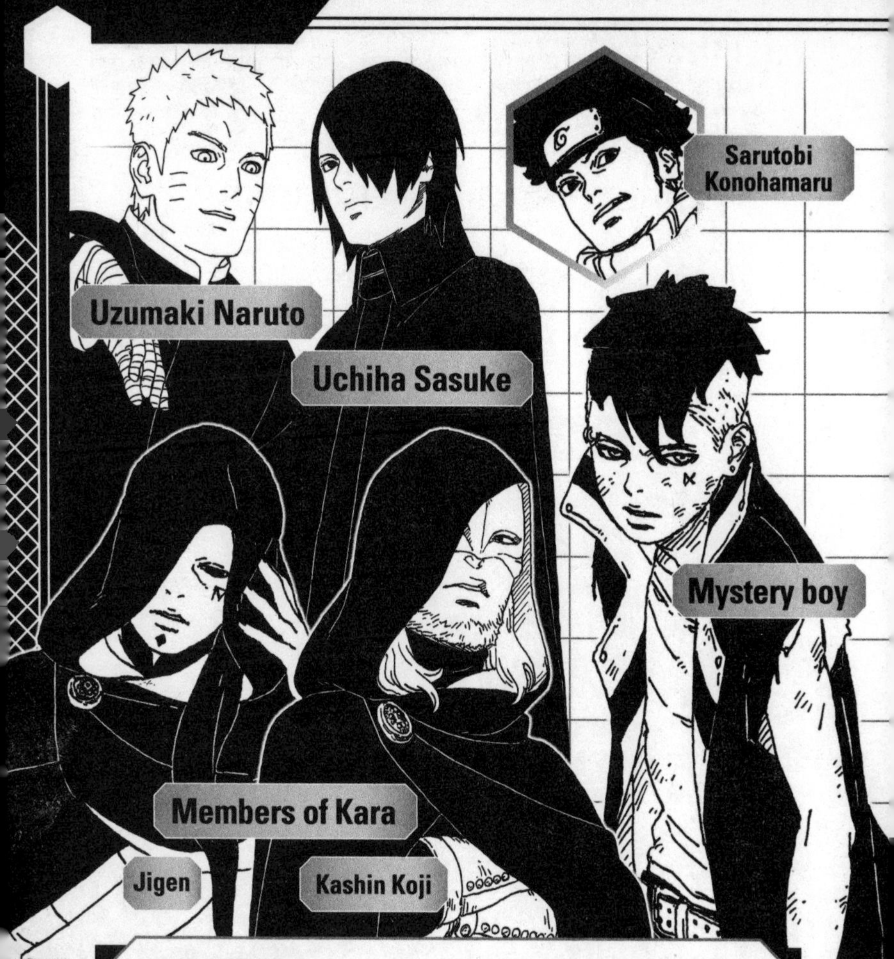
Sarutobi Konohamaru
Uzumaki Naruto
Uchiha Sasuke
Mystery boy
Members of Kara
Jigen
Kashin Koji

STORY

The Great Ninja War that shook the world and shed much blood is now history. Naruto has become the Seventh Hokage, and the people of Konohagakure Village are enjoying peace. Yet Naruto's son Uzumaki Boruto has a glum life, perhaps due to his father's too-great influence.

Rebelling against Naruto while simultaneously craving his praise, Boruto decides to enter the Chunin Exam along with his teammates Sarada and Mitsuki. However, Boruto ends up secretly using a prohibited Scientific Ninja Tool and is stripped of his shinobi status by his father.

Just then, members of the Ohtsutsuki Clan attack the arena! Boruto faces off against them alongside Naruto, Sasuke, and others, and they achieve victory with a Rasengan that father and son weave together. However, a strange mark appears on Boruto's right palm…

During a search mission to find Konohamaru, Boruto and his teammates are attacked by former Mist Ninja Ao. Prevailing in the fierce battle, Boruto gains a new perspective on Scientific Ninja Tools, but then Kashin Koji of Kara shows up. Boruto unconsciously activates the power of his mark and absorbs Koji's jutsu, causing the Kara member to retreat for the time being. However, on the way home to Konoha, they find a boy passed out who bears the same mark as Boruto…?!

BORUTO

-NARUTO NEXT GENERATIONS-

VOLUME 7
KAWAKI

CONTENTS

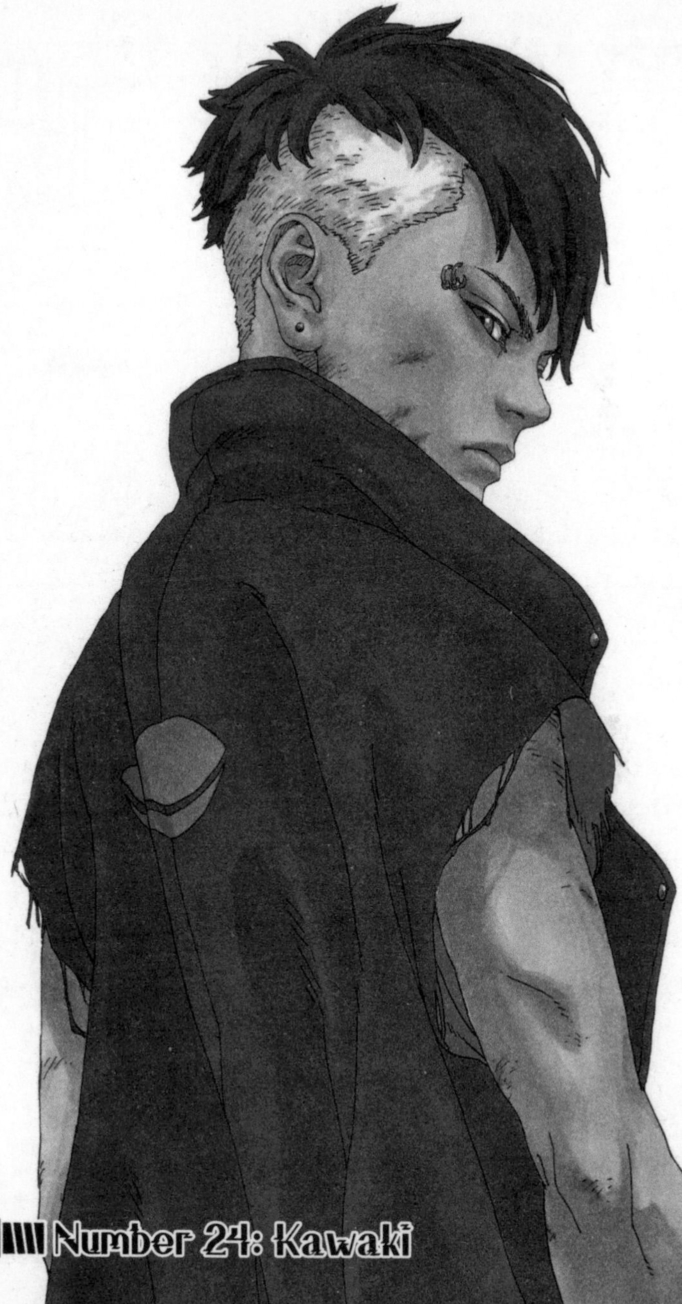

Number 24: Kawaki

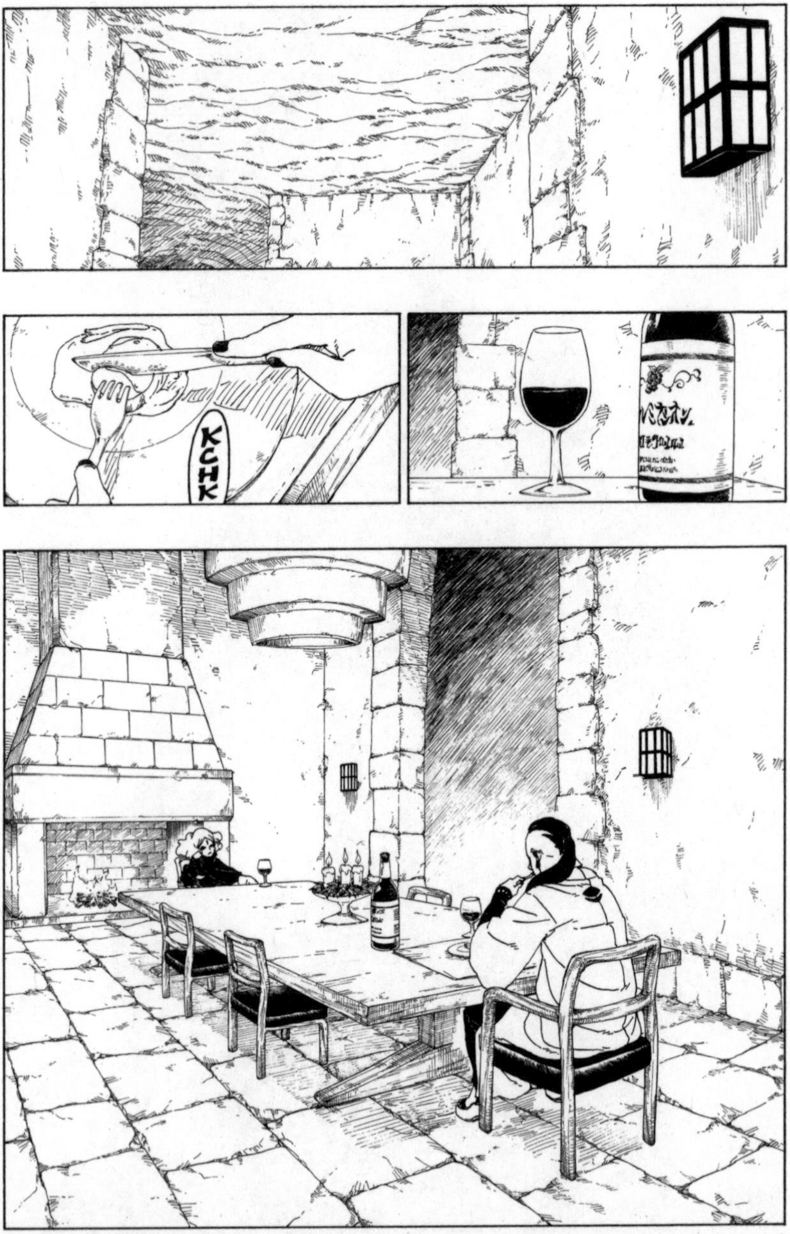
KCHK

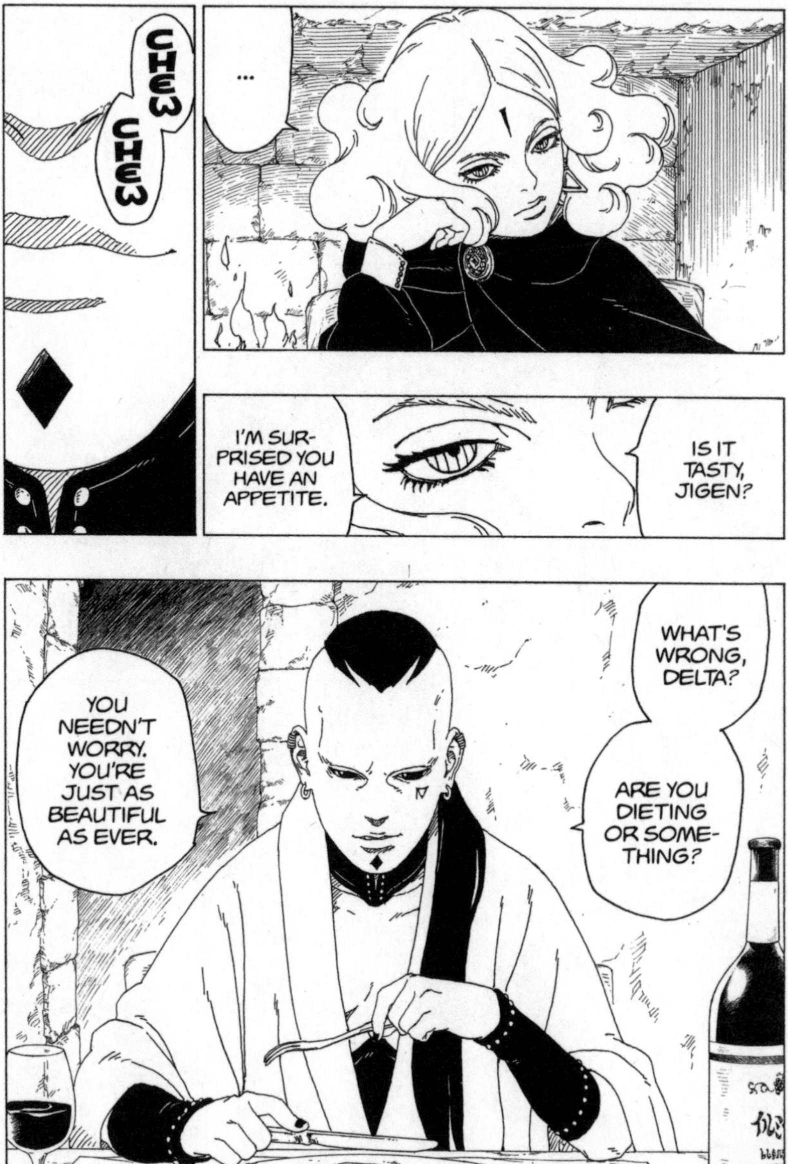
...
IS IT TASTY, JIGEN?
I'M SUR-PRISED YOU HAVE AN APPETITE.
CHEW CHEW
WHAT'S WRONG, DELTA?
ARE YOU DIETING OR SOME-THING?
YOU NEEDN'T WORRY. YOU'RE JUST AS BEAUTIFUL AS EVER.

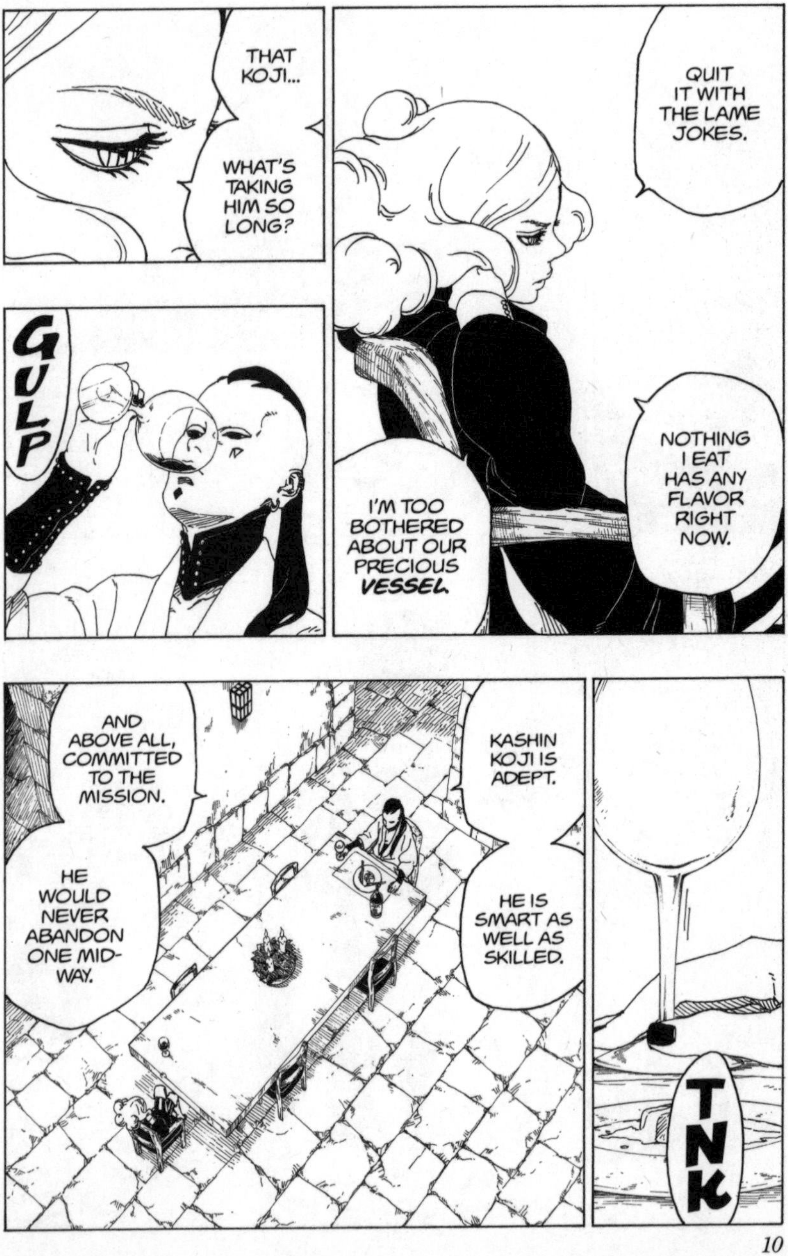
QUIT IT WITH THE LAME JOKES.
NOTHING I EAT HAS ANY FLAVOR RIGHT NOW.
I'M TOO BOTHERED ABOUT OUR PRECIOUS *VESSEL*.
THAT KOJI...
WHAT'S TAKING HIM SO LONG?
GULP
TNK
KASHIN KOJI IS ADEPT.
HE IS SMART AS WELL AS SKILLED.
AND ABOVE ALL, COMMITTED TO THE MISSION.
HE WOULD NEVER ABANDON ONE MID-WAY.

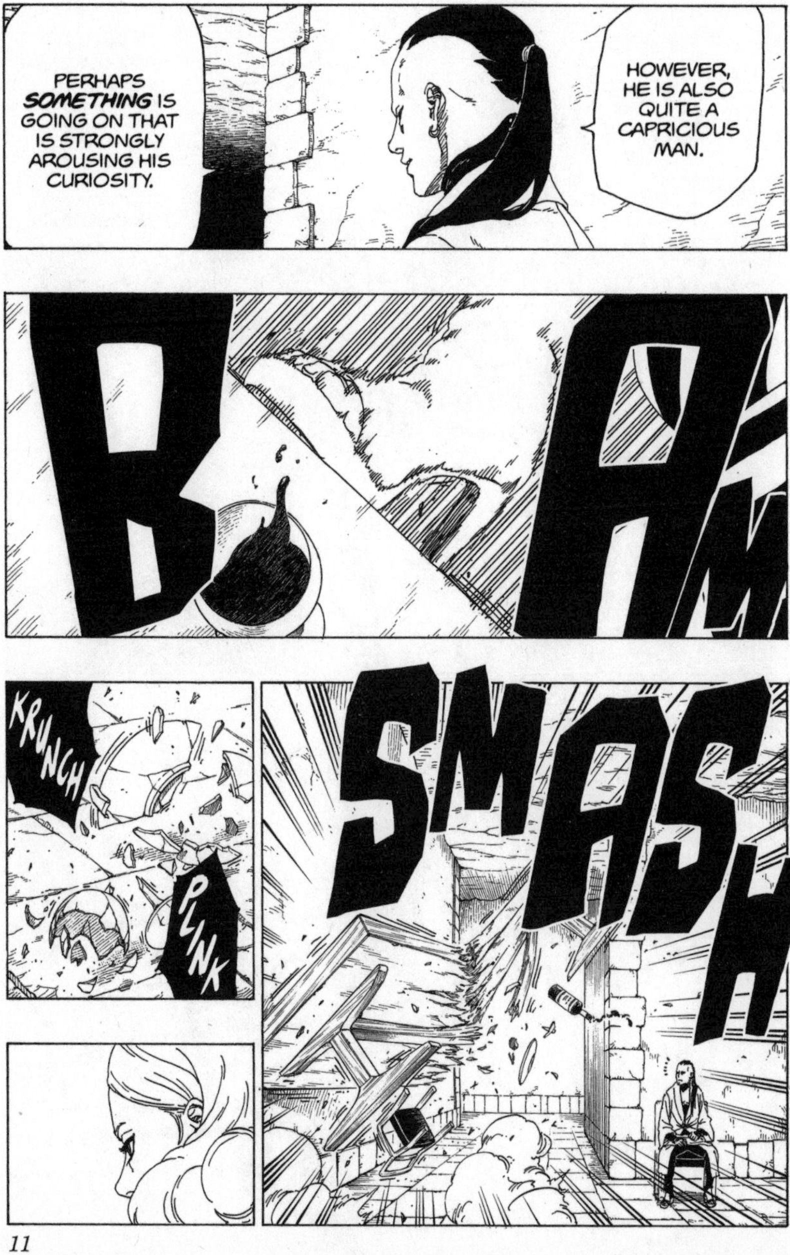
HOWEVER, HE IS ALSO QUITE A CAPRICIOUS MAN.
PERHAPS SOMETHING IS GOING ON THAT IS STRONGLY AROUSING HIS CURIOSITY.
BAM
SMASH
KRUNCH
PLINK

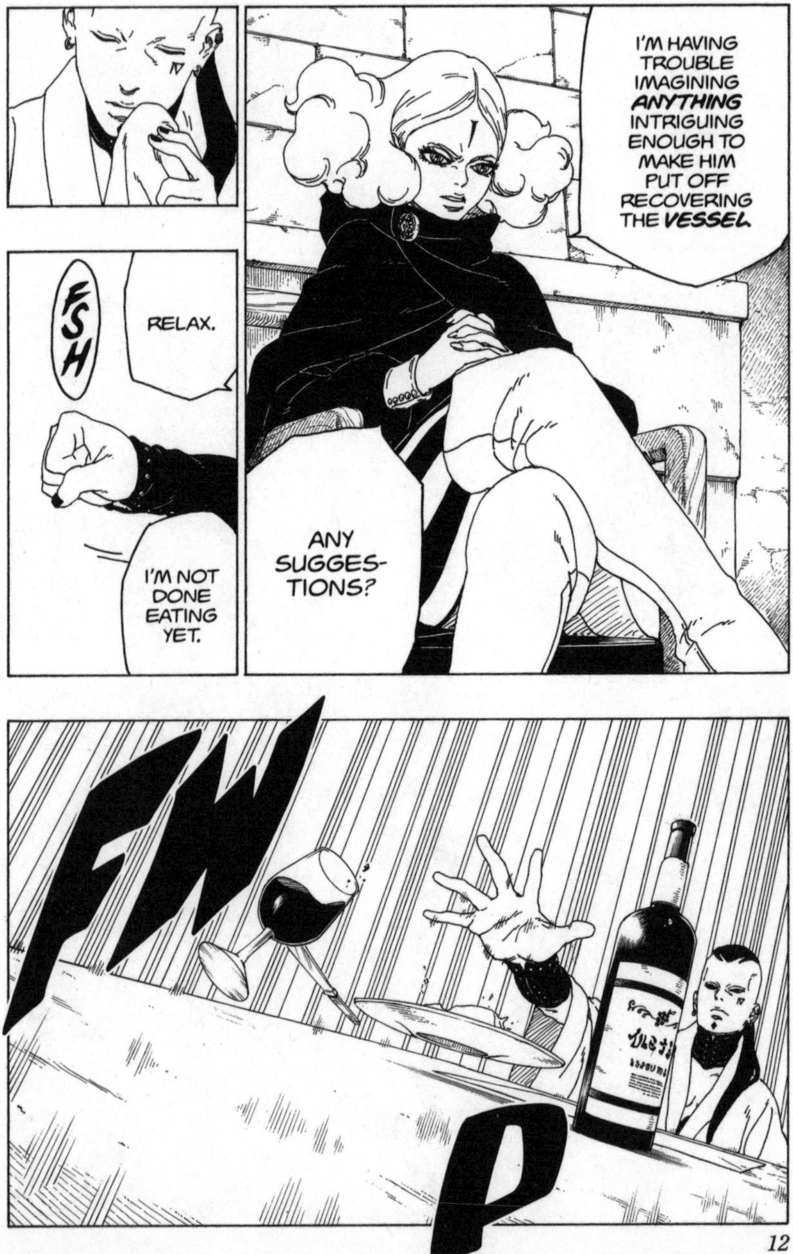
I'M HAVING TROUBLE IMAGINING ANYTHING INTRIGUING ENOUGH TO MAKE HIM PUT OFF RECOVERING THE VESSEL.
ANY SUGGES-TIONS?
RELAX.
FSH
I'M NOT DONE EATING YET.
FWP

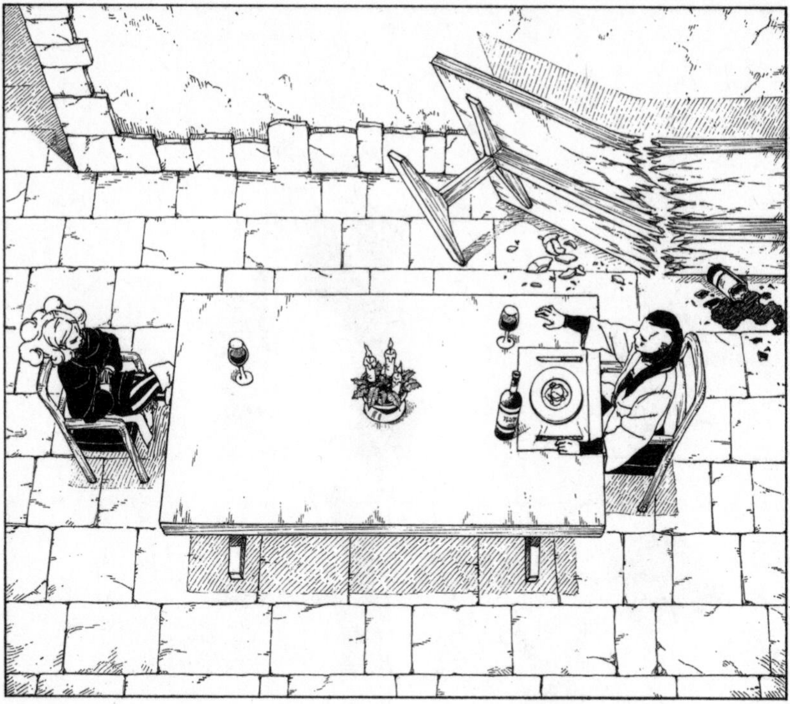

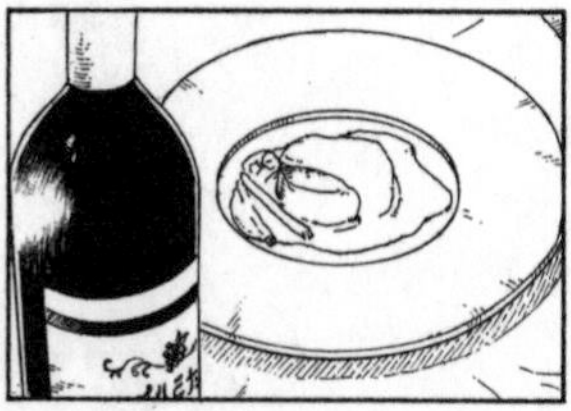

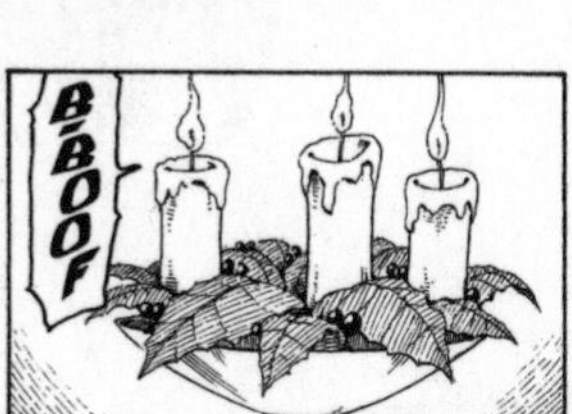
B-BOOF

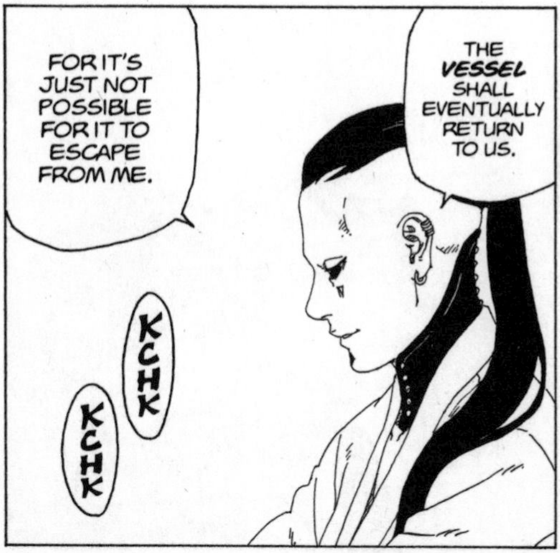
THE *VESSEL* SHALL EVENTUALLY RETURN TO US.
FOR IT'S JUST NOT POSSIBLE FOR IT TO ESCAPE FROM ME.
KCHK
KCHK

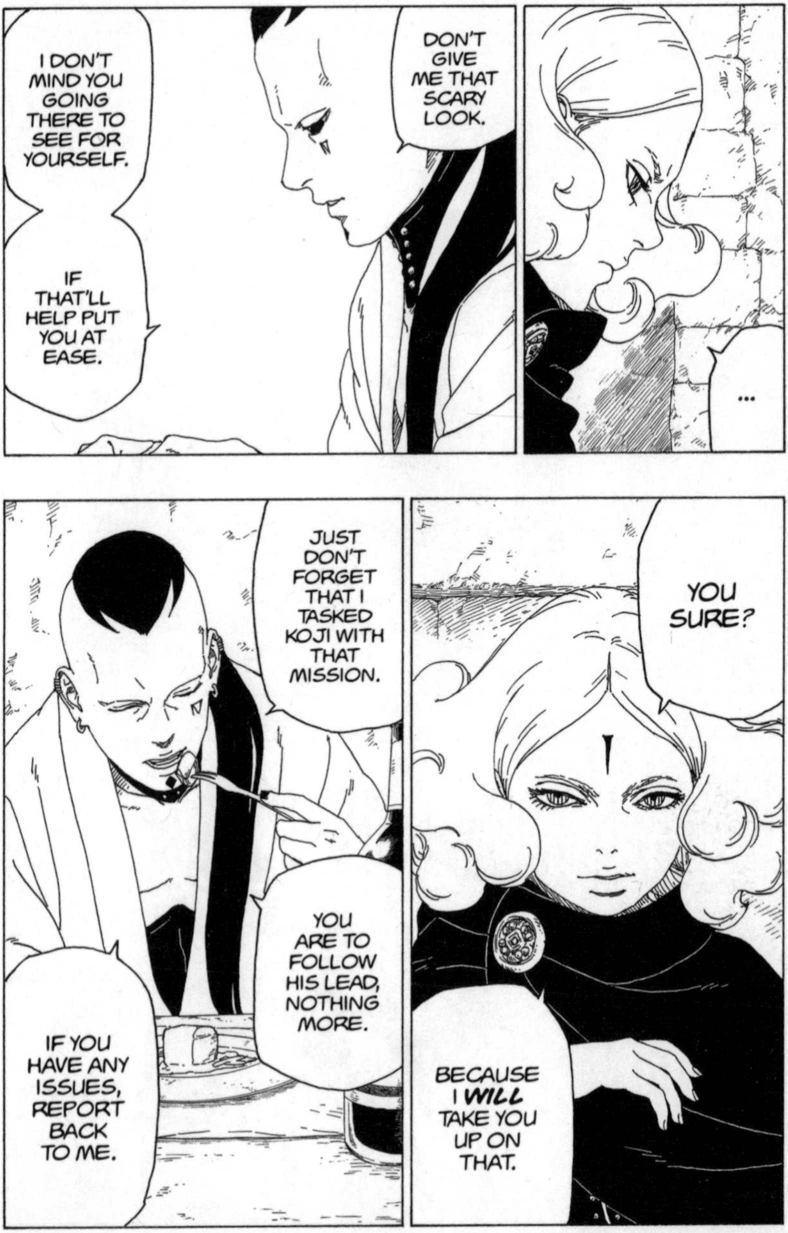
...
DON'T GIVE ME THAT SCARY LOOK.
I DON'T MIND YOU GOING THERE TO SEE FOR YOURSELF.
IF THAT'LL HELP PUT YOU AT EASE.
YOU SURE?
BECAUSE I **WILL** TAKE YOU UP ON THAT.
JUST DON'T FORGET THAT I TASKED KOJI WITH THAT MISSION.
YOU ARE TO FOLLOW HIS LEAD, NOTHING MORE.
IF YOU HAVE ANY ISSUES, REPORT BACK TO ME.

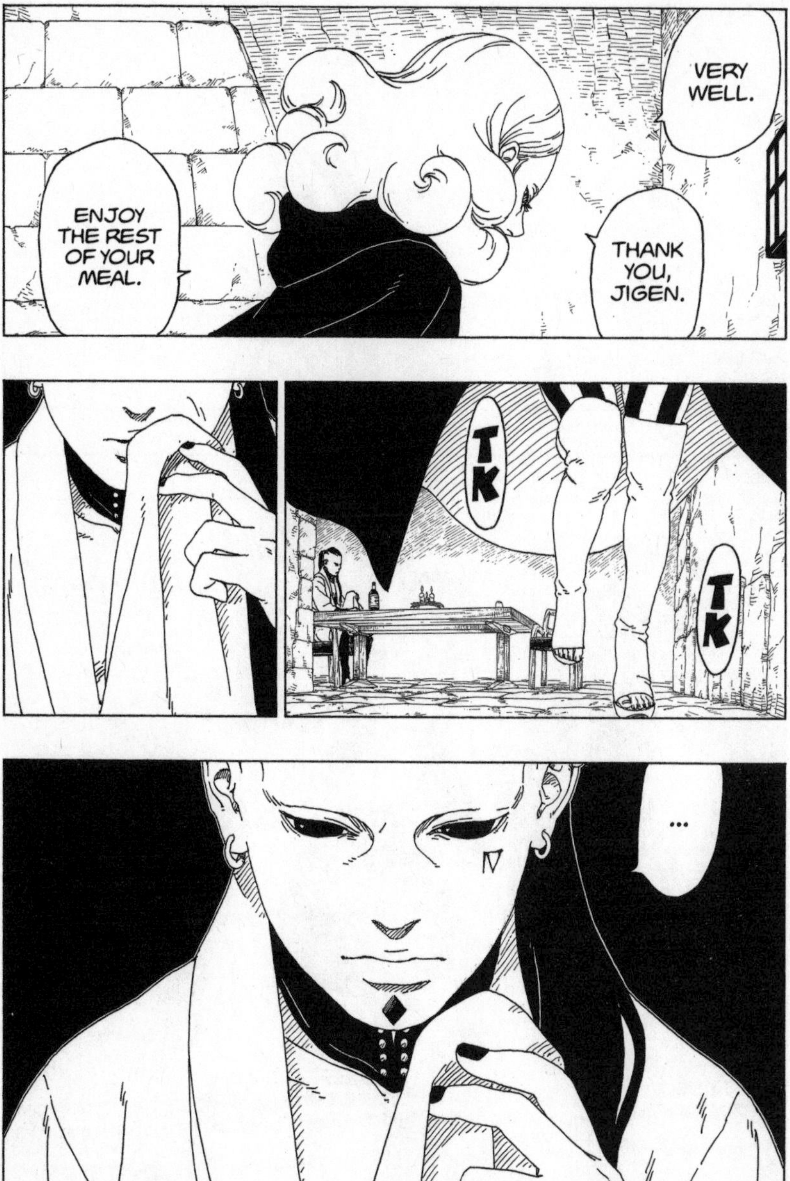
VERY WELL.
THANK YOU, JIGEN.
ENJOY THE REST OF YOUR MEAL.
TK
TK
...

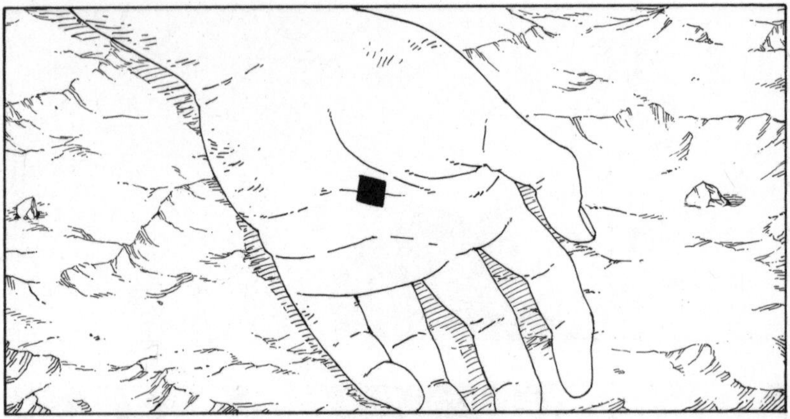

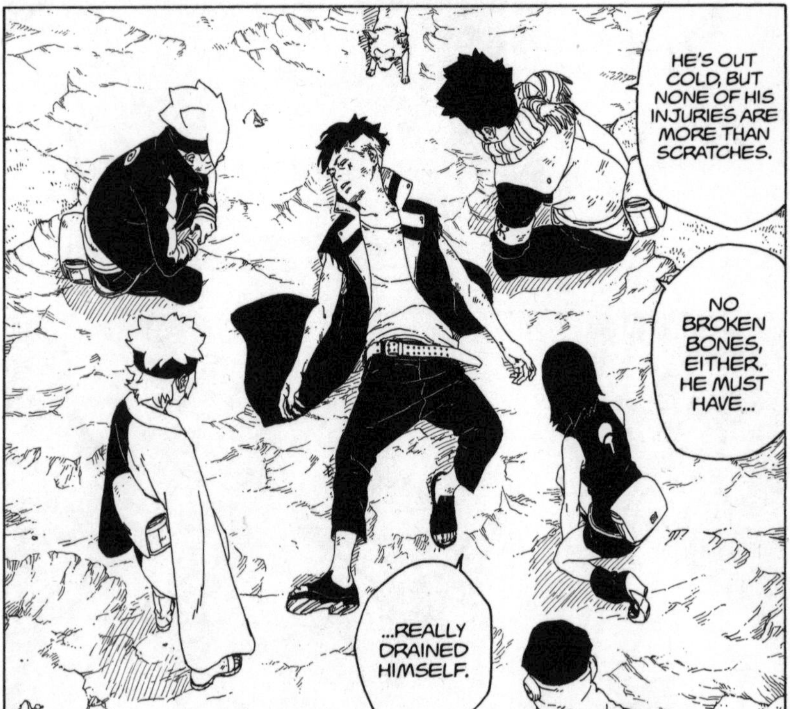
HE'S OUT COLD, BUT NONE OF HIS INJURIES ARE MORE THAN SCRATCHES.
NO BROKEN BONES, EITHER. HE MUST HAVE...
...REALLY DRAINED HIMSELF.

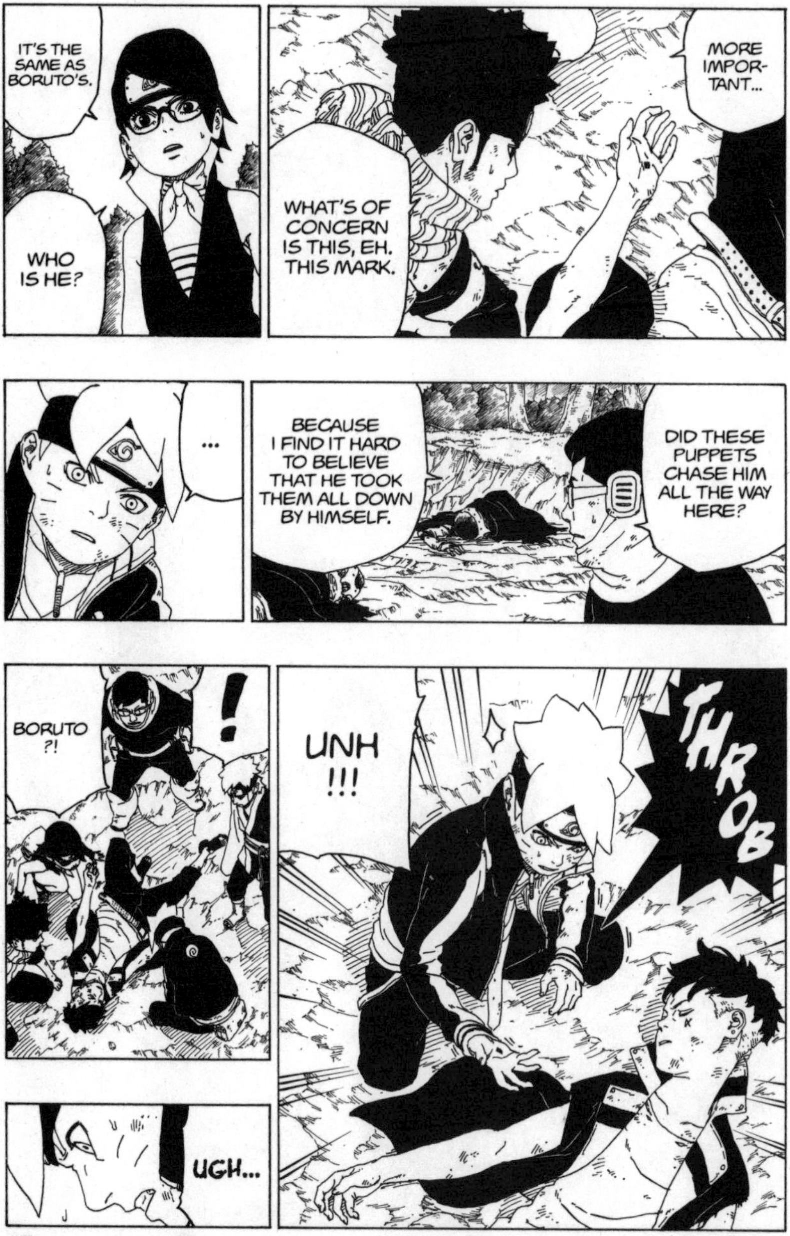
MORE IMPORTANT...
WHAT'S OF CONCERN IS THIS, EH. THIS MARK.
IT'S THE SAME AS BORUTO'S.
WHO IS HE?
DID THESE PUPPETS CHASE HIM ALL THE WAY HERE?
BECAUSE I FIND IT HARD TO BELIEVE THAT HE TOOK THEM ALL DOWN BY HIMSELF.
...
THROB
UNH !!!
!
BORUTO ?!
UGH...

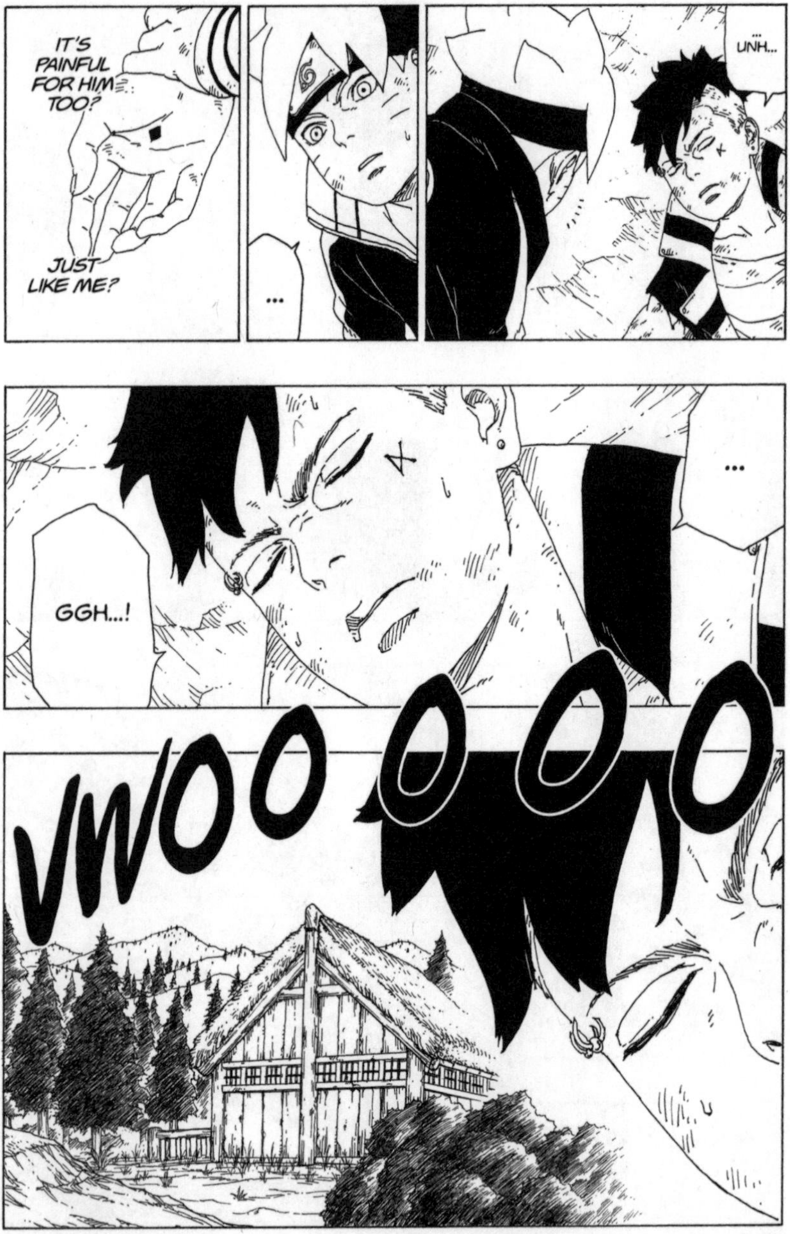
... UNH...
...
IT'S PAINFUL FOR HIM TOO?
JUST LIKE ME?
...
GGH...!
VWOOOOO

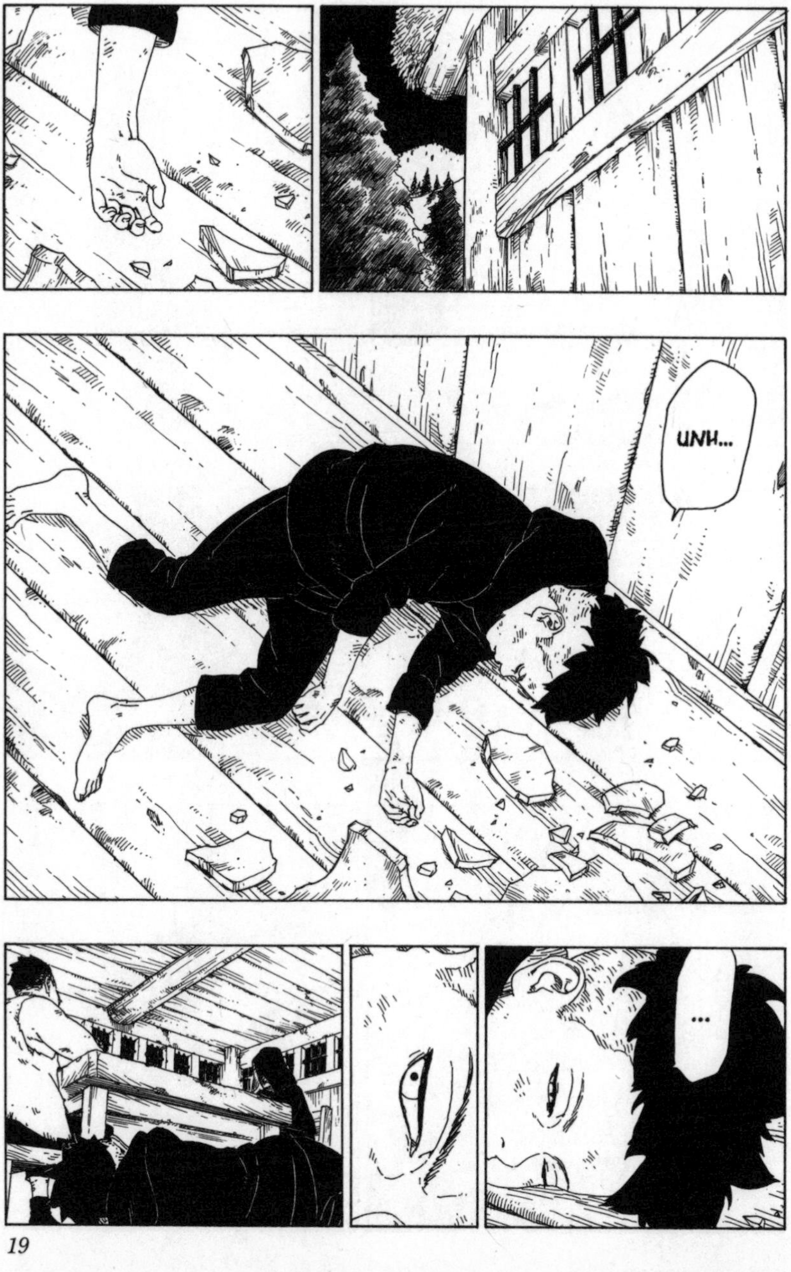
UNH...
...

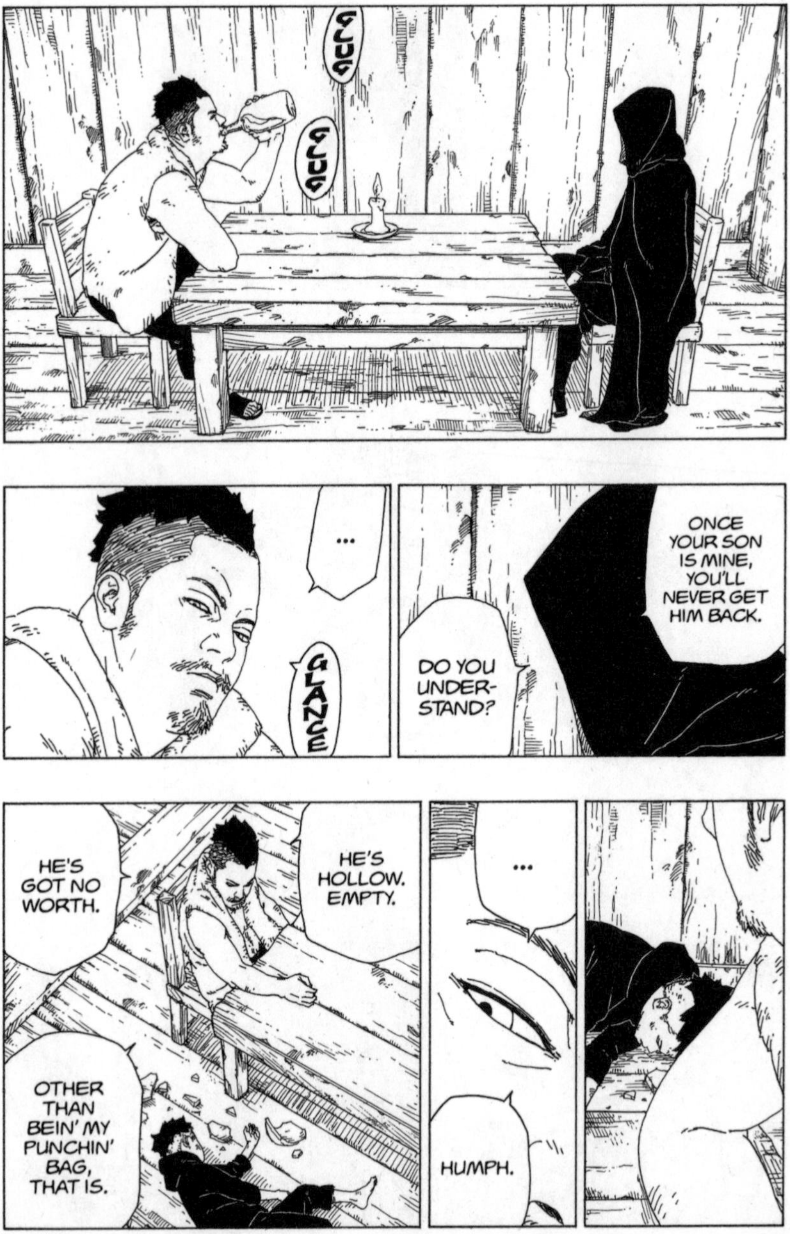
GLUG
GLUG
ONCE YOUR SON IS MINE, YOU'LL NEVER GET HIM BACK.
DO YOU UNDER-STAND?
...
GLANCE
...
HUMPH.
HE'S HOLLOW. EMPTY.
HE'S GOT NO WORTH.
OTHER THAN BEIN' MY PUNCHIN' BAG, THAT IS.

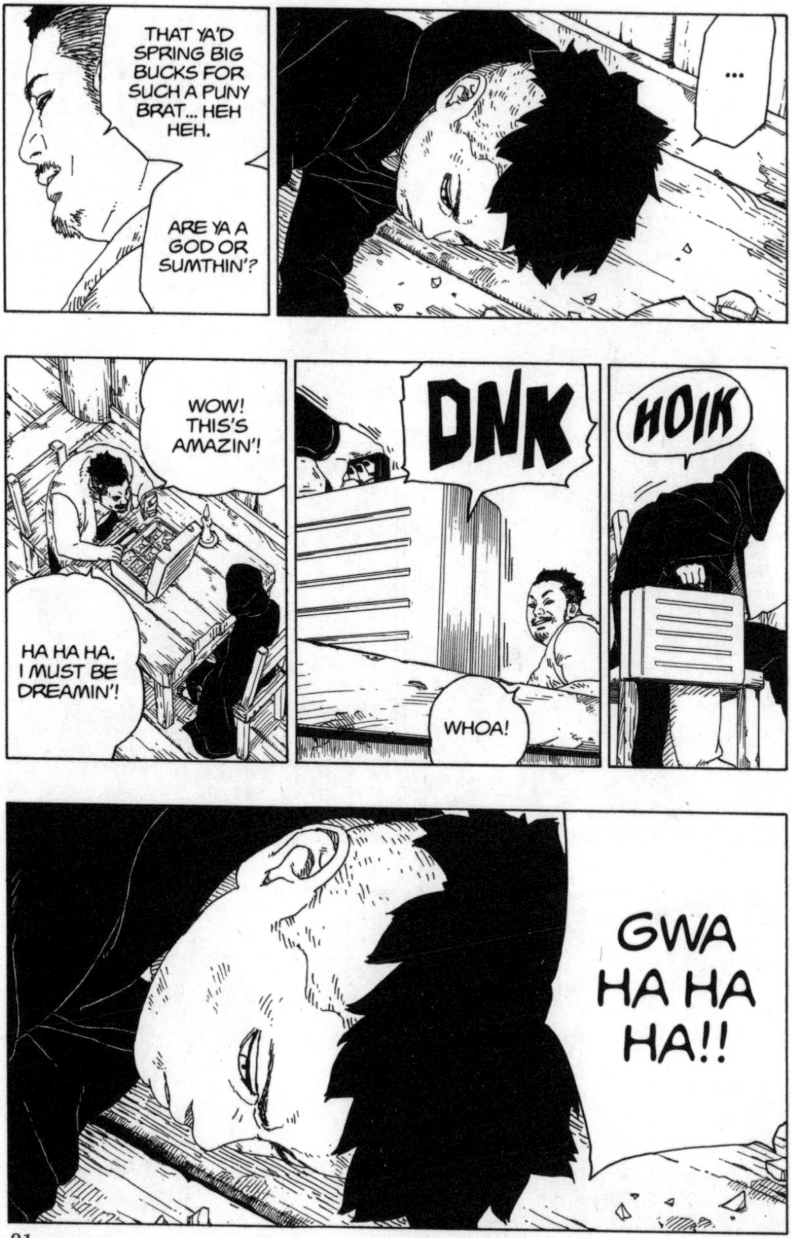
...
THAT YA'D SPRING BIG BUCKS FOR SUCH A PUNY BRAT... HEH HEH.
ARE YA A GOD OR SUMTHIN'?
HOIK
DNK
WHOA!
WOW! THIS'S AMAZIN'!
HA HA HA. I MUST BE DREAMIN'!
GWA HA HA HA!!

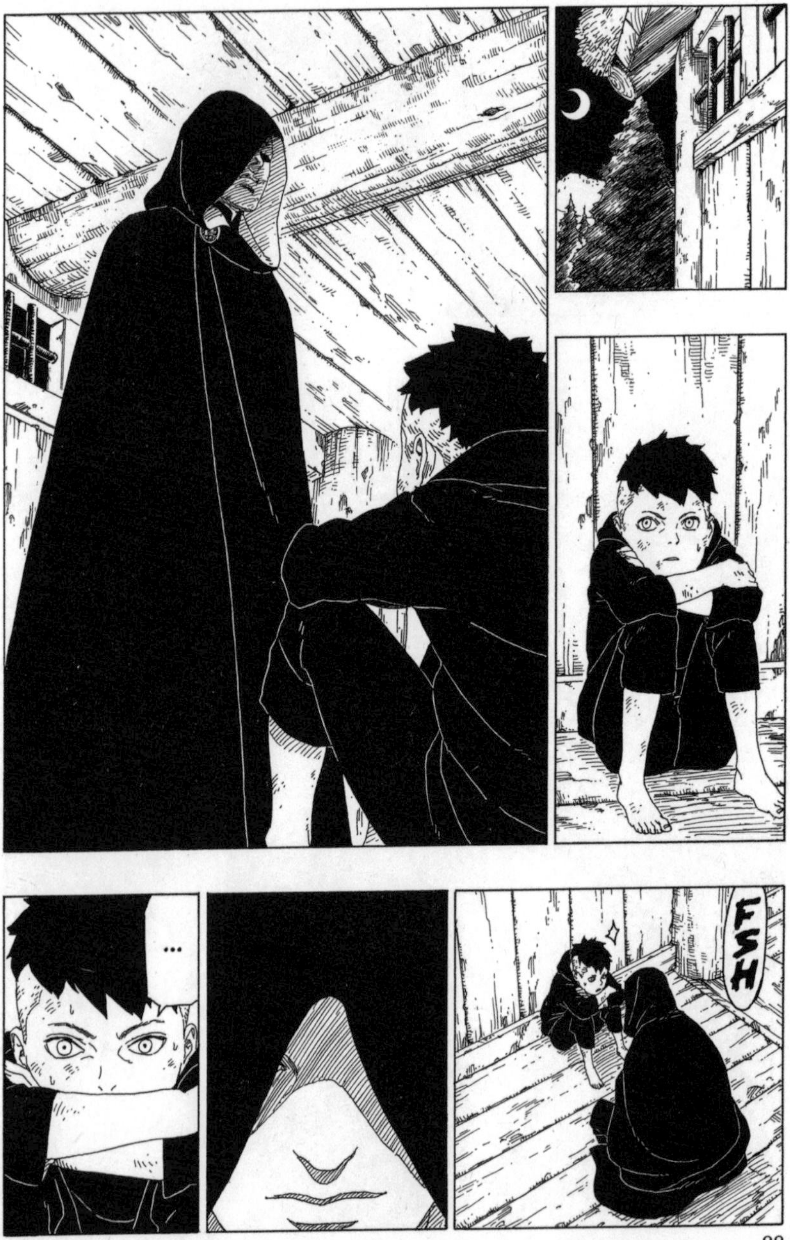
FSH
...

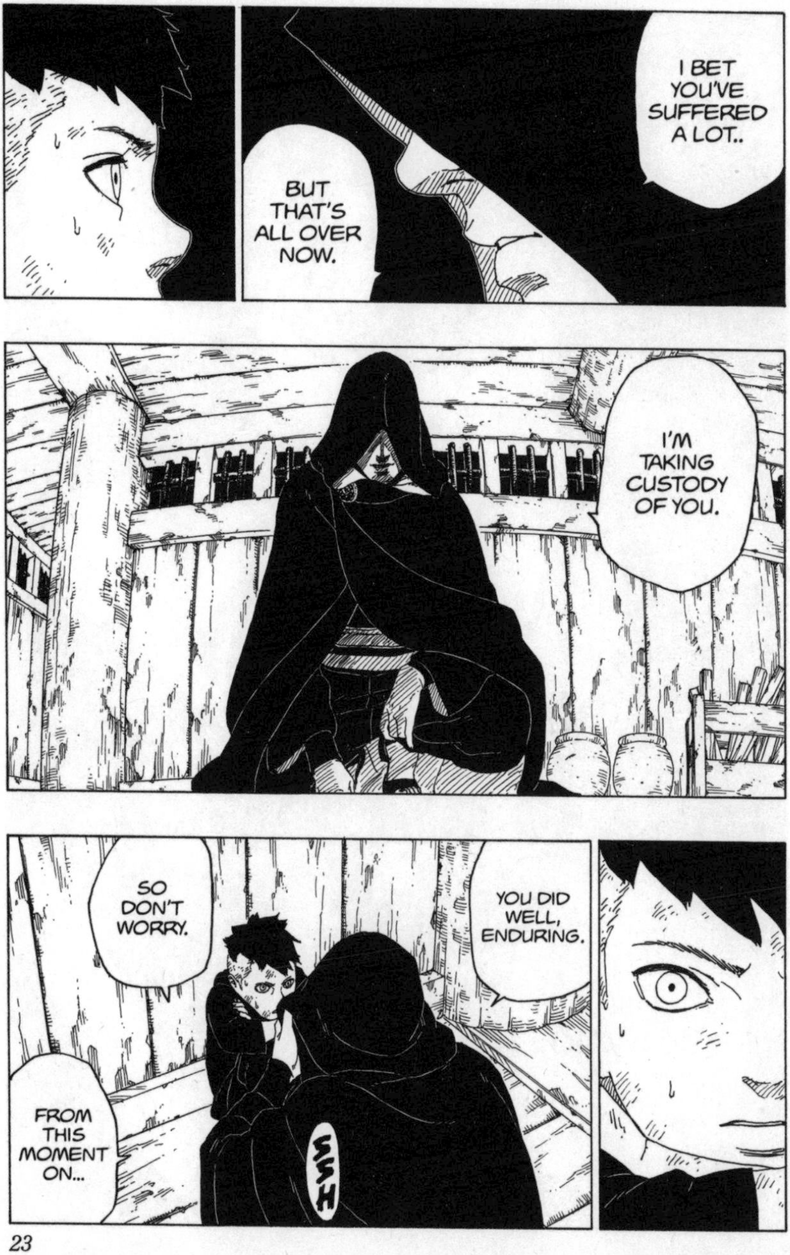
I BET YOU'VE SUFFERED A LOT..
BUT THAT'S ALL OVER NOW.
I'M TAKING CUSTODY OF YOU.
YOU DID WELL, ENDURING.
SO DON'T WORRY.
SSH
FROM THIS MOMENT ON...

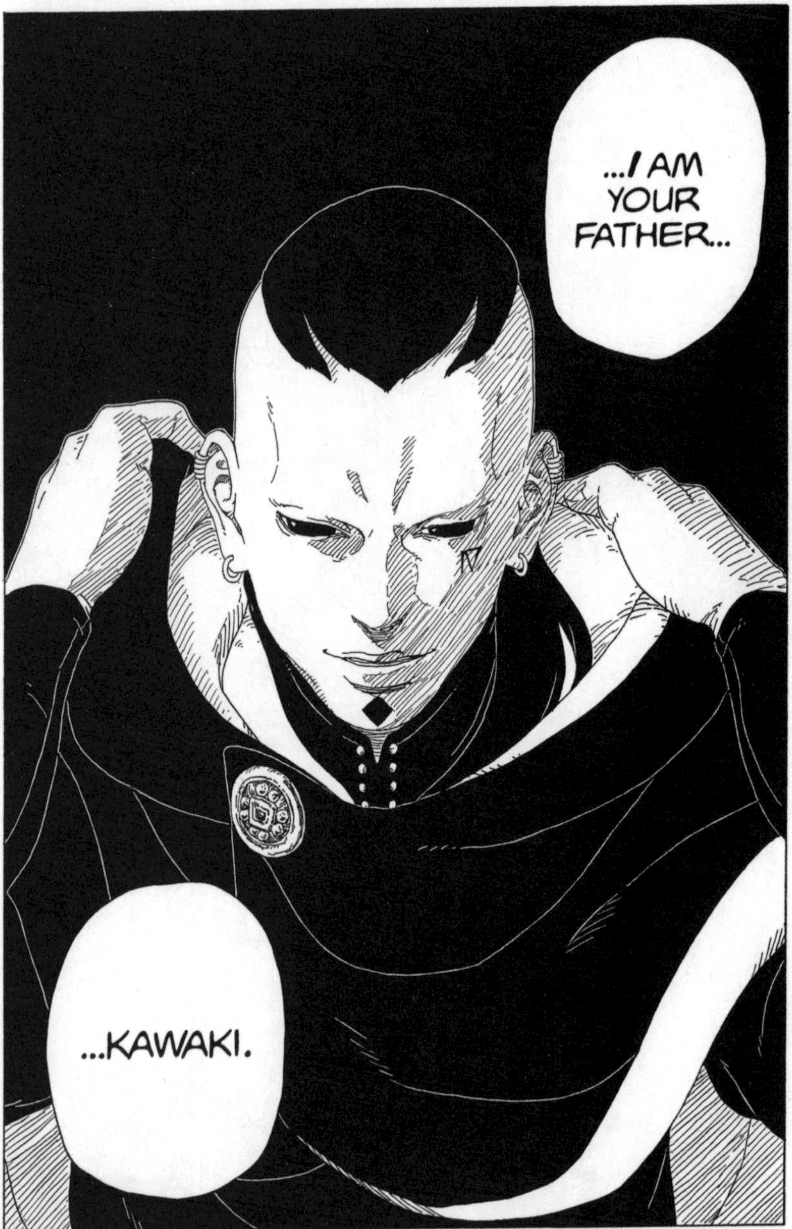
...I AM YOUR FATHER...
...KAWAKI.

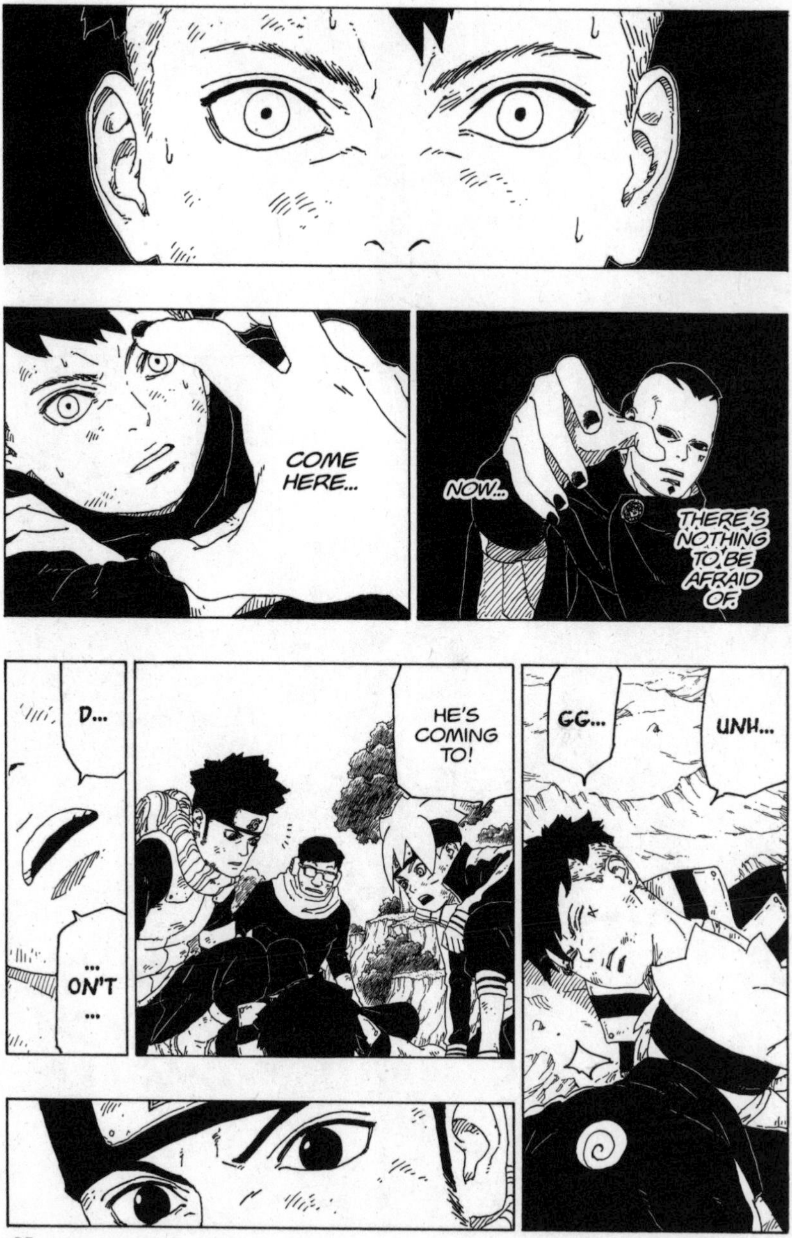
NOW...
THERE'S NOTHING TO BE AFRAID OF.
COME HERE...
UNH...
GG...
HE'S COMING TO!
D...
...ON'T...

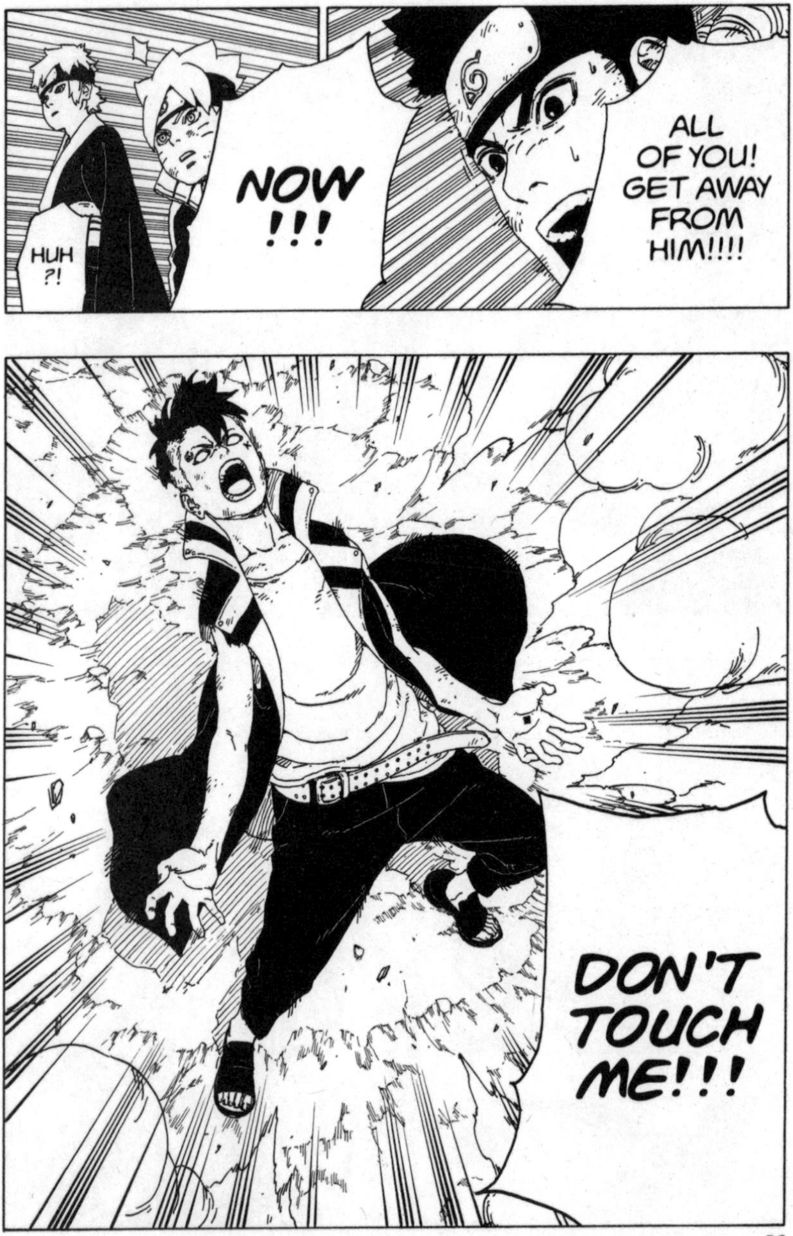
ALL OF YOU! GET AWAY FROM HIM!!!!
NOW !!!
HUH ?!
DON'T TOUCH ME!!!

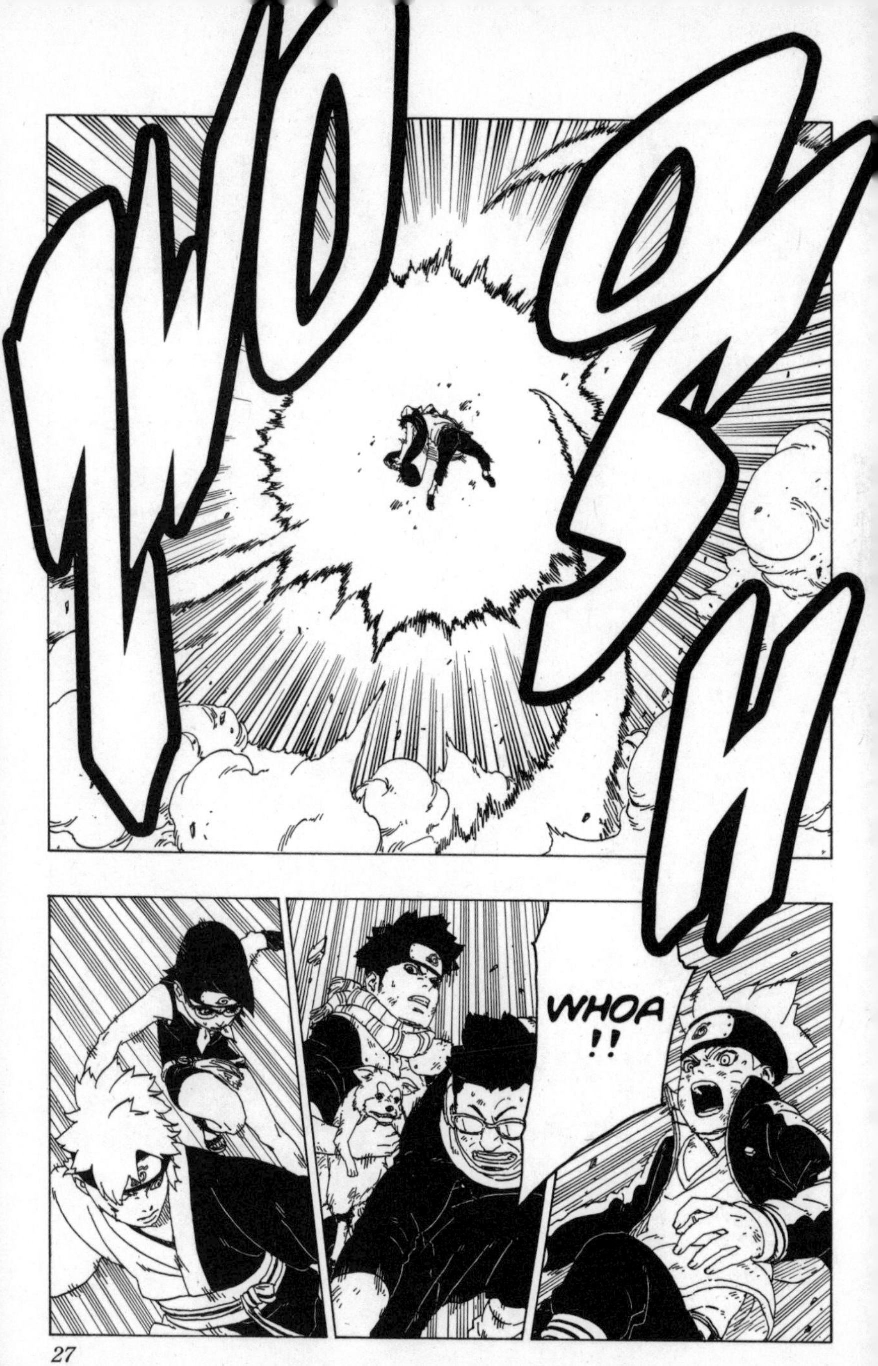
WHOOSH
WHOA!!

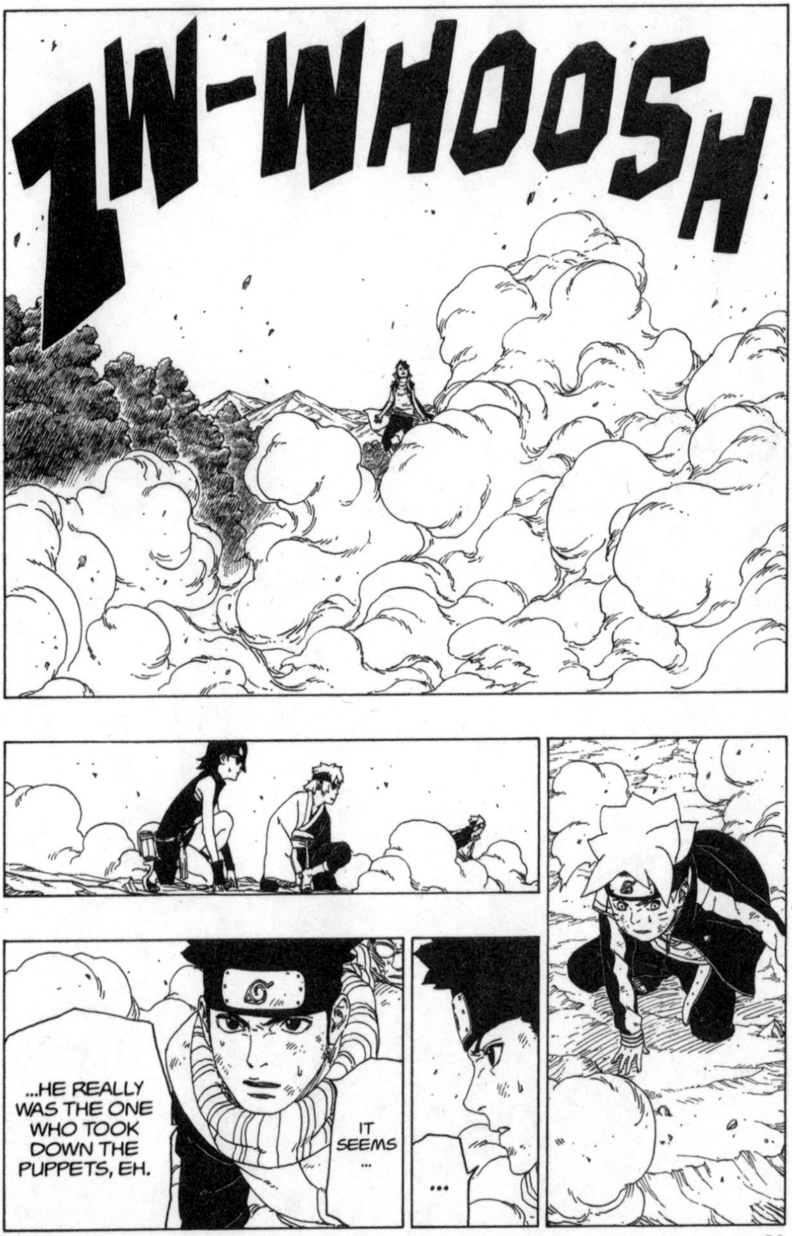
ZW-WHOOSH
...
IT SEEMS ...
...HE REALLY WAS THE ONE WHO TOOK DOWN THE PUPPETS, EH.

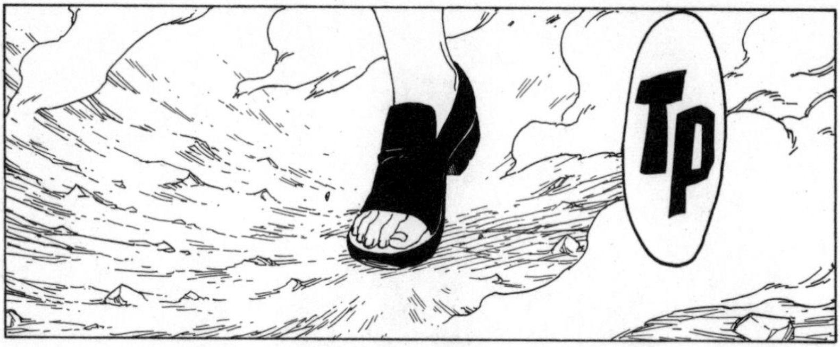
TP
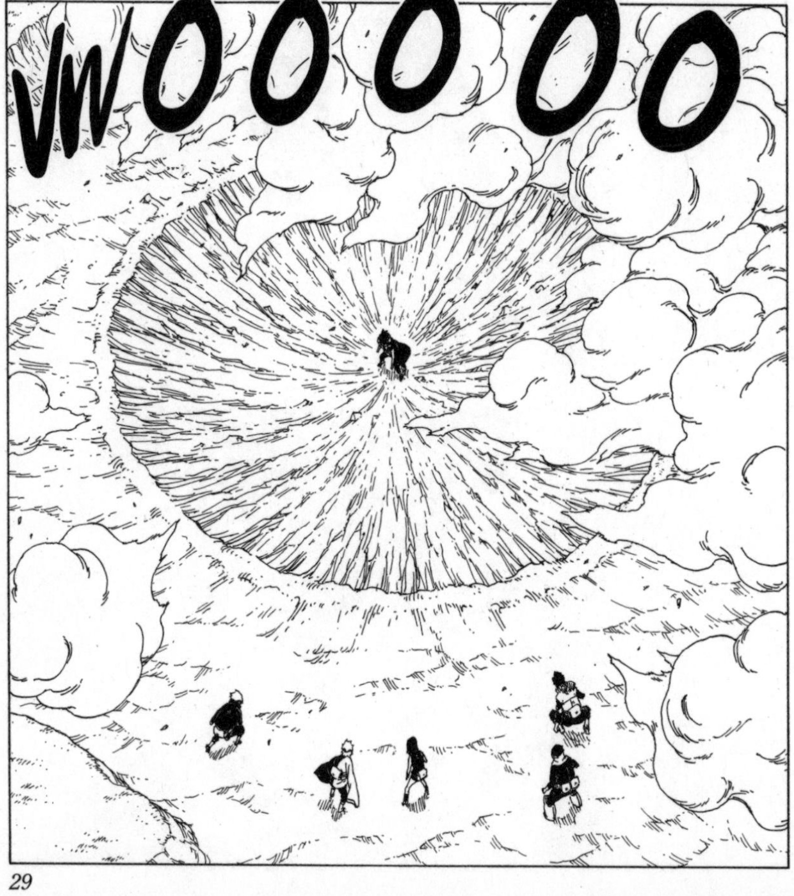
VWOOOOO

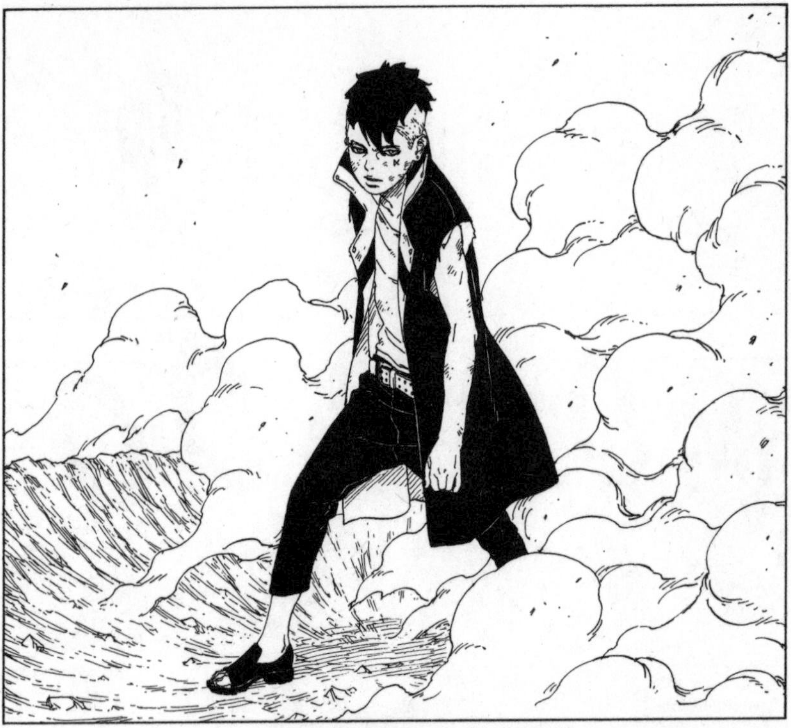

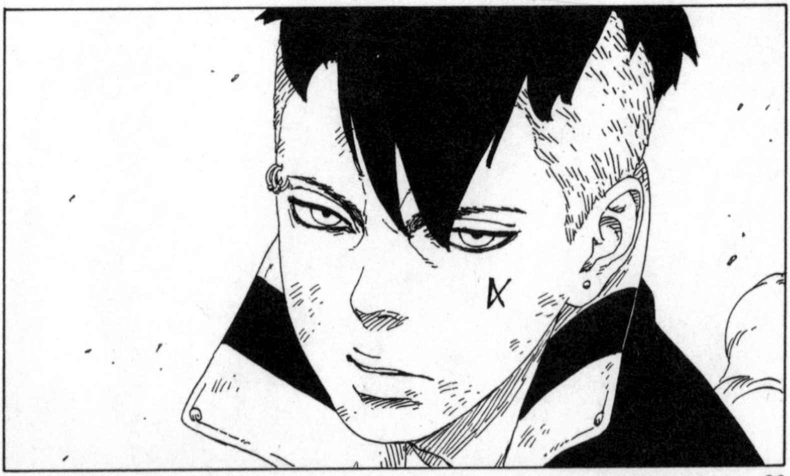

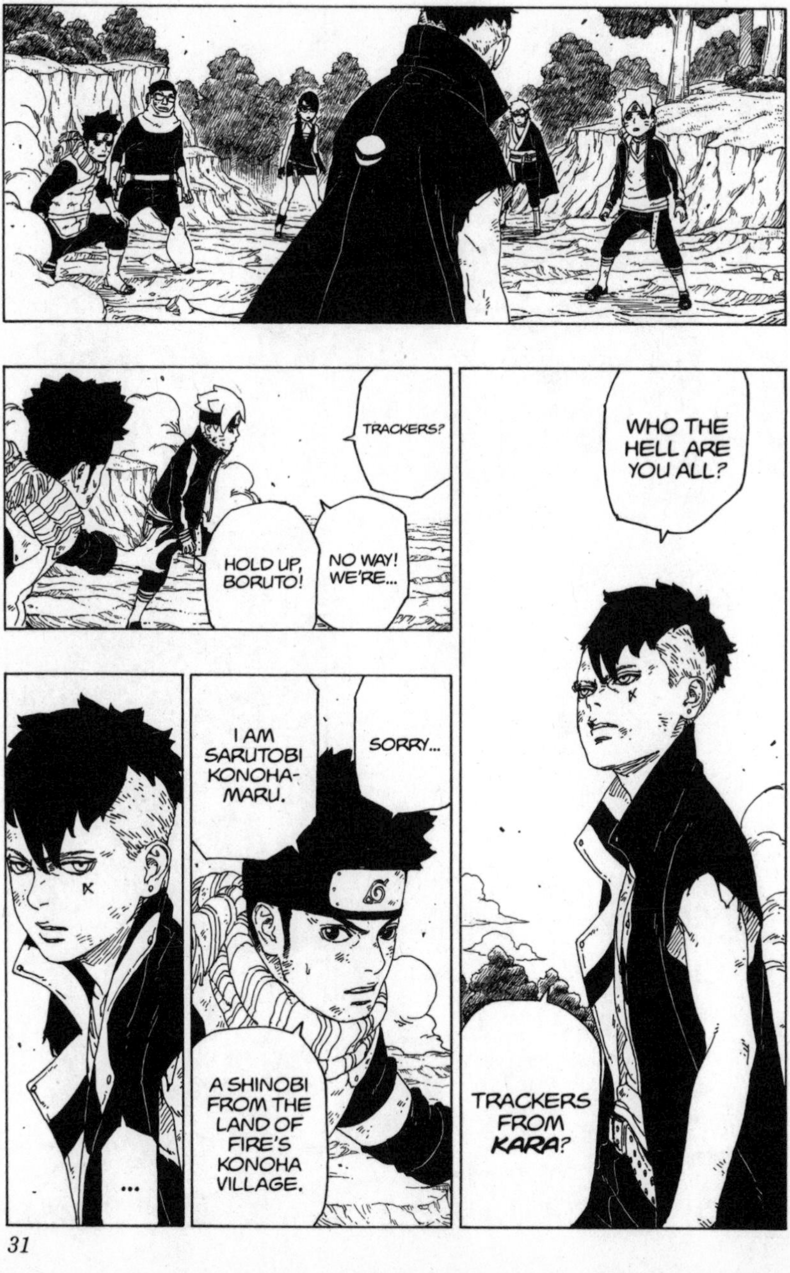

WHO THE HELL ARE YOU ALL?
TRACKERS FROM KARA?
TRACKERS?
NO WAY! WE'RE...
HOLD UP, BORUTO!
SORRY...
I AM SARUTOBI KONOHA-MARU.
A SHINOBI FROM THE LAND OF FIRE'S KONOHA VILLAGE.
...

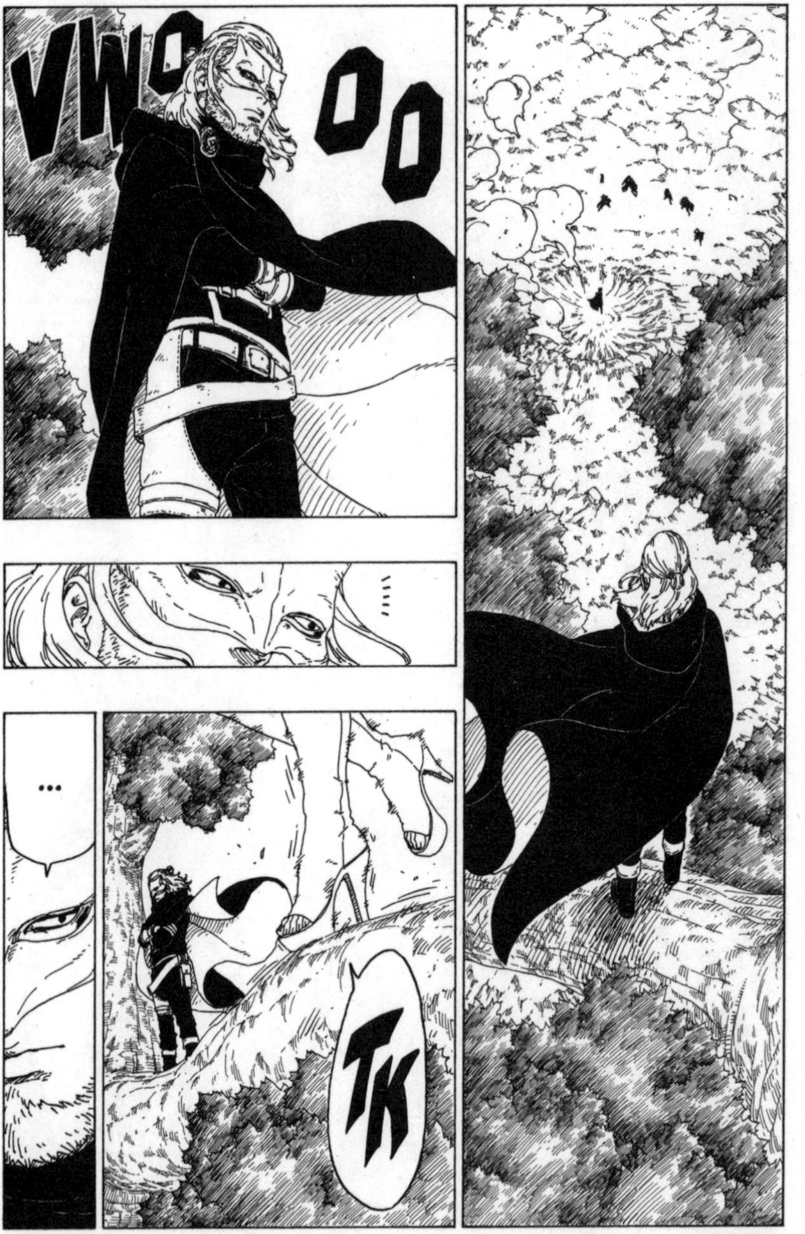
VWOOO
TK
...

ALWAYS SUCH AN EXPRESSIVE FACE, KOJI.

YOU LOOK RATHER ANNOYED. I'M OFFENDED.

WHAT A PLEASURE, DELTA.

THOUGH I DON'T RECALL INVITING YOU.

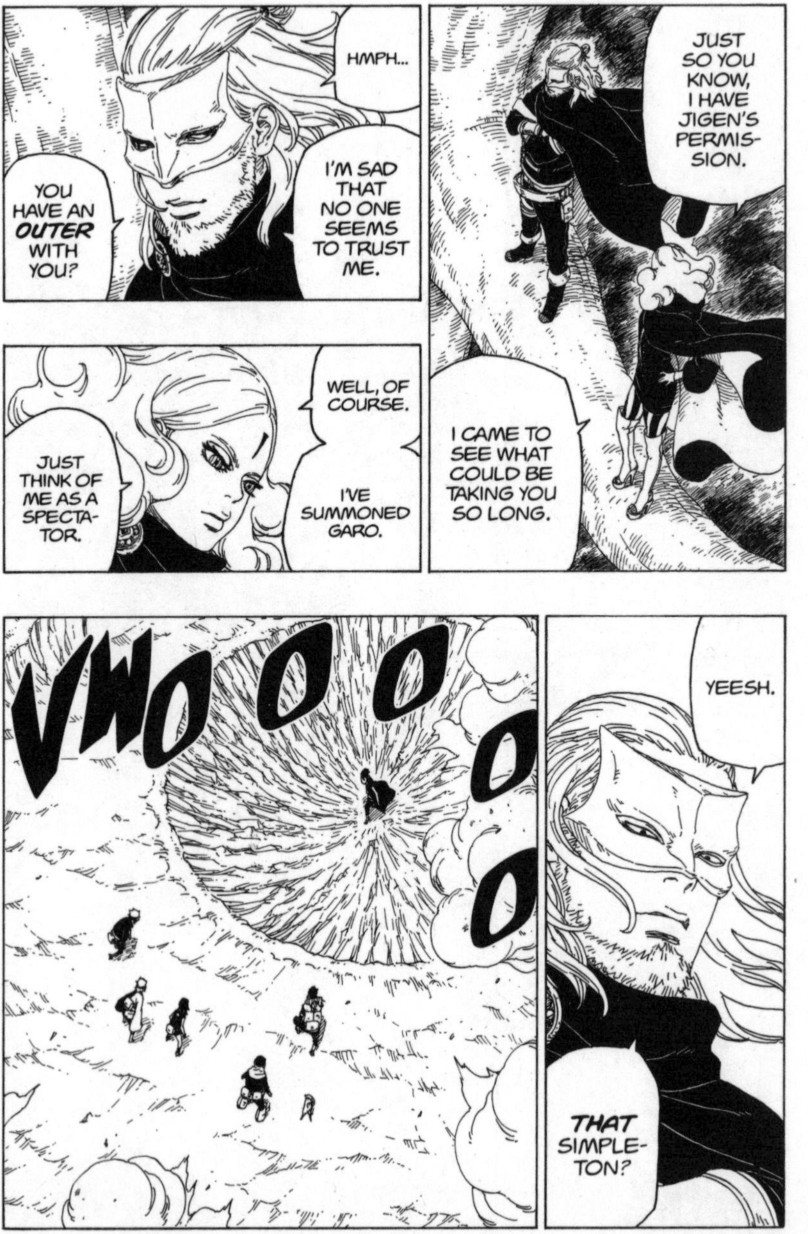
JUST SO YOU KNOW, I HAVE JIGEN'S PERMISSION.
I CAME TO SEE WHAT COULD BE TAKING YOU SO LONG.
HMPH...
I'M SAD THAT NO ONE SEEMS TO TRUST ME.
YOU HAVE AN *OUTER* WITH YOU?
WELL, OF COURSE.
I'VE SUMMONED GARO.
JUST THINK OF ME AS A SPECTATOR.
YEESH.
THAT SIMPLETON?
VWOOOOOO

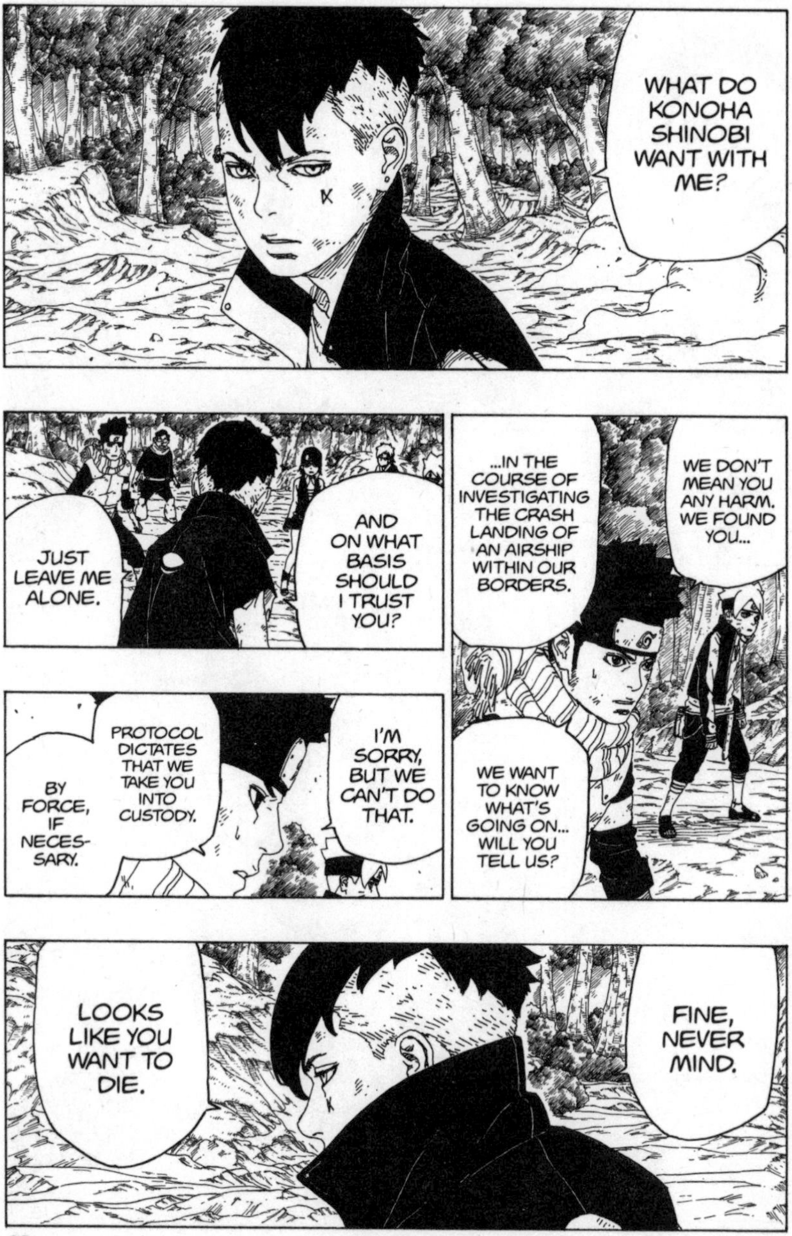
WHAT DO KONOHA SHINOBI WANT WITH ME?
WE DON'T MEAN YOU ANY HARM. WE FOUND YOU...
...IN THE COURSE OF INVESTIGATING THE CRASH LANDING OF AN AIRSHIP WITHIN OUR BORDERS.
WE WANT TO KNOW WHAT'S GOING ON... WILL YOU TELL US?
AND ON WHAT BASIS SHOULD I TRUST YOU?
JUST LEAVE ME ALONE.
I'M SORRY, BUT WE CAN'T DO THAT.
PROTOCOL DICTATES THAT WE TAKE YOU INTO CUSTODY.
BY FORCE, IF NECES-SARY.
FINE, NEVER MIND.
LOOKS LIKE YOU WANT TO DIE.

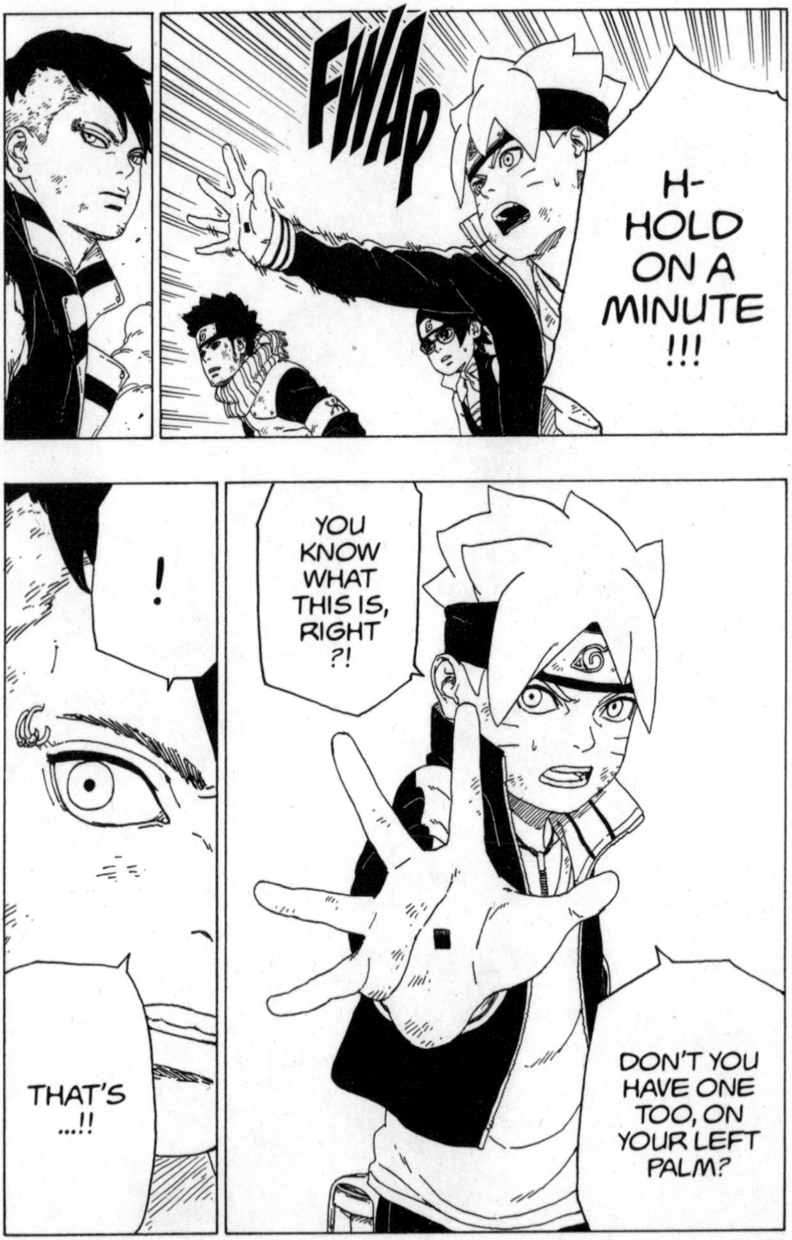
FWAP
H-HOLD ON A MINUTE!!!
YOU KNOW WHAT THIS IS, RIGHT?!
DON'T YOU HAVE ONE TOO, ON YOUR LEFT PALM?
!
THAT'S ...!!

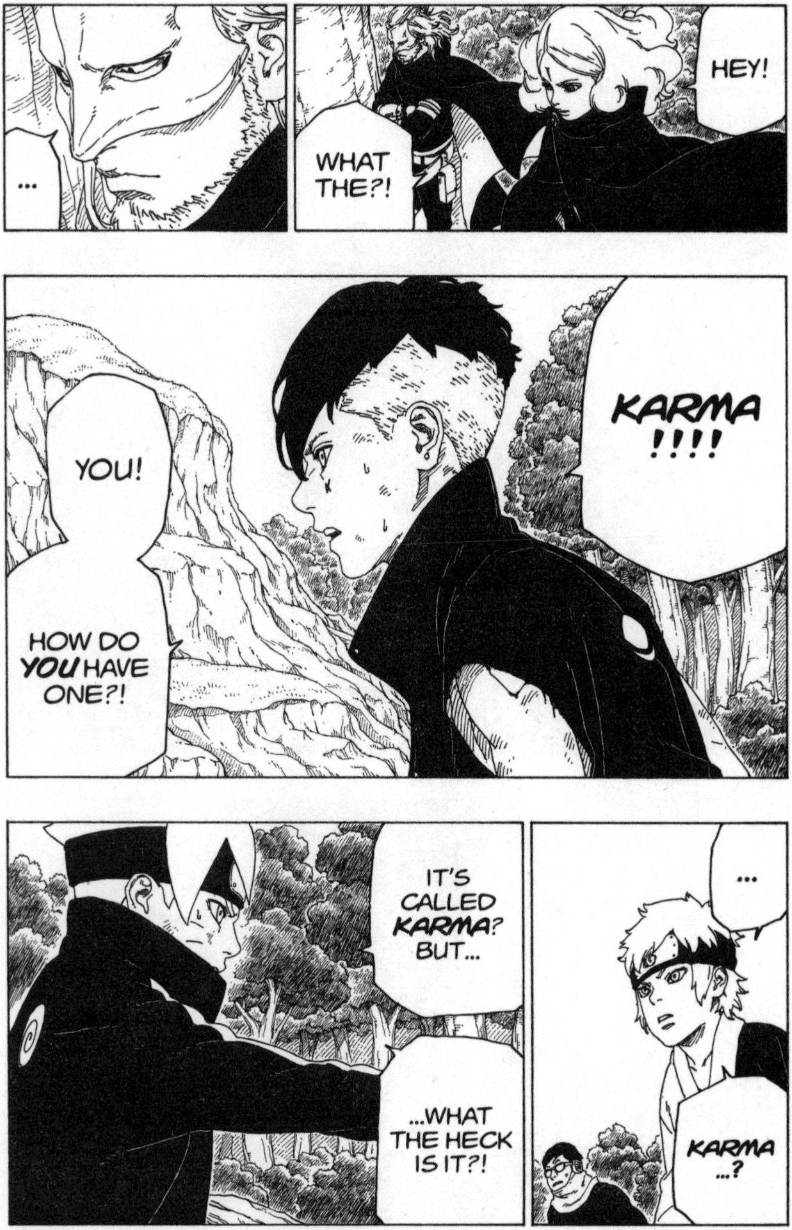
HEY!
WHAT THE?!
...
KARMA!!!!
YOU!
HOW DO YOU HAVE ONE?!
...
KARMA...?
IT'S CALLED KARMA? BUT...
...WHAT THE HECK IS IT?!

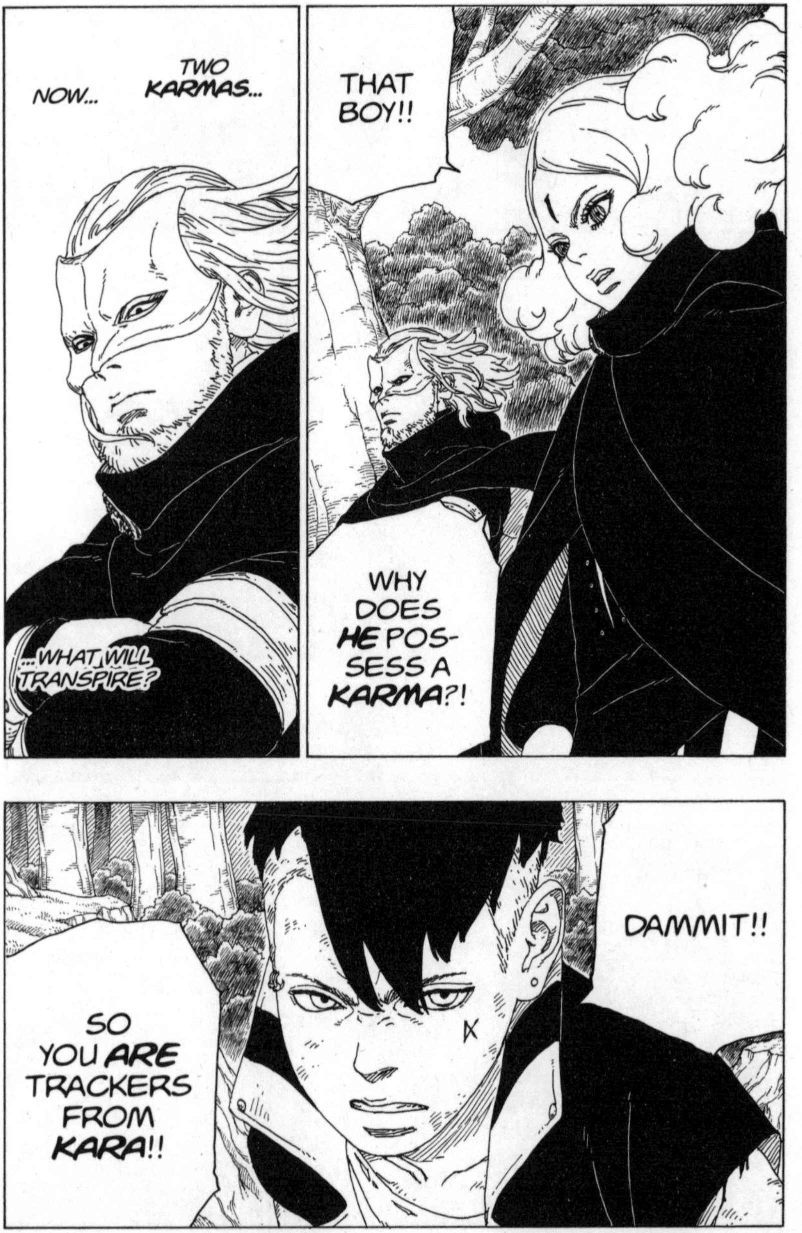
THAT BOY!!
WHY DOES HE POSSESS A KARMA?!
NOW...
TWO KARMAS...
...WHAT WILL TRANSPIRE?
DAMMIT!!
SO YOU ARE TRACKERS FROM KARA!!

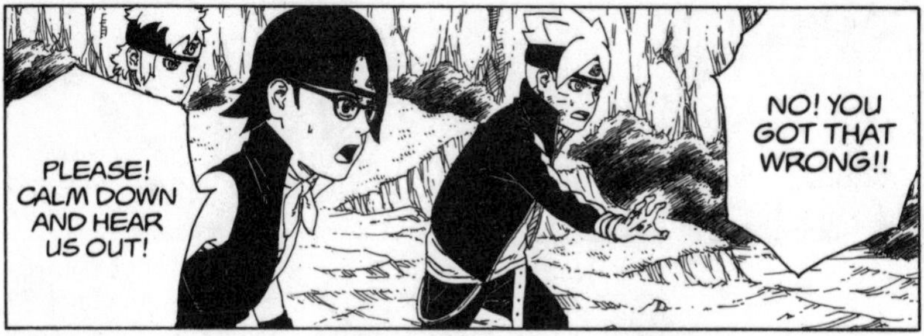
NO! YOU GOT THAT WRONG!!
PLEASE! CALM DOWN AND HEAR US OUT!

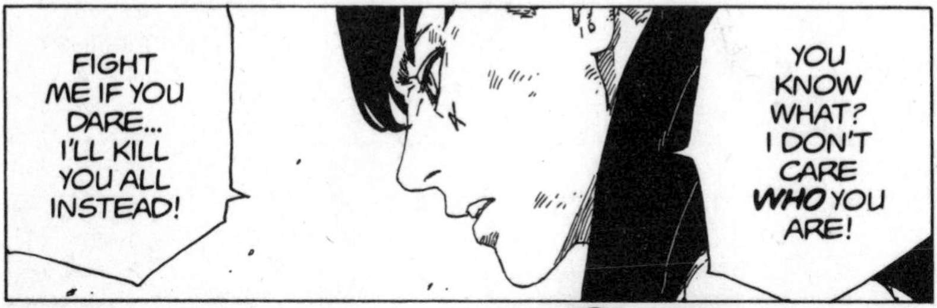
YOU KNOW WHAT? I DON'T CARE ***WHO*** YOU ARE!
FIGHT ME IF YOU DARE... I'LL KILL YOU ALL INSTEAD!

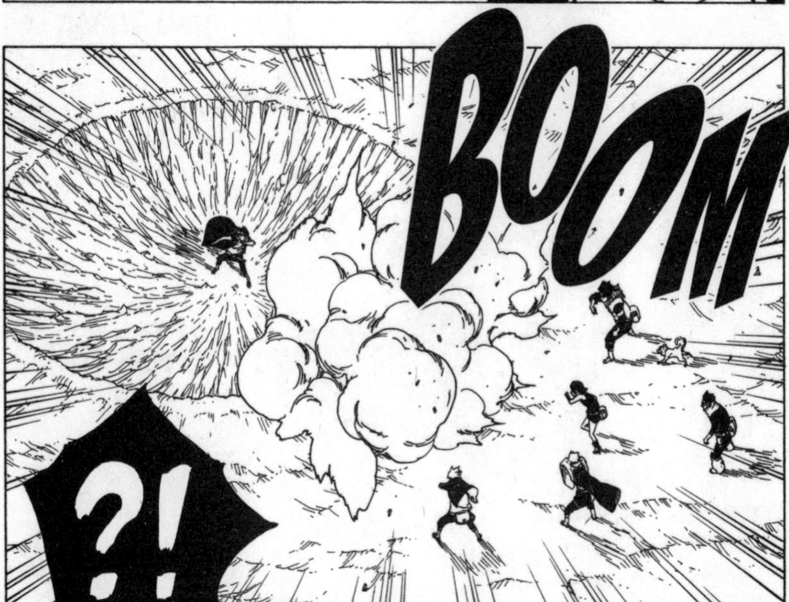
BOOM
?!

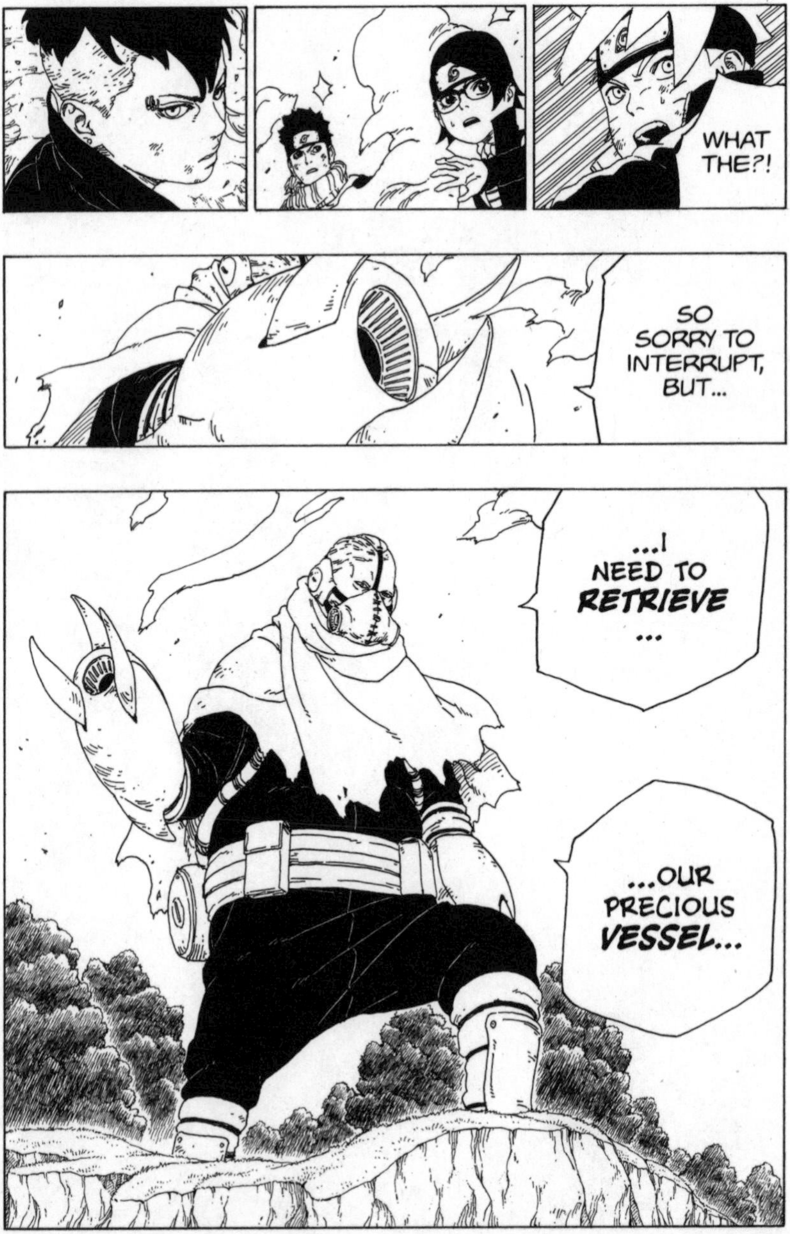
WHAT THE?!
SO SORRY TO INTERRUPT, BUT...
...I NEED TO RETRIEVE ...
...OUR PRECIOUS VESSEL...

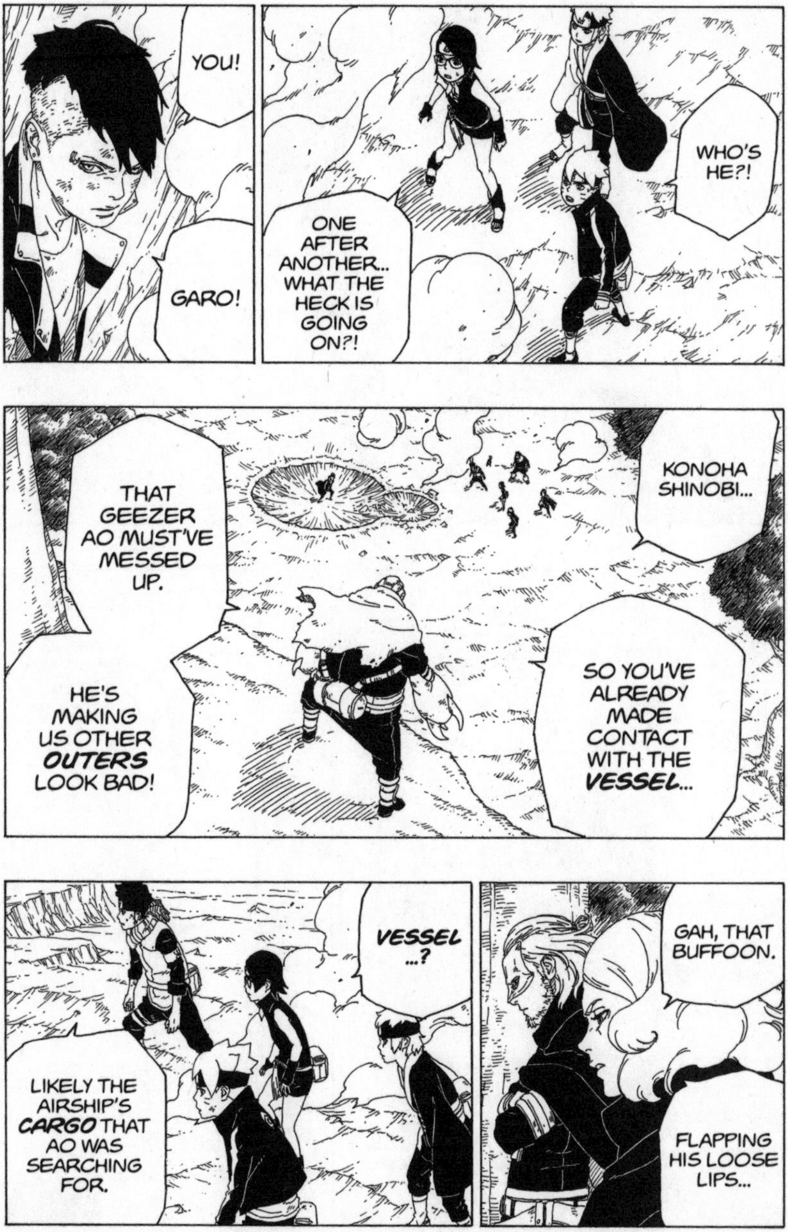
WHO'S HE?!
ONE AFTER ANOTHER... WHAT THE HECK IS GOING ON?!
YOU!
GARO!
KONOHA SHINOBI...
SO YOU'VE ALREADY MADE CONTACT WITH THE VESSEL...
THAT GEEZER AO MUST'VE MESSED UP.
HE'S MAKING US OTHER OUTERS LOOK BAD!
GAH, THAT BUFFOON.
FLAPPING HIS LOOSE LIPS...
VESSEL ...?
LIKELY THE AIRSHIP'S CARGO THAT AO WAS SEARCHING FOR.

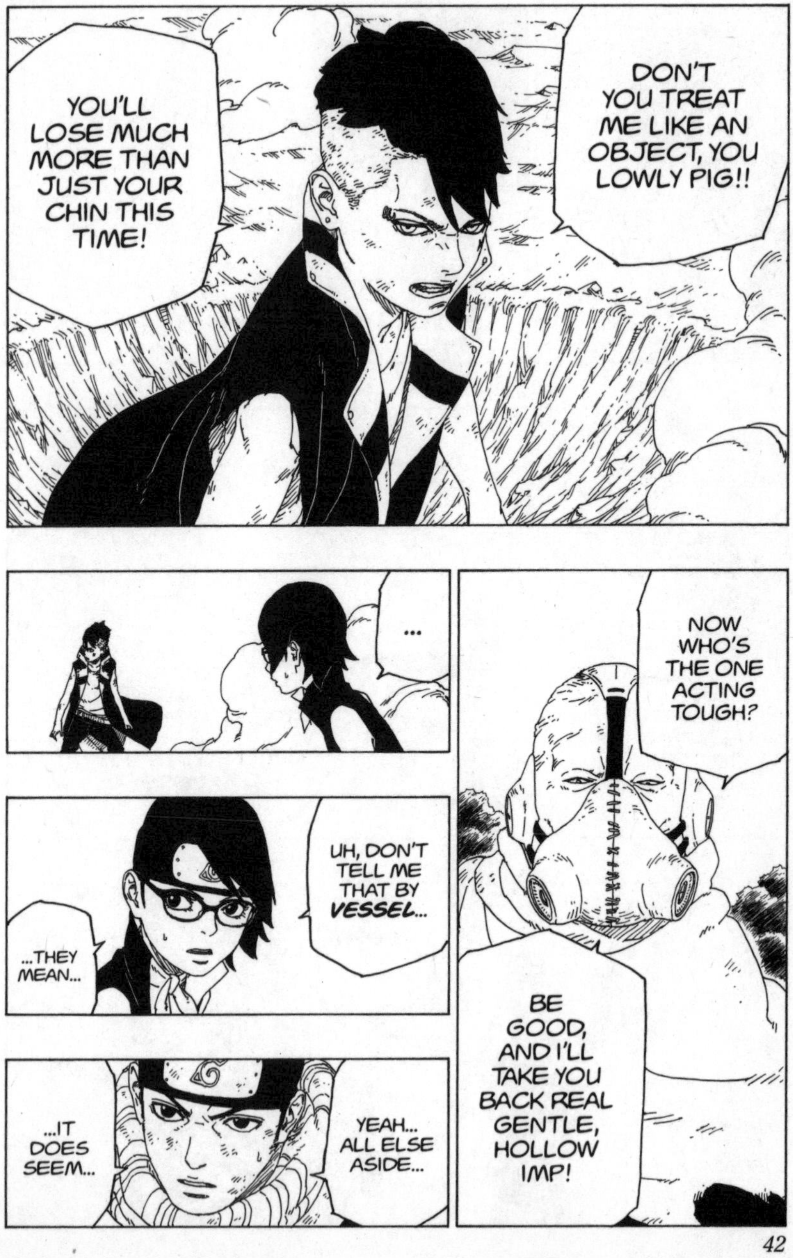
DON'T YOU TREAT ME LIKE AN OBJECT, YOU LOWLY PIG!!
YOU'LL LOSE MUCH MORE THAN JUST YOUR CHIN THIS TIME!
NOW WHO'S THE ONE ACTING TOUGH?
BE GOOD, AND I'LL TAKE YOU BACK REAL GENTLE, HOLLOW IMP!
...
UH, DON'T TELL ME THAT BY *VESSEL*...
...THEY MEAN...
YEAH... ALL ELSE ASIDE...
...IT DOES SEEM...

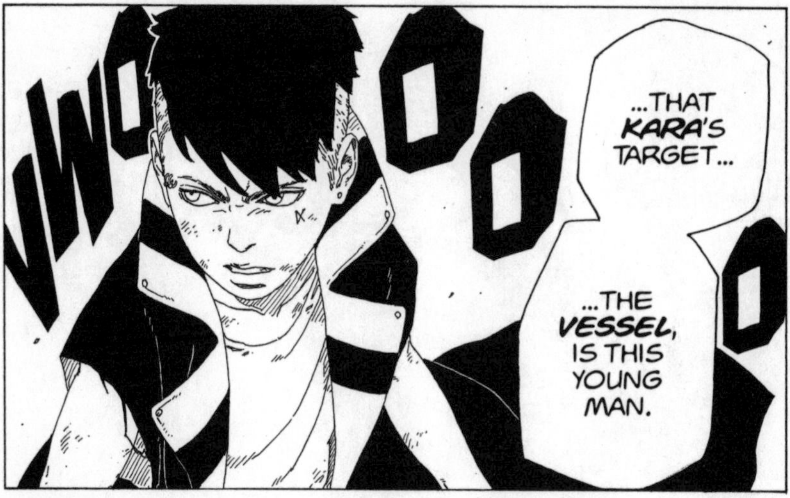
...THAT KARA'S TARGET...
...THE VESSEL, IS THIS YOUNG MAN.
VWOOOOOO

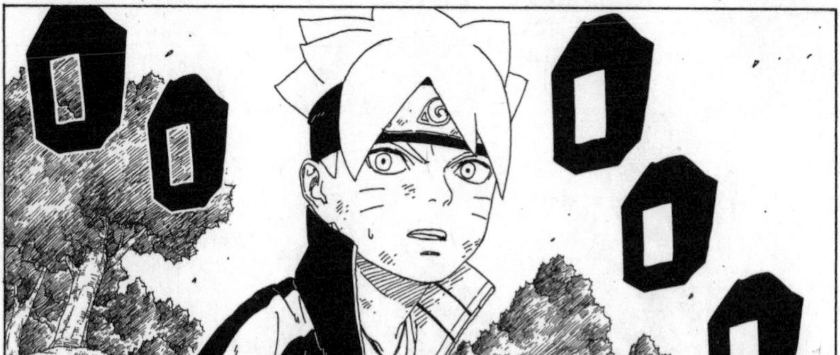
OOOOOOO

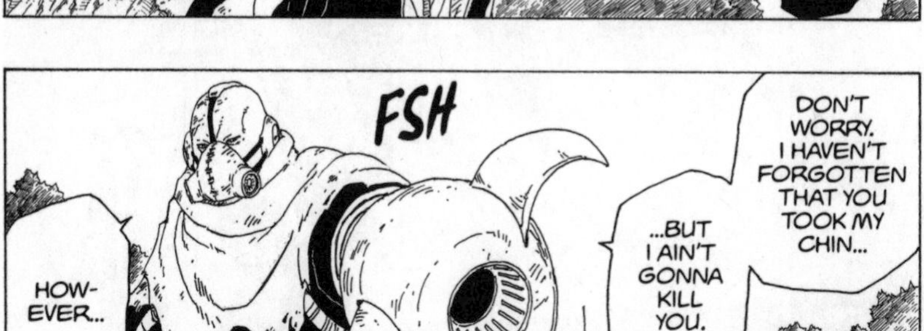
DON'T WORRY. I HAVEN'T FORGOTTEN THAT YOU TOOK MY CHIN...
...BUT I AIN'T GONNA KILL YOU.
FSH
HOW-EVER...

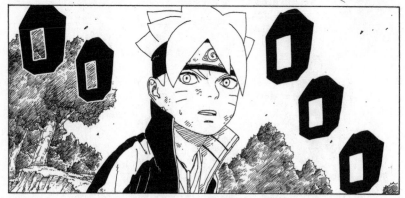

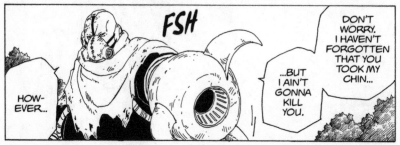

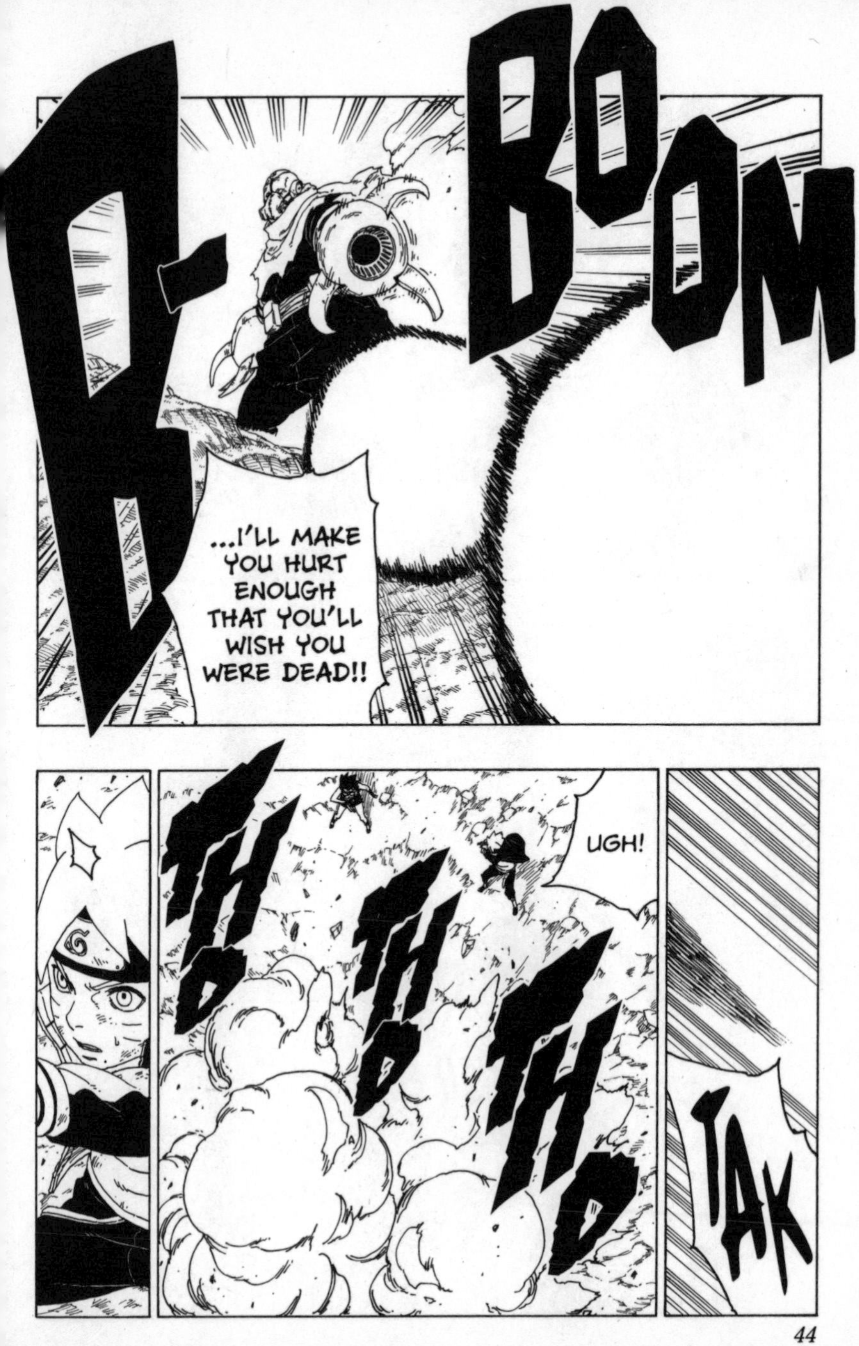
B-BOOM
...I'LL MAKE YOU HURT ENOUGH THAT YOU'LL WISH YOU WERE DEAD!!
TAK
UGH!
THD
THD
THD

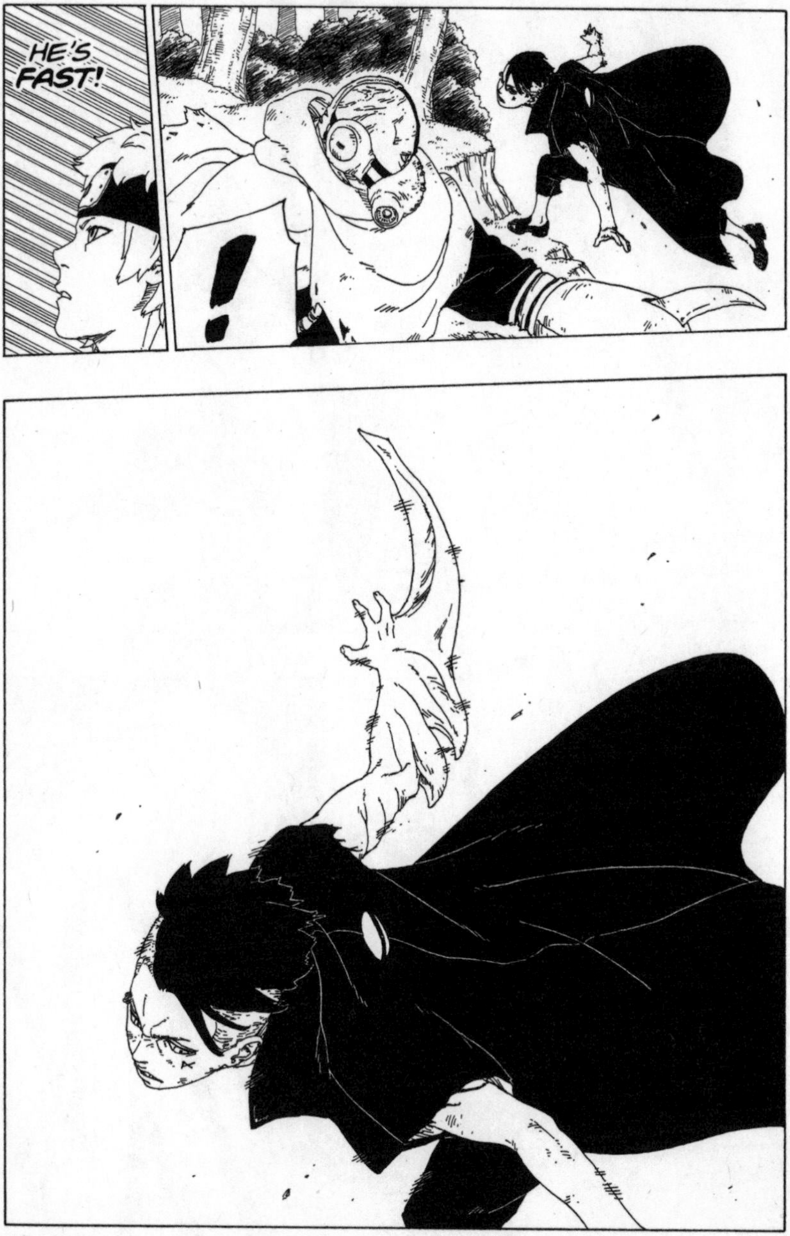
HE'S FAST!

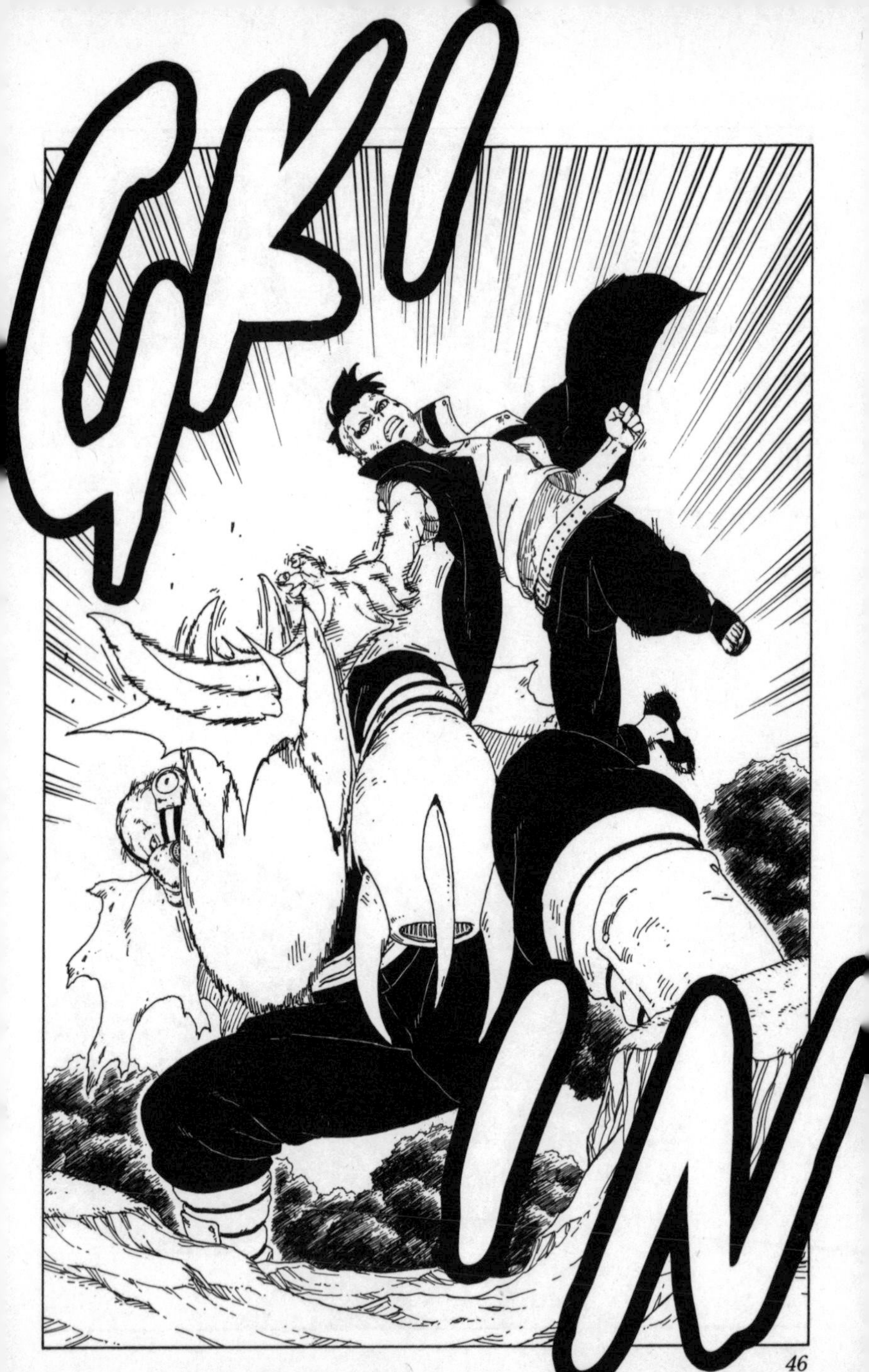

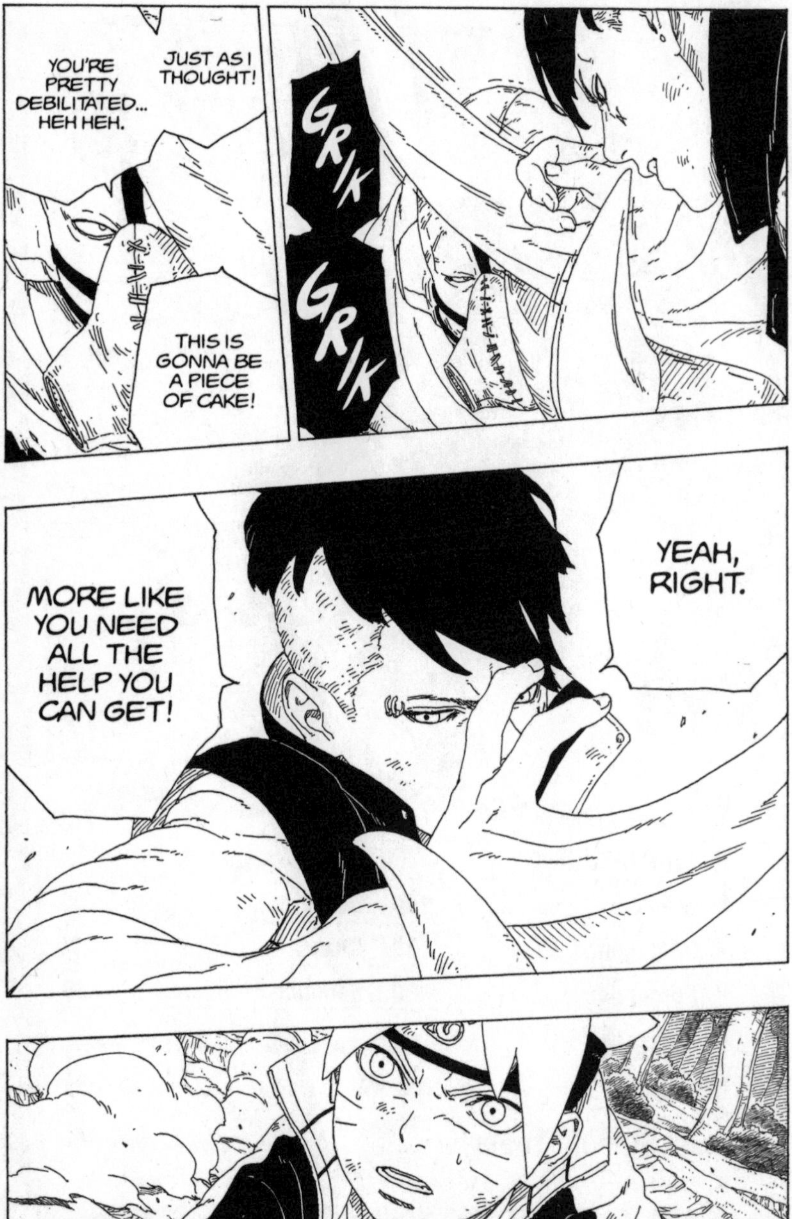
GRIK
GRIK
JUST AS I THOUGHT!
YOU'RE PRETTY DEBILITATED... HEH HEH.
THIS IS GONNA BE A PIECE OF CAKE!
YEAH, RIGHT.
MORE LIKE YOU NEED ALL THE HELP YOU CAN GET!

NINJA ENCYCLOPEDIA · ENTRY 19

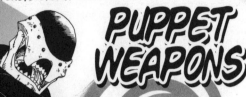

PUPPET WEAPONS

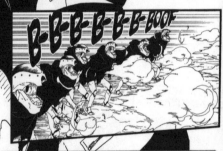

B-B-B-B-B-B-BOOF

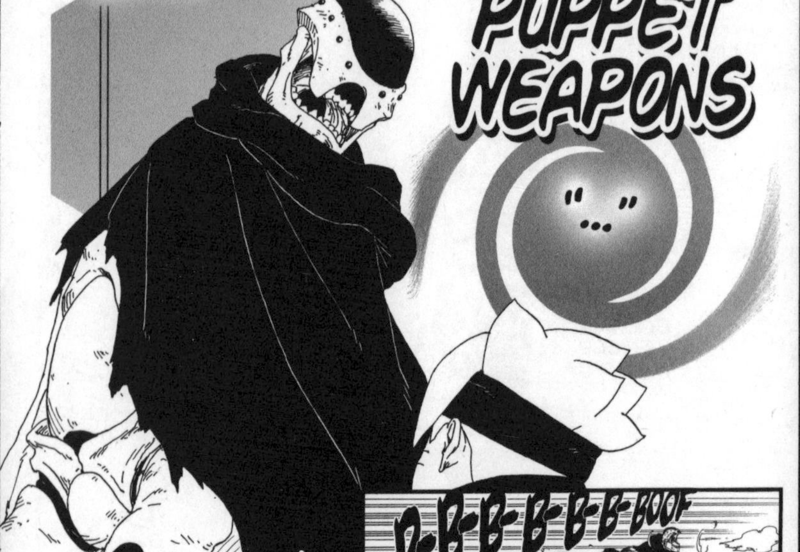

Attributes

Strength	100	Dexterity	100
Intelligence	30	Chakra	0*
Perception	80	Negotiation	10

Skills

Movement ☆☆☆ Marksmanship ☆☆☆ Combat ☆☆☆

Shinobi Tools

Katon bombs, Taijutsu: Hardening Nerves, Exterior Type Rapid-Firing Shuriken Launchers, etc.

*Average attribute value is 60 for ordinary people and 90 for genin. Skill values range from 1 to 5☆ with 5☆ signifying super top-notch. *Puppet Weapons use chakra that has been stored in their condensers.

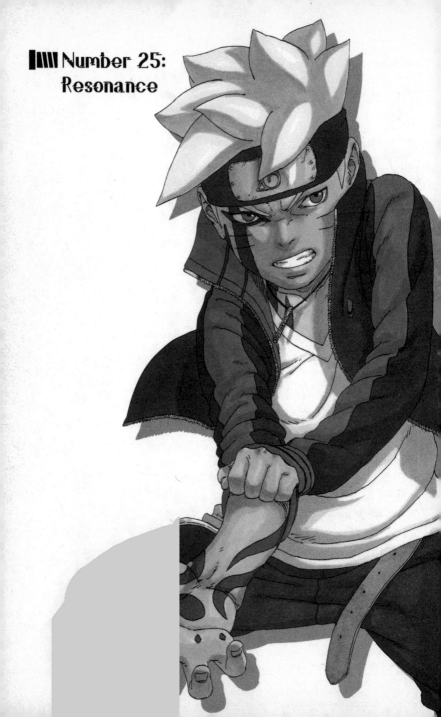

Number 25: Resonance

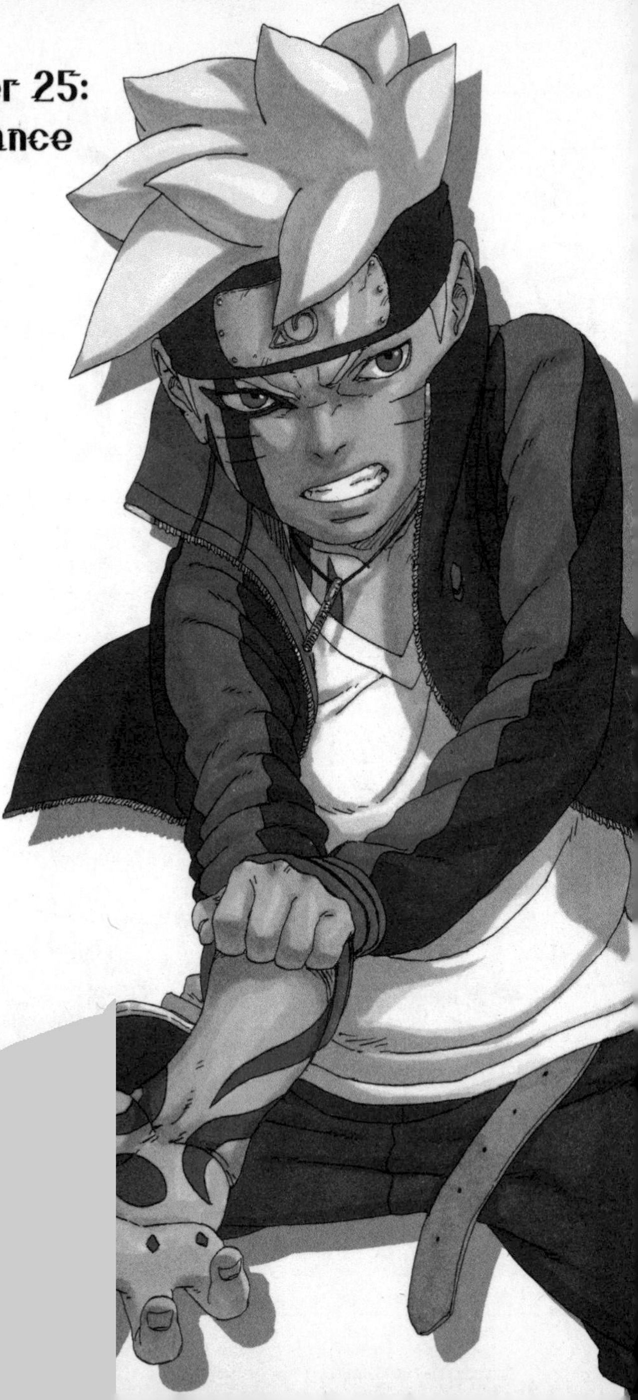

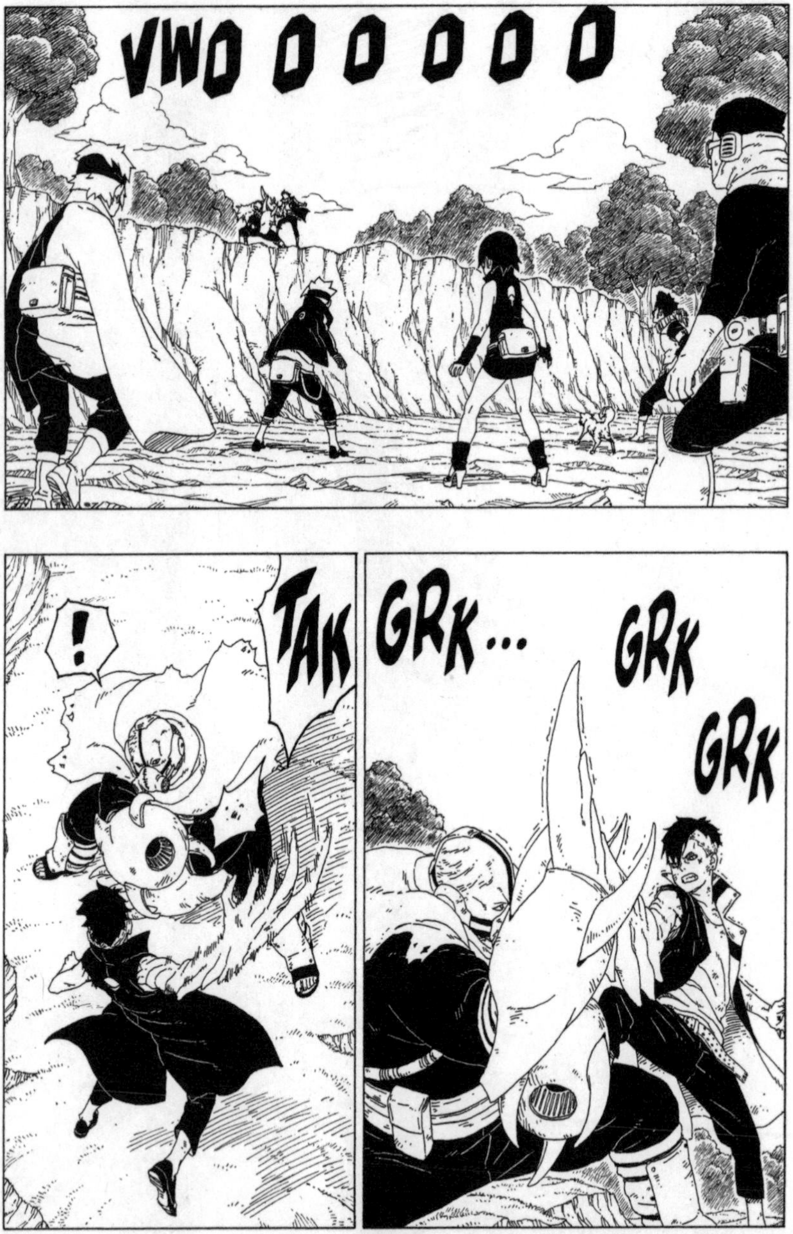
VWO O O O O O
GRK...
GRK
GRK
TAK
!

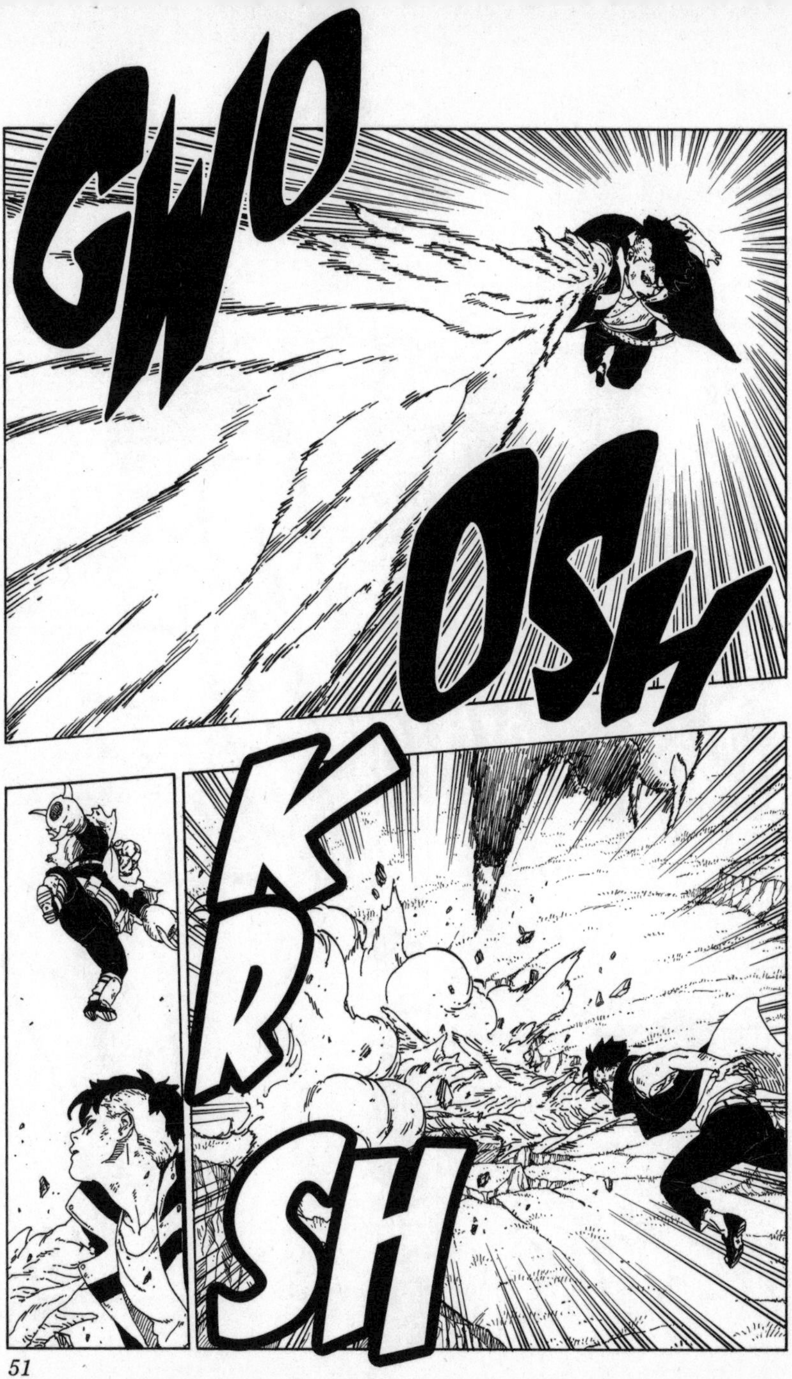
GWOOSH
K'RSH

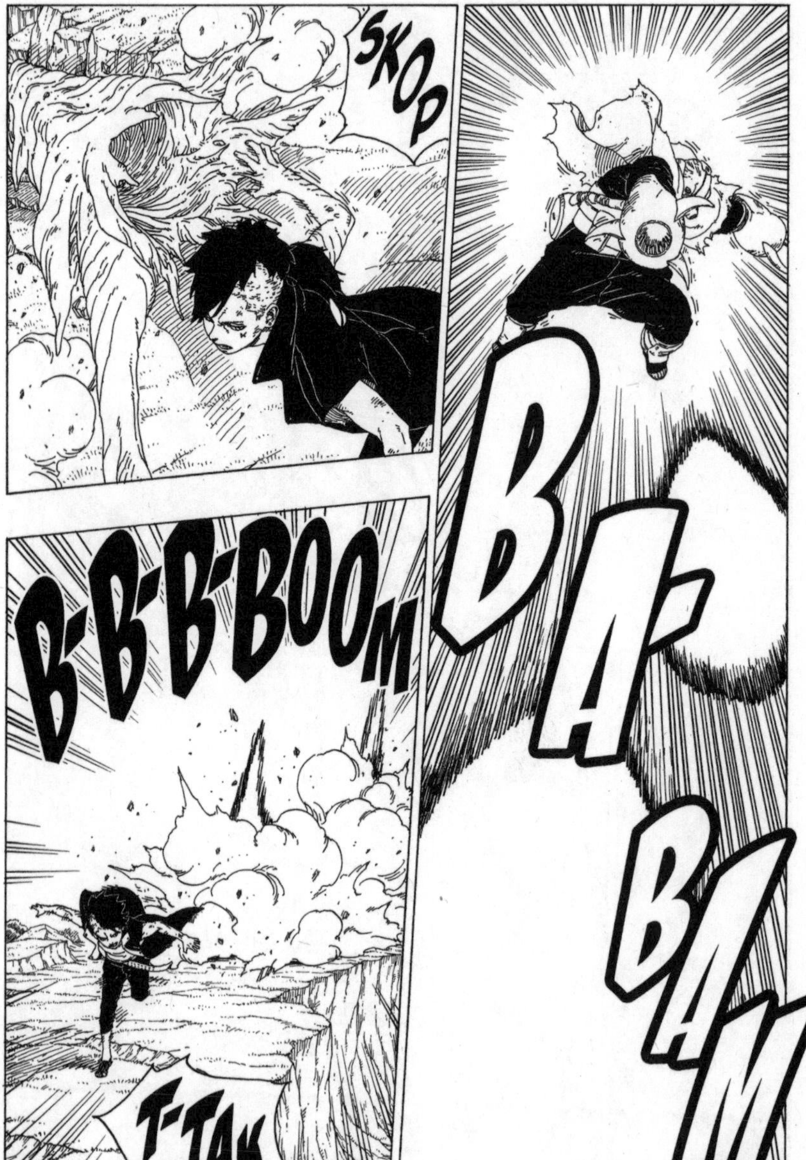
BA-BAM
SKOP
B-B-B-BOOM
T-TAK

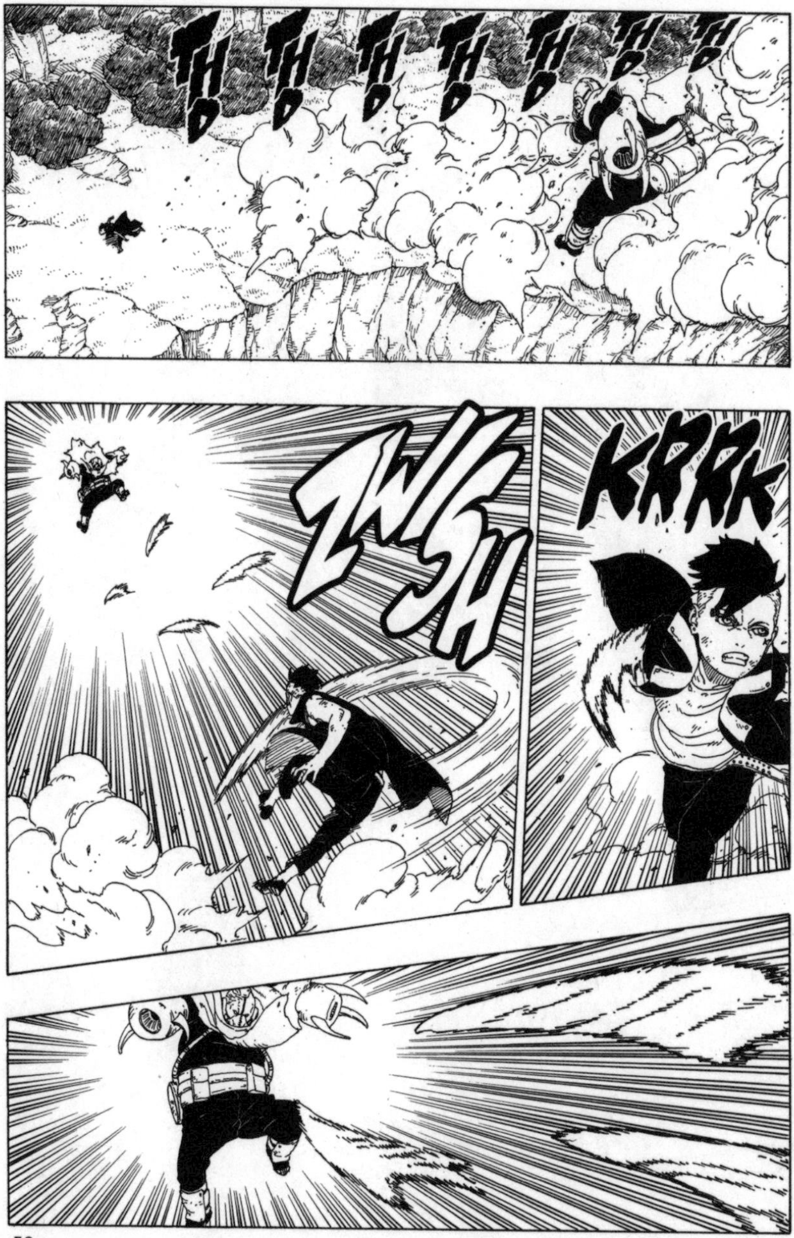
THD THD THD THD THD THD THD
KRRK
ZWISH

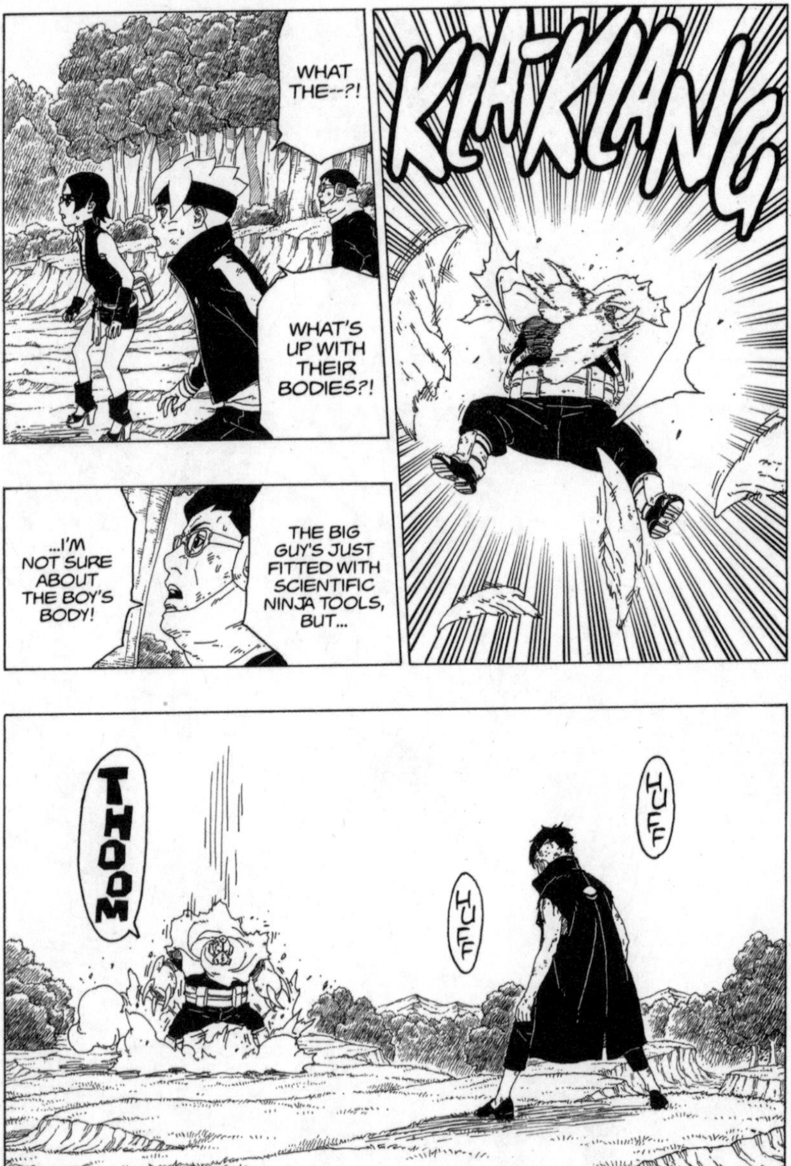
KLA-KLANG
WHAT THE--?!
WHAT'S UP WITH THEIR BODIES?!
THE BIG GUY'S JUST FITTED WITH SCIENTIFIC NINJA TOOLS, BUT...
...I'M NOT SURE ABOUT THE BOY'S BODY!
HUFF
HUFF
THOOM

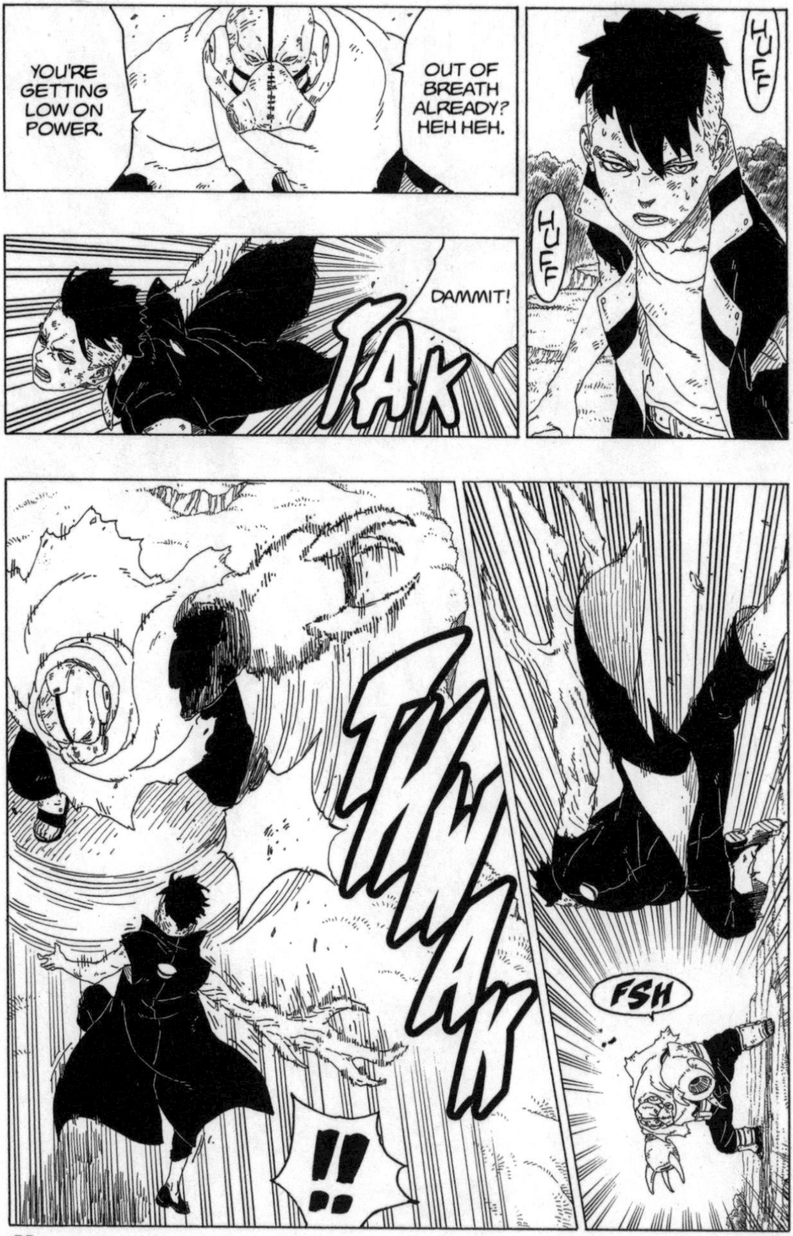
HUFF
HUFF
OUT OF BREATH ALREADY? HEH HEH.
YOU'RE GETTING LOW ON POWER.
DAMMIT!
TAK
FSH
THWAK
!!

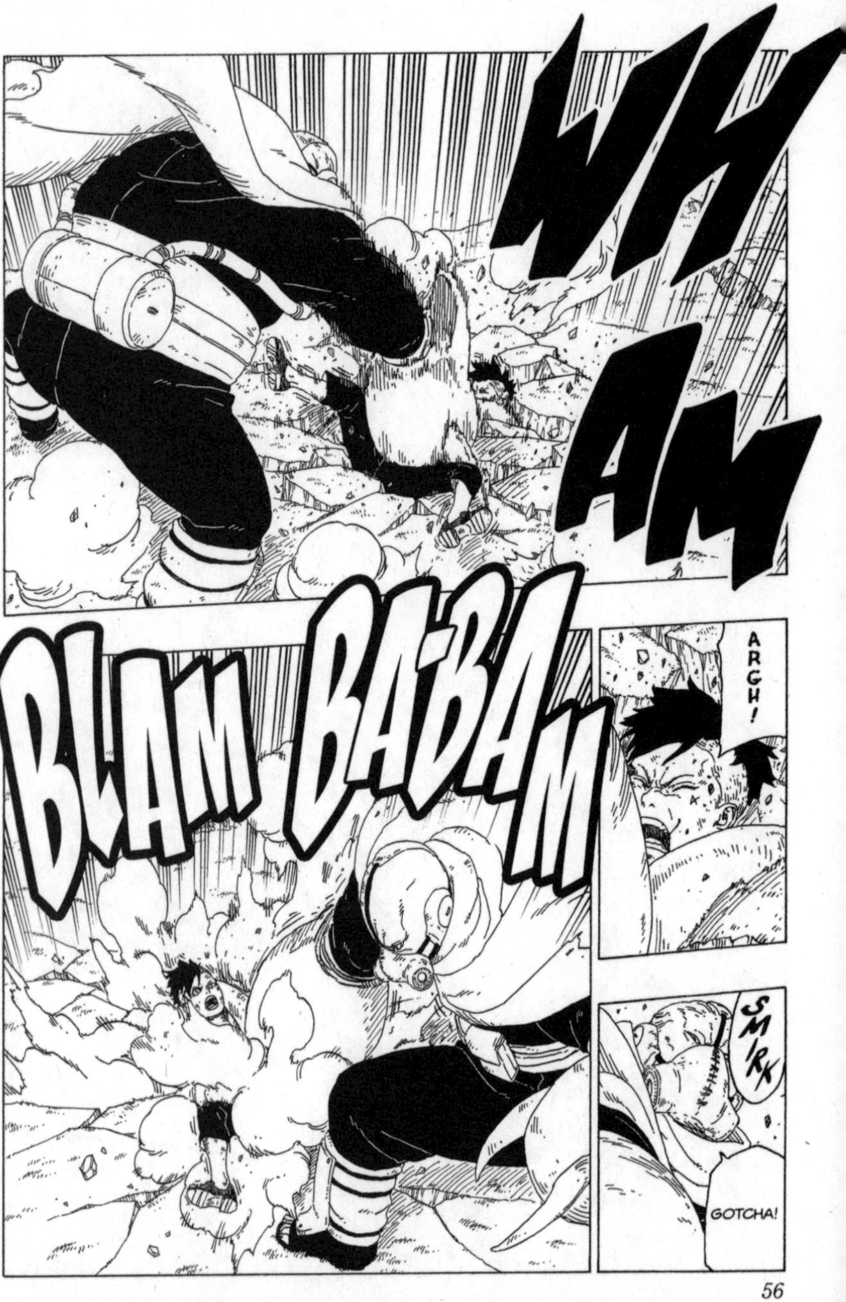
WHAMAM
ARGH!
SMIRK
GOTCHA!
BLAM
BA-BAM

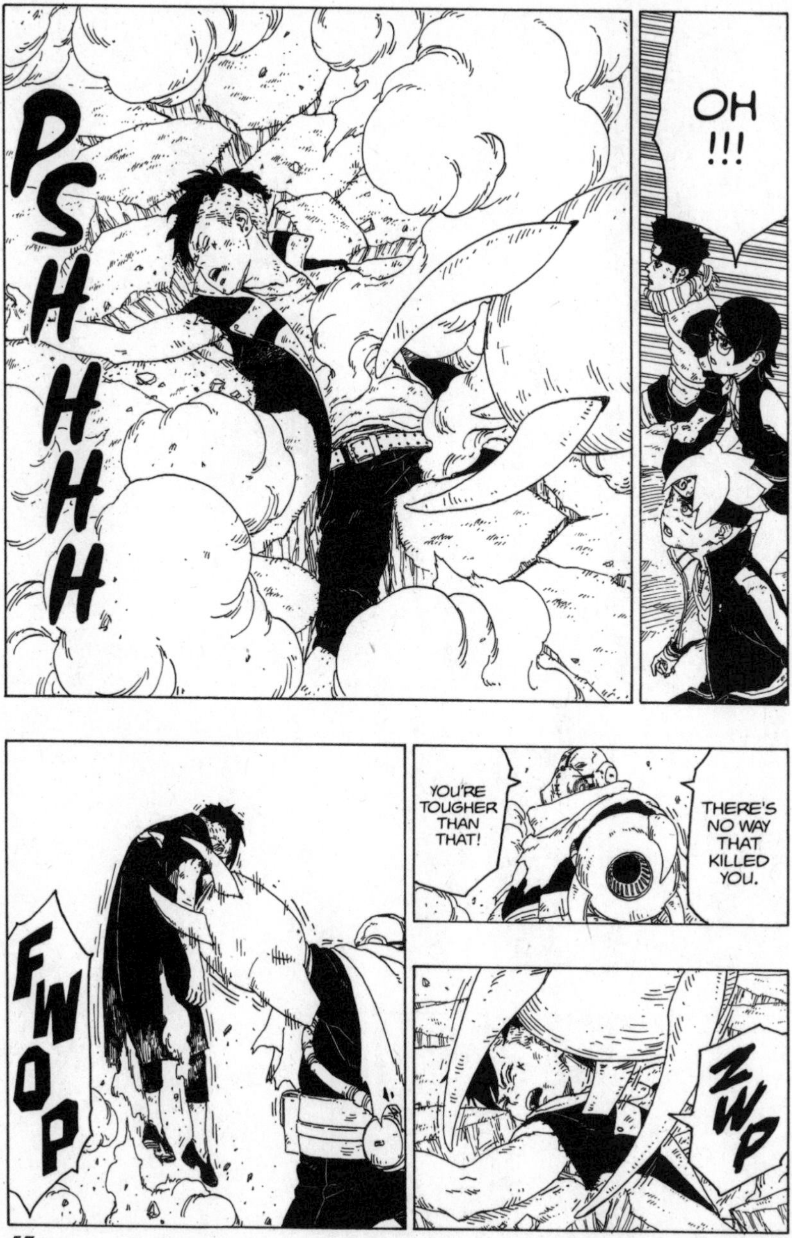
OH !!!
PSHHHHH
THERE'S NO WAY THAT KILLED YOU.
YOU'RE TOUGHER THAN THAT!
ZWP
FWOP

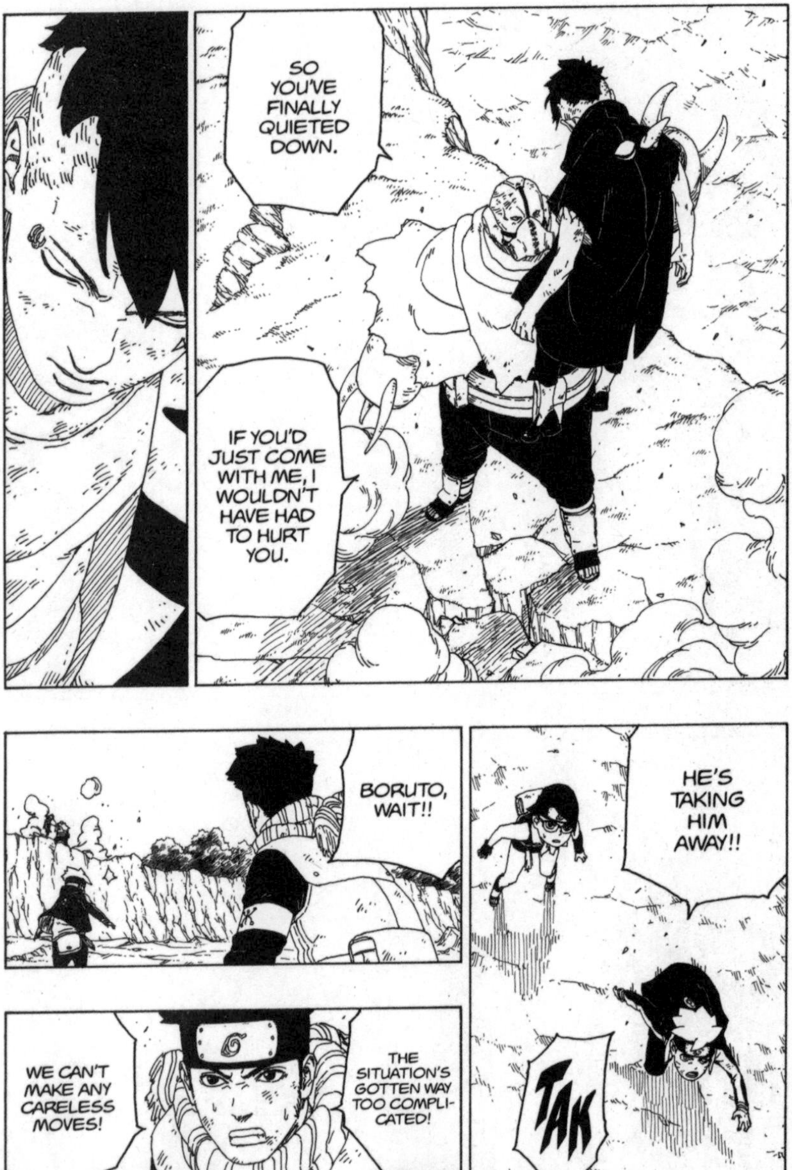
SO YOU'VE FINALLY QUIETED DOWN.
IF YOU'D JUST COME WITH ME, I WOULDN'T HAVE HAD TO HURT YOU.
HE'S TAKING HIM AWAY!!
TAK
BORUTO, WAIT!!
THE SITUATION'S GOTTEN WAY TOO COMPLI-CATED!
WE CAN'T MAKE ANY CARELESS MOVES!

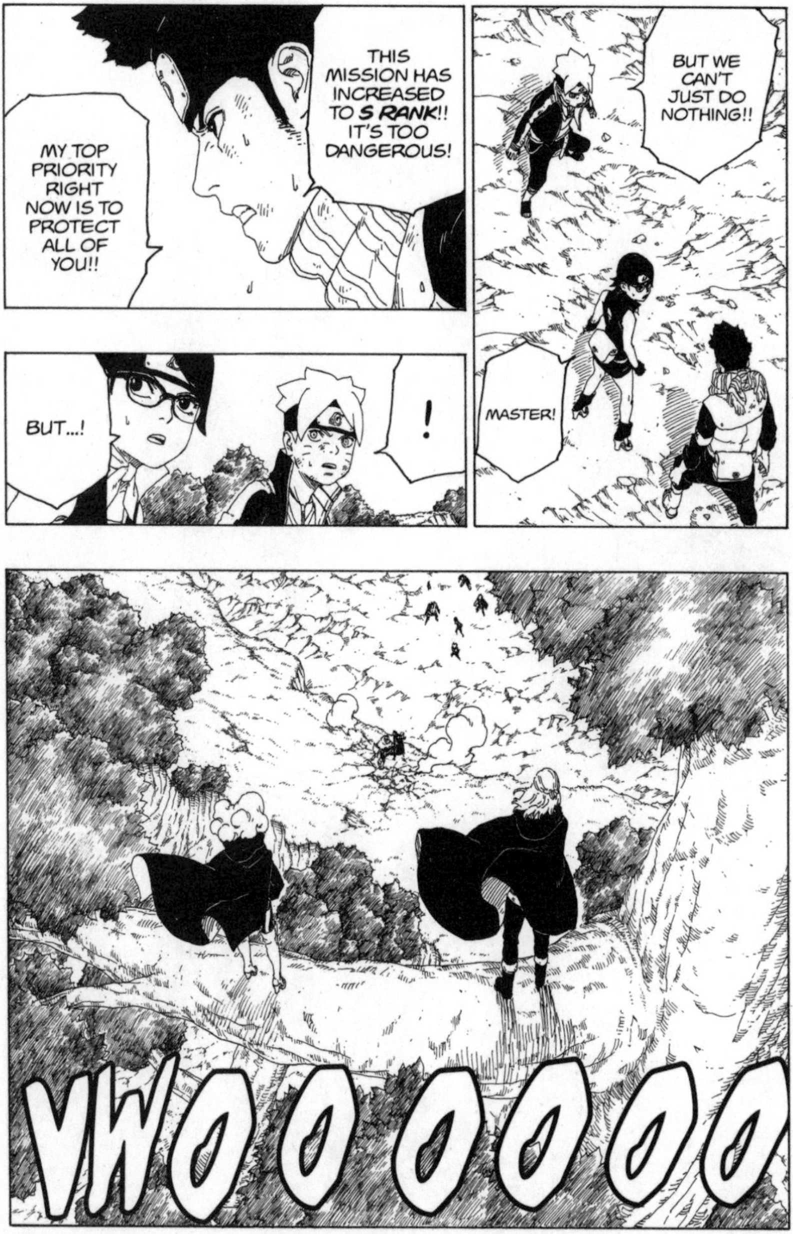
BUT WE CAN'T JUST DO NOTHING!!
MASTER!
THIS MISSION HAS INCREASED TO S RANK!! IT'S TOO DANGEROUS!
MY TOP PRIORITY RIGHT NOW IS TO PROTECT ALL OF YOU!!
!
BUT...!
VWOOOOOO

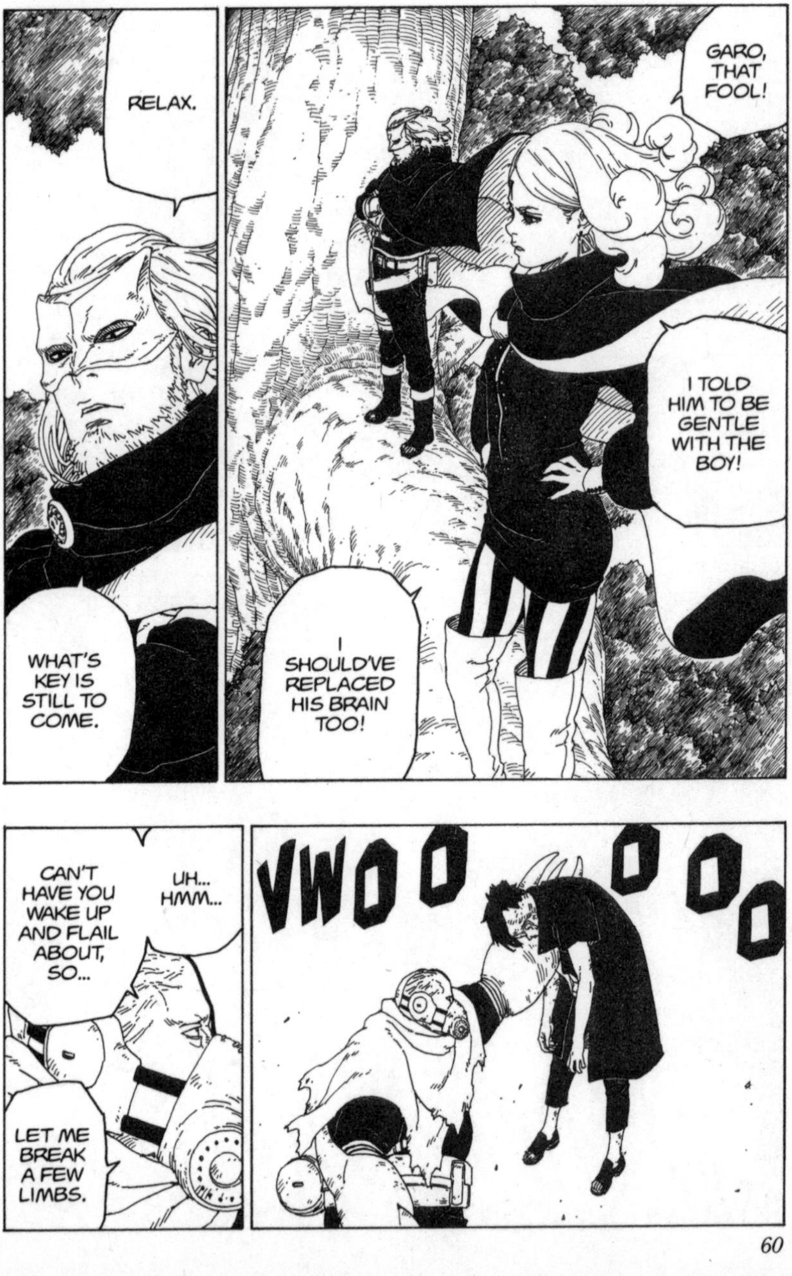
GARO, THAT FOOL!
I TOLD HIM TO BE GENTLE WITH THE BOY!
I SHOULD'VE REPLACED HIS BRAIN TOO!
RELAX.
WHAT'S KEY IS STILL TO COME.
VWOOOOOO
UH... HMM...
CAN'T HAVE YOU WAKE UP AND FLAIL ABOUT, SO...
LET ME BREAK A FEW LIMBS.

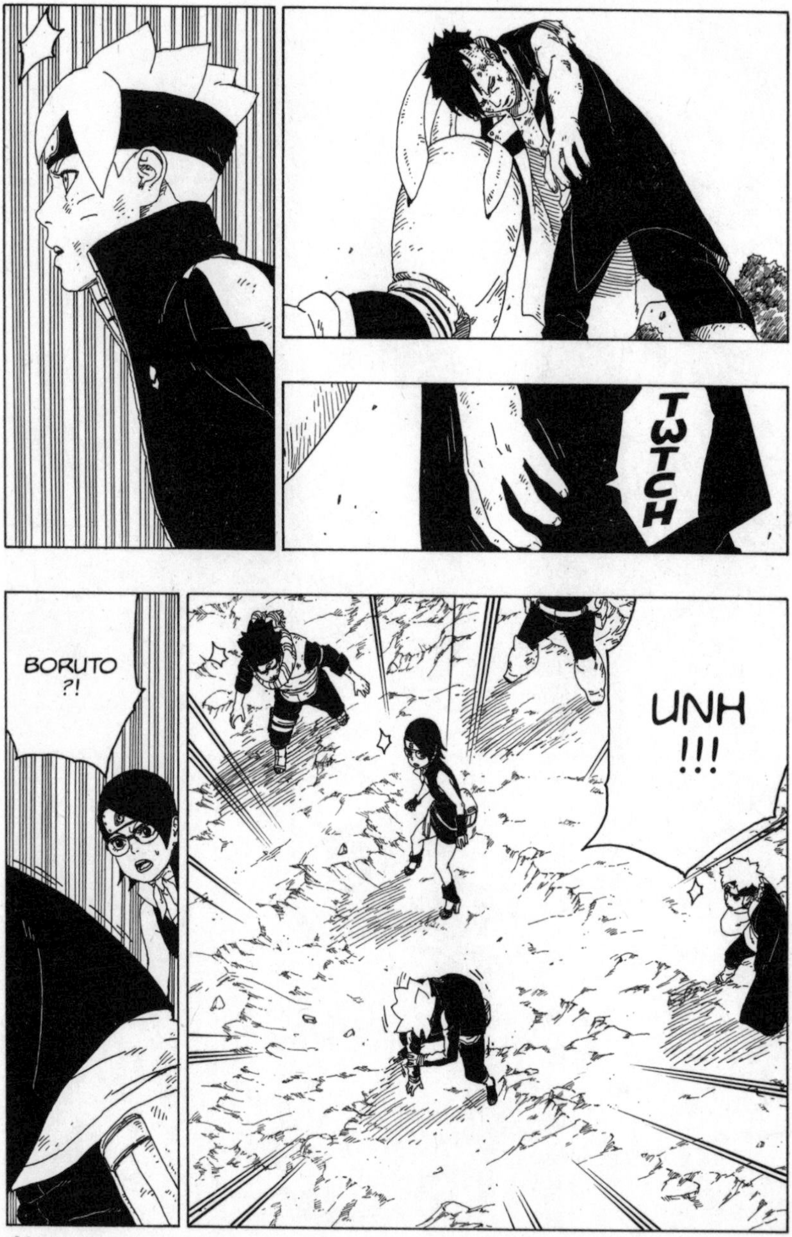
TWTCH
UNH !!!
BORUTO ?!

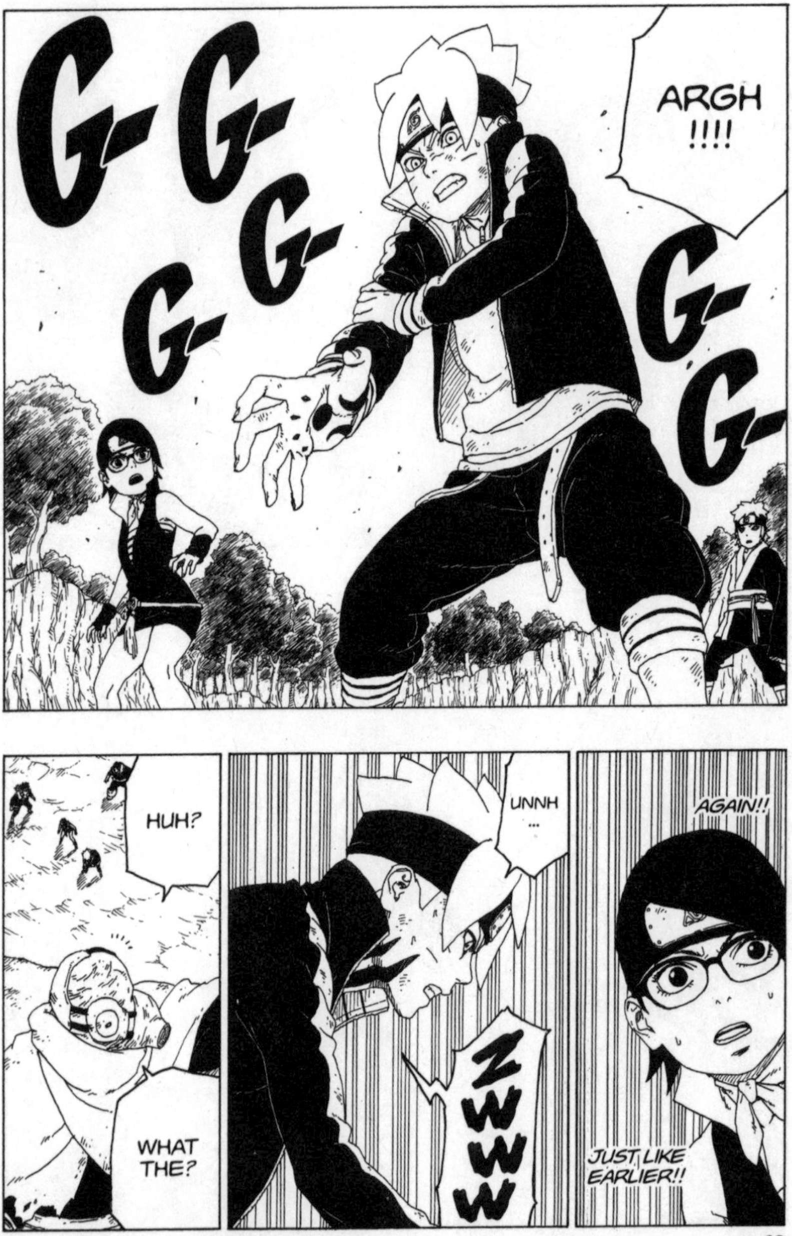
ARGH !!!!
G-G-
G-G-G-G-
AGAIN!!
JUST LIKE EARLIER!!
UNNH ...
ZWWW
HUH?
WHAT THE?

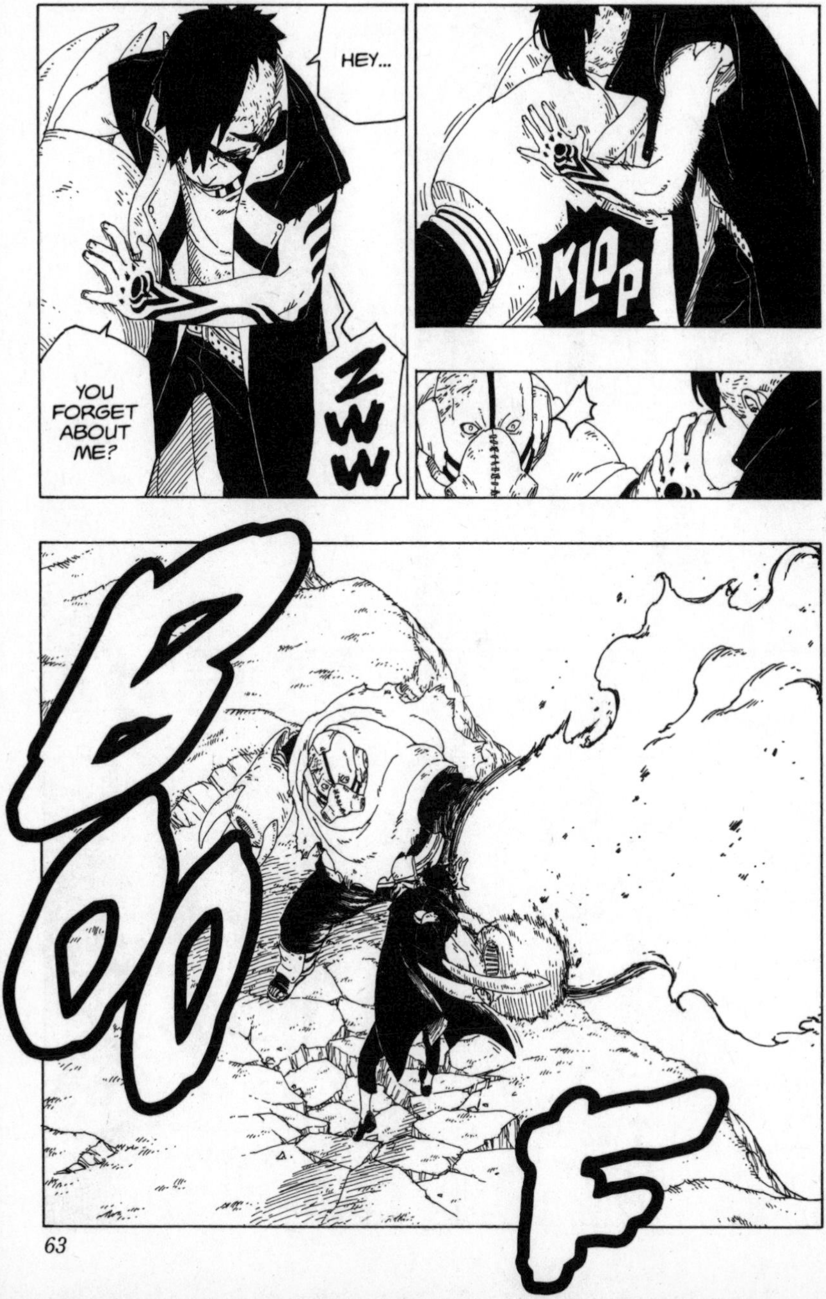
KLOP
HEY...
YOU FORGET ABOUT ME?
ZWWW
BOOF

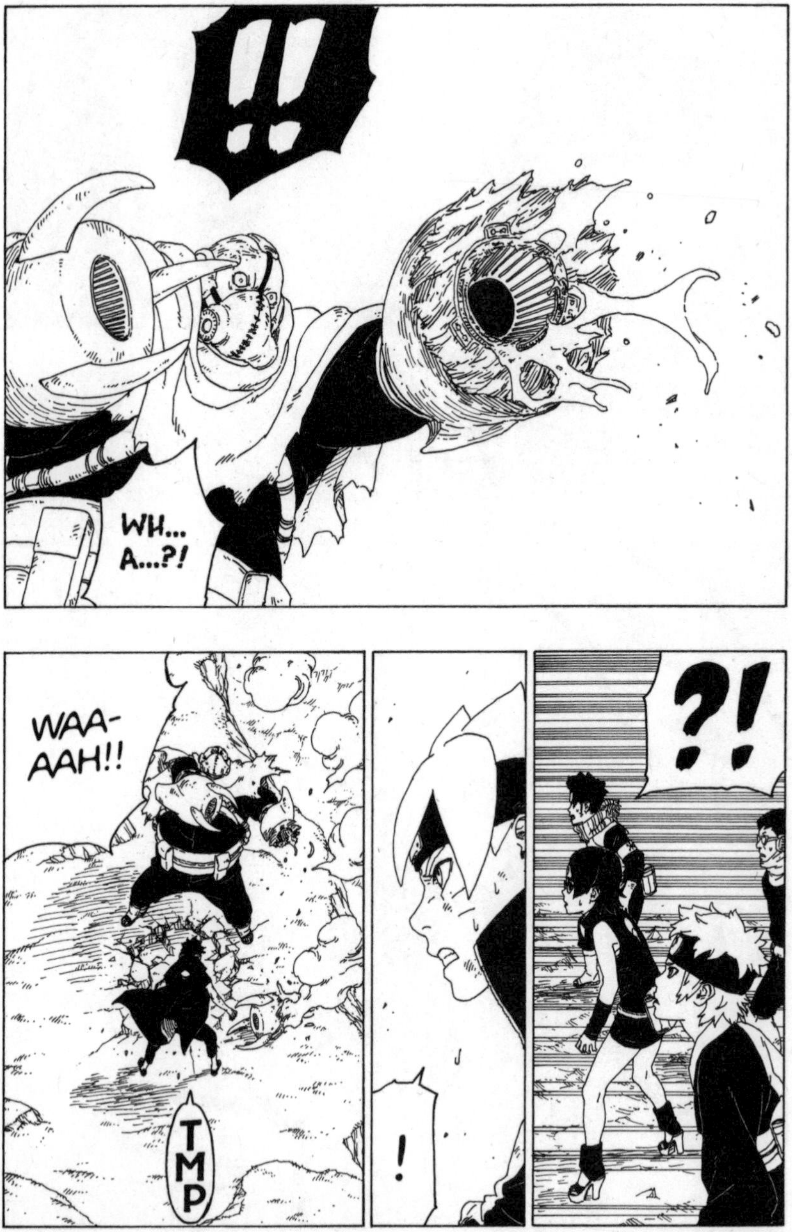
!!
WH... A...?!
?!
!
WAA-AAH!!
TMP

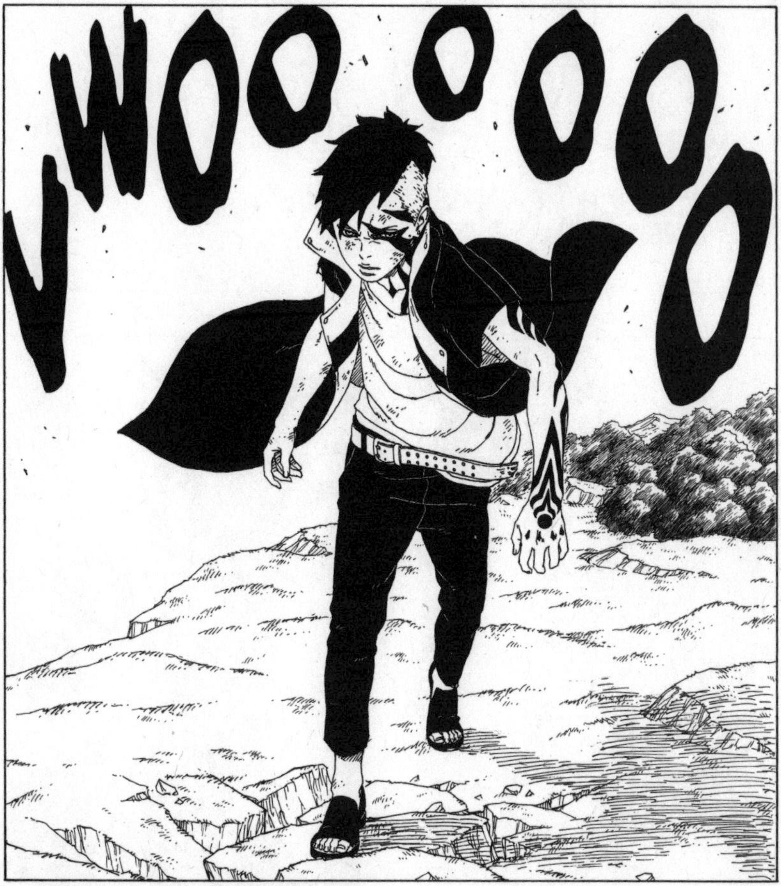
VWOOOOOOO

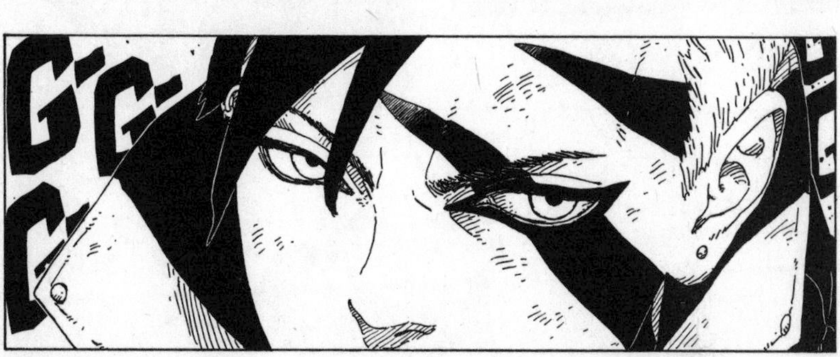
G-G-G-

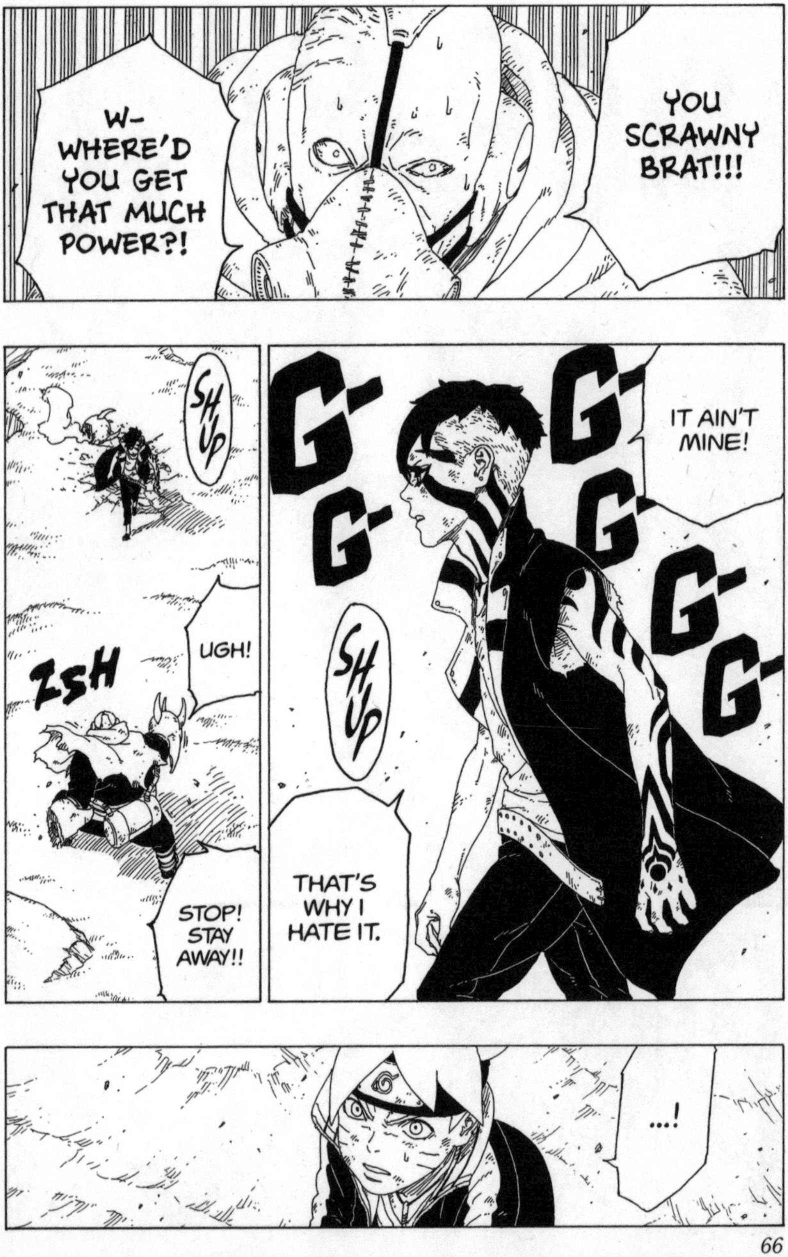
YOU SCRAWNY BRAT!!!
W- WHERE'D YOU GET THAT MUCH POWER?!
G-G-G-
G-G-G-
IT AIN'T MINE!
SHUP
THAT'S WHY I HATE IT.
SHUP
UGH!
ZSH
STOP! STAY AWAY!!
...!

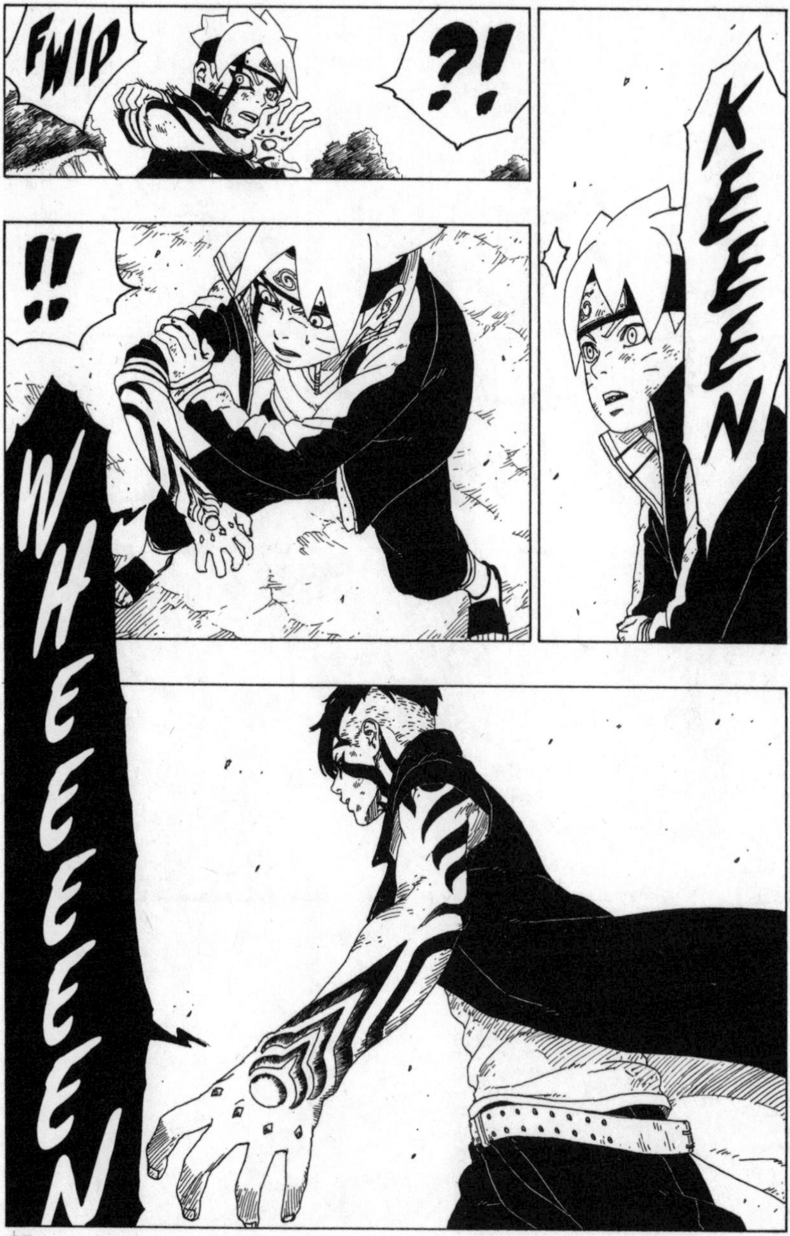
KEEEEN
FWIP
?!
!!
WHEEEEEEN

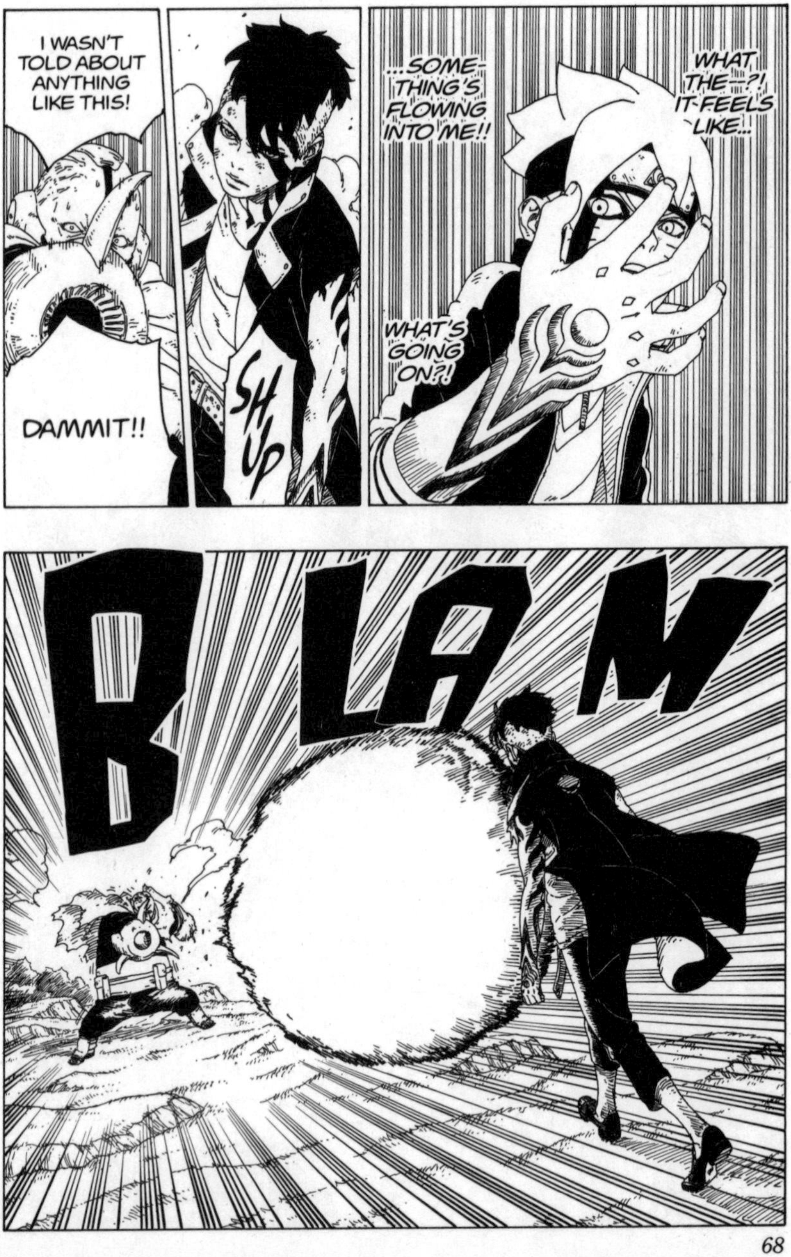
WHAT THE--?! IT FEELS LIKE...
...SOMETHING'S FLOWING INTO ME!!
WHAT'S GOING ON?!
SHUP
I WASN'T TOLD ABOUT ANYTHING LIKE THIS!
DAMMIT!!
BLAM

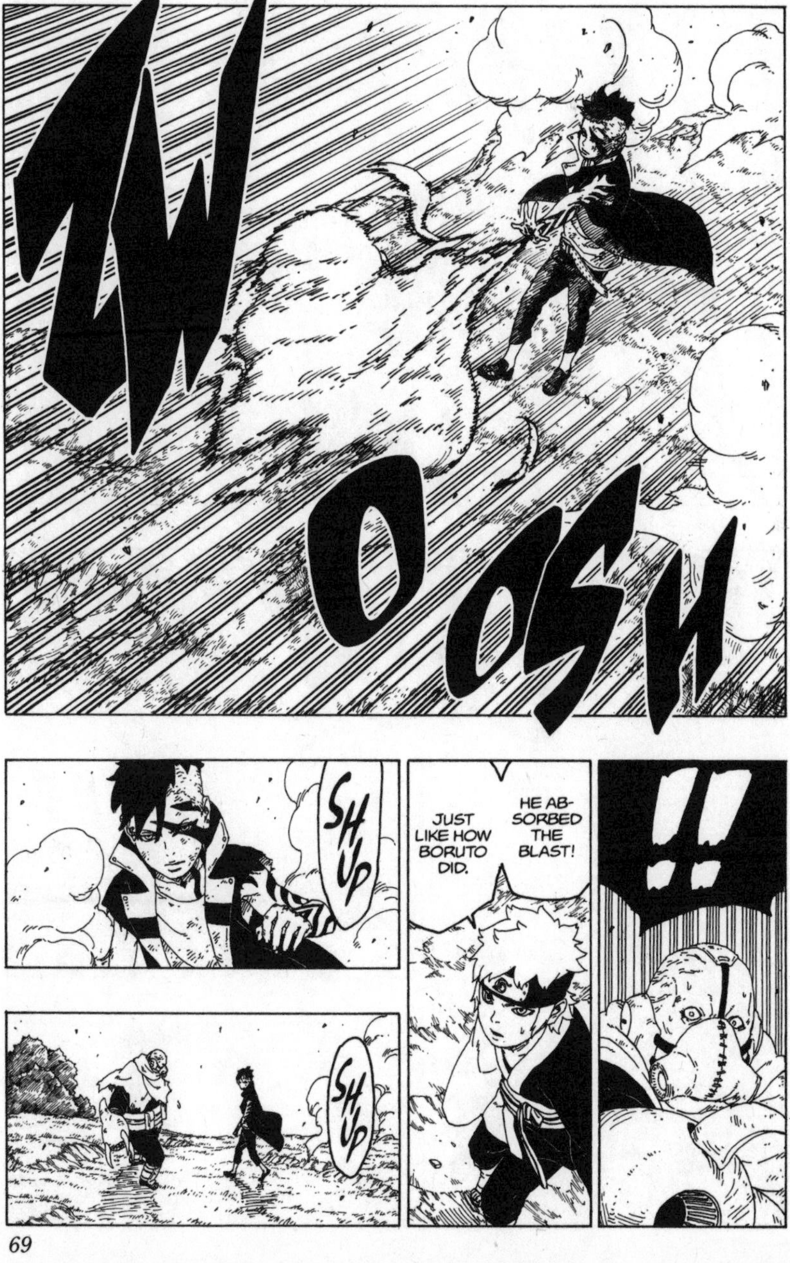
ZWOOSH
!!
HE ABSORBED THE BLAST!
JUST LIKE HOW BORUTO DID.
SHUP
SHUP

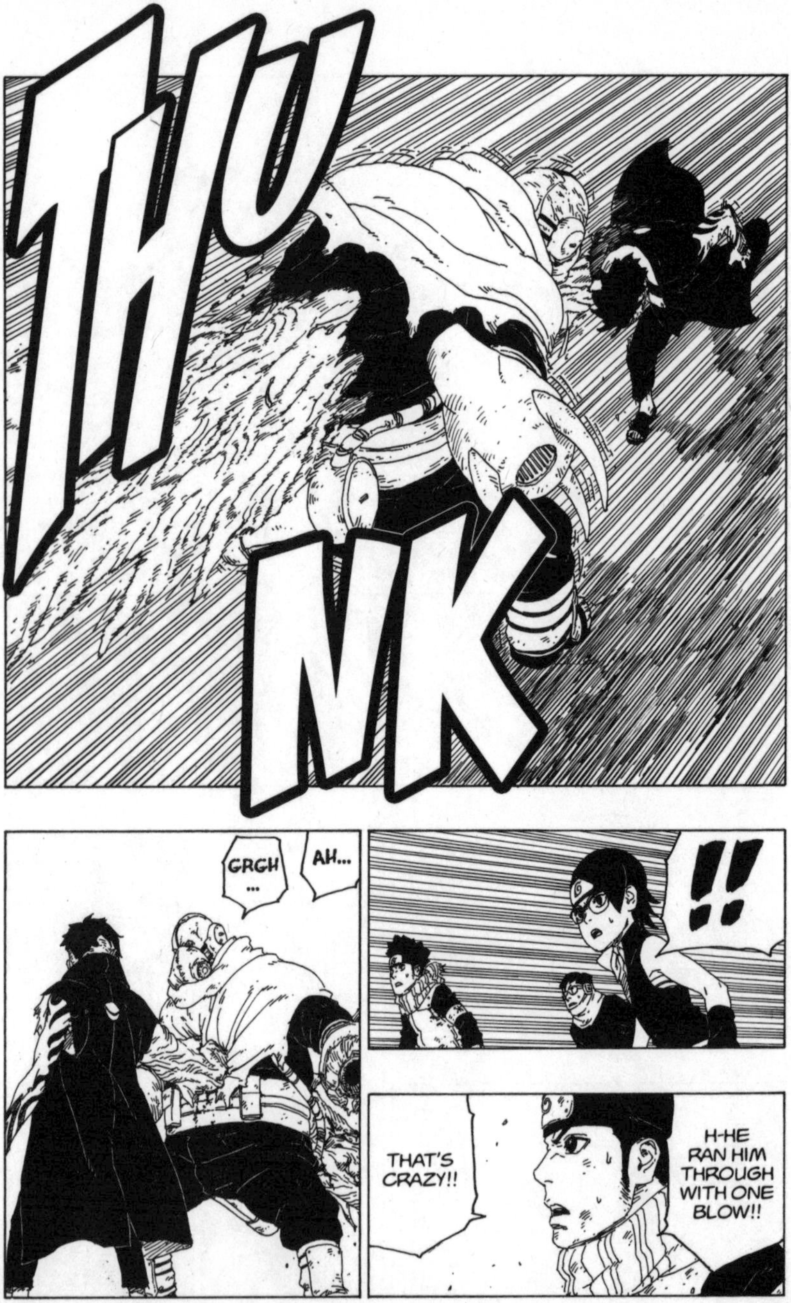
THUNK
!!
H-HE RAN HIM THROUGH WITH ONE BLOW!!
THAT'S CRAZY!!
AH...
GRGH...

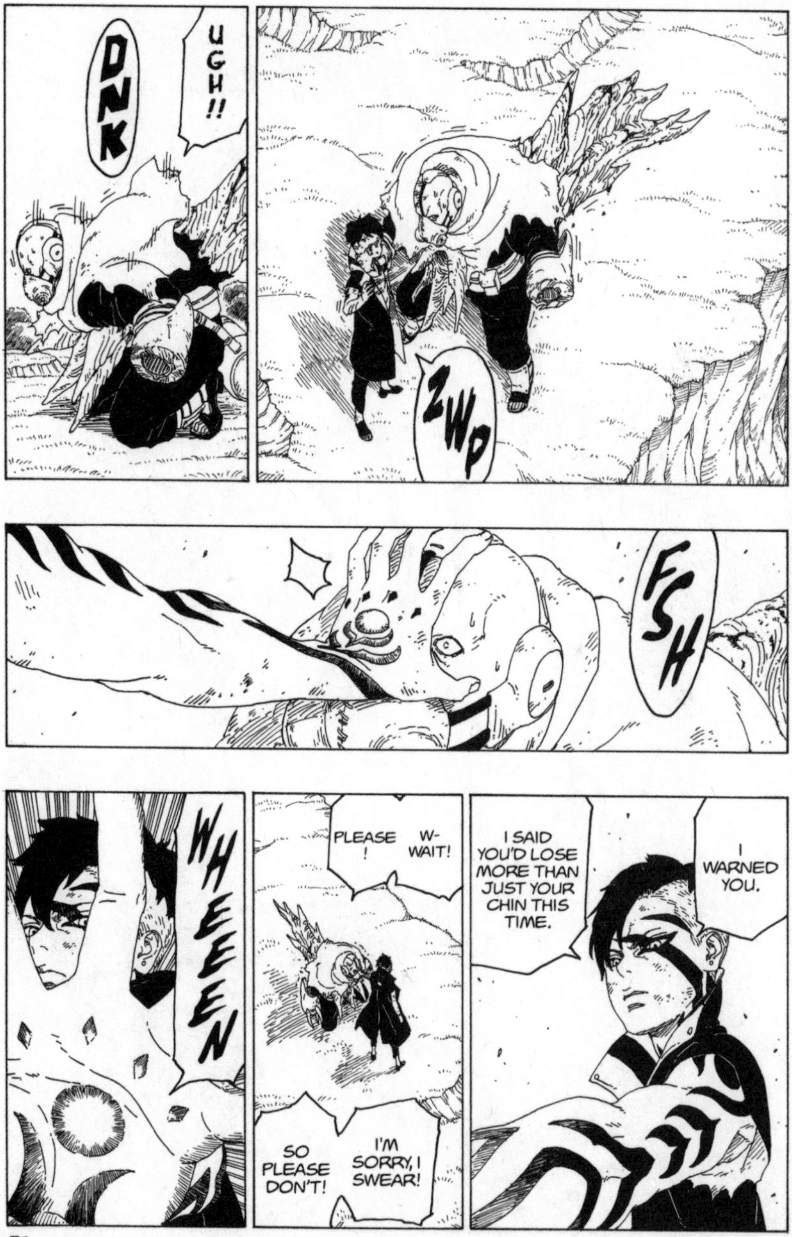
ZWP
UGH!!
DNK
FSH
I WARNED YOU.
I SAID YOU'D LOSE MORE THAN JUST YOUR CHIN THIS TIME.
W-WAIT!
PLEASE!
I'M SORRY, I SWEAR!
SO PLEASE DON'T!
WHEEEEN

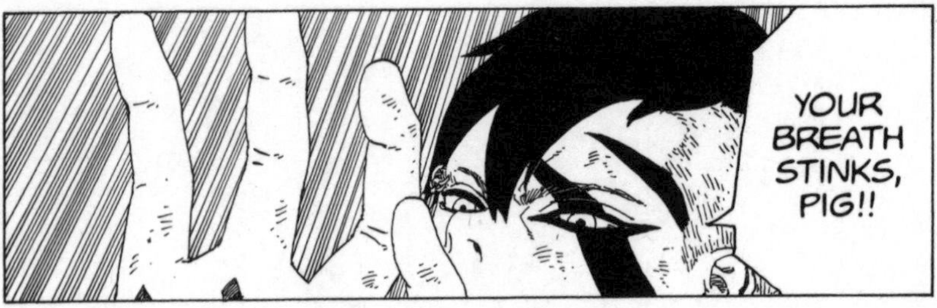
YOUR BREATH STINKS, PIG!!
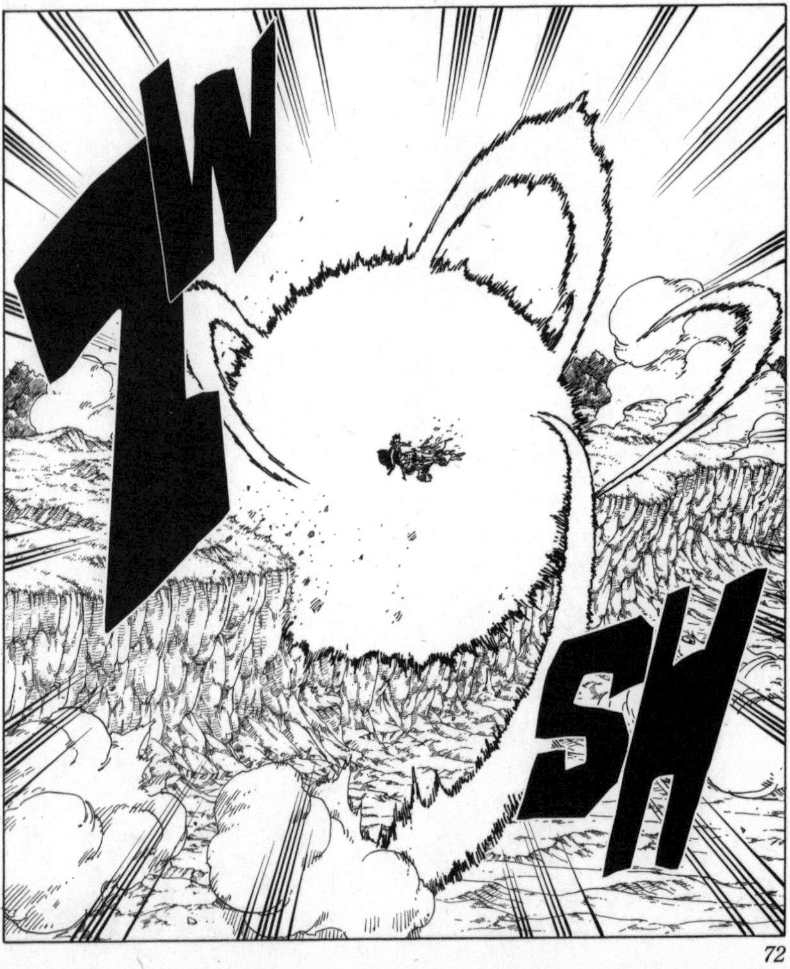
ZWISH

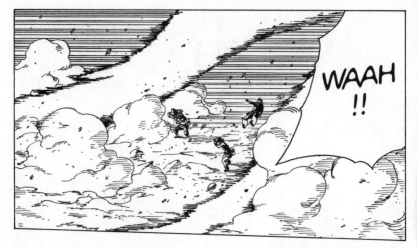

WAAH
!!

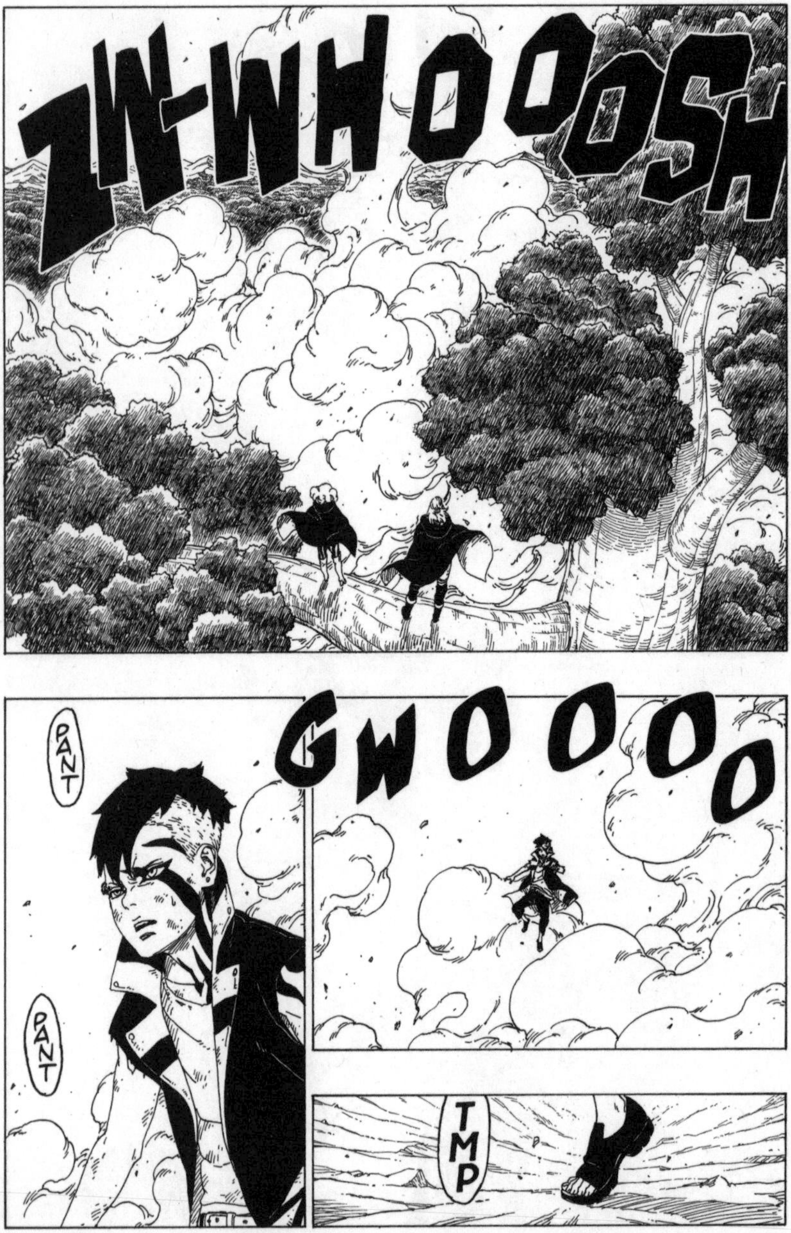
ZN-WHOOOSH
GWOOOOO
TMP
PANT
PANT

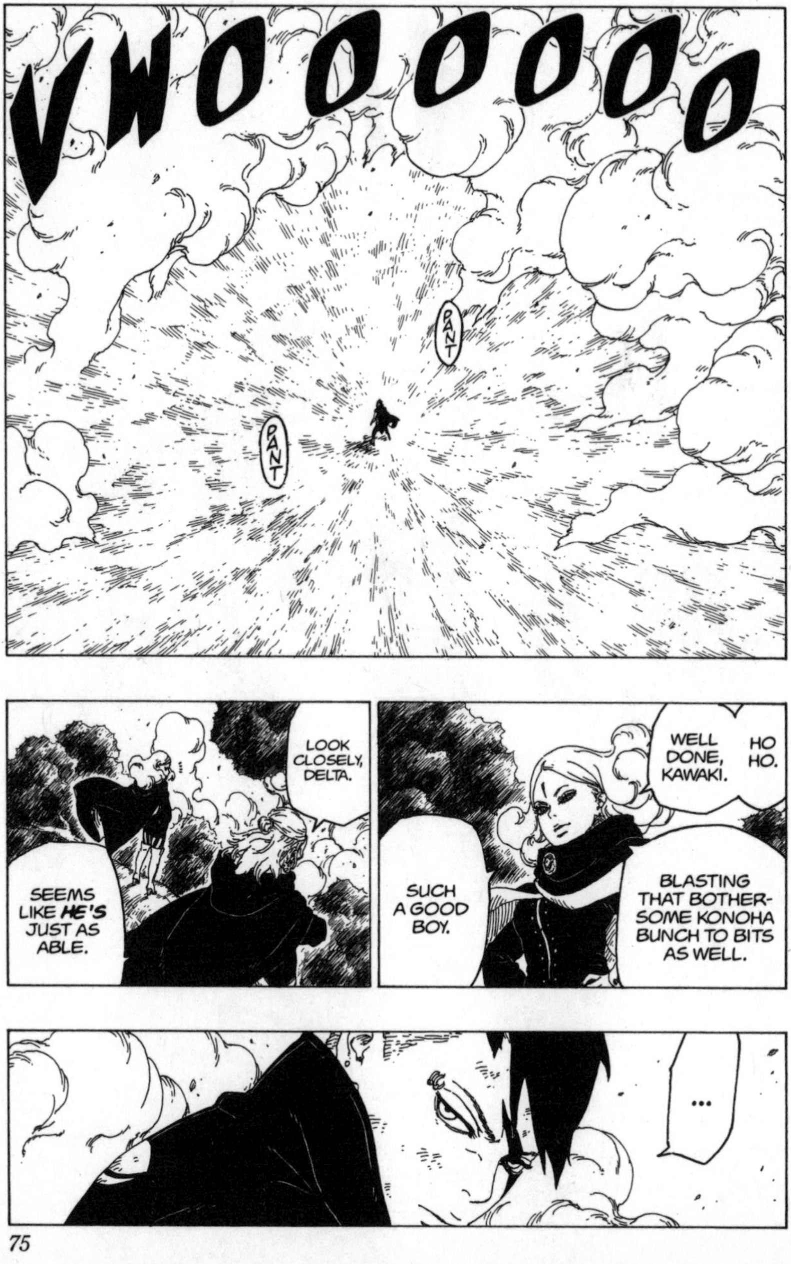
VWOOOOOO
PANT
PANT
HO HO.
WELL DONE, KAWAKI.
BLASTING THAT BOTHER-SOME KONOHA BUNCH TO BITS AS WELL.
SUCH A GOOD BOY.
LOOK CLOSELY, DELTA.
SEEMS LIKE HE'S JUST AS ABLE.
...

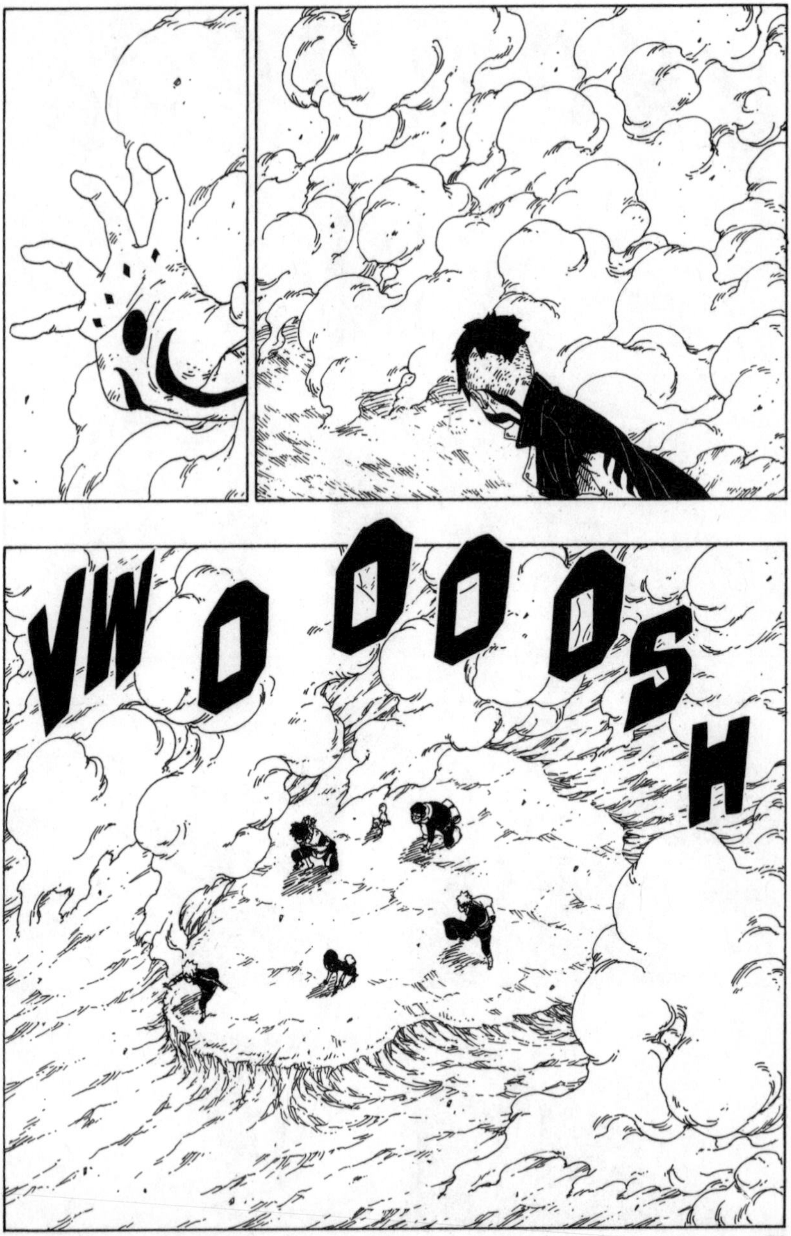
VWOOOOSH

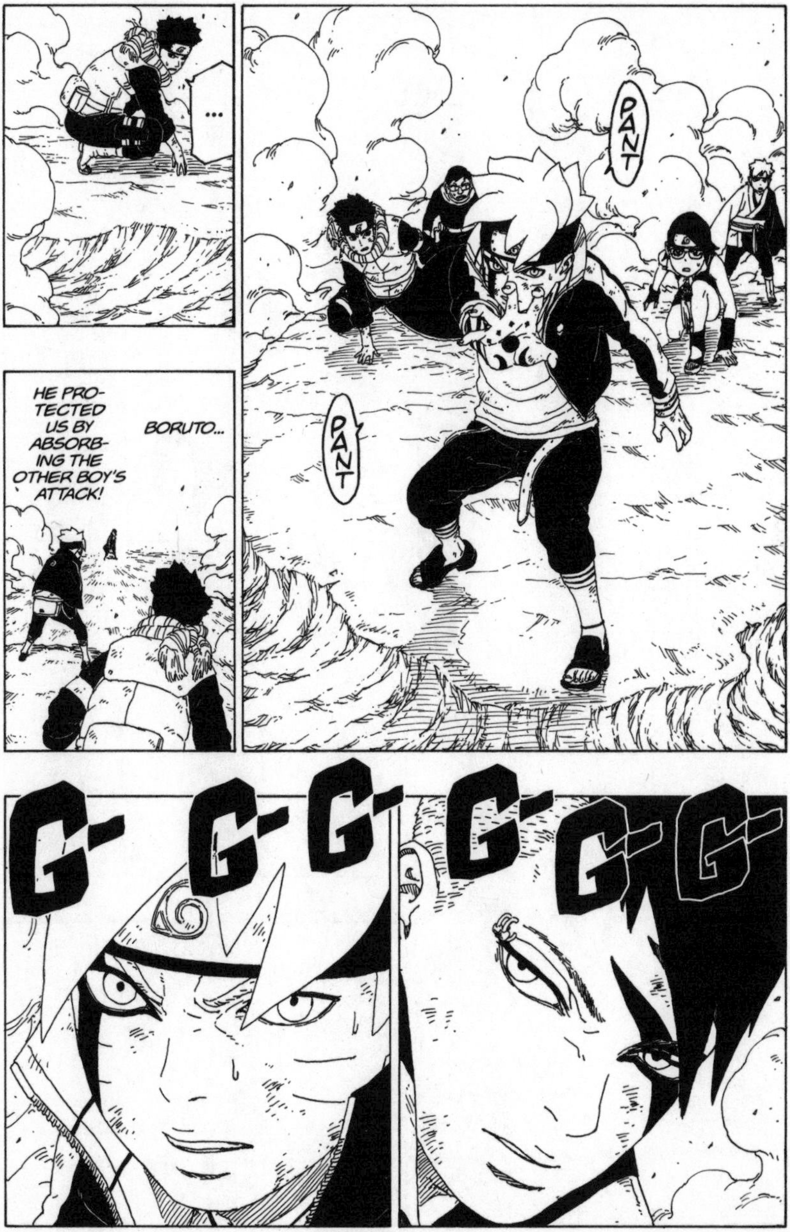
PANT
PANT
...
BORUTO...
HE PROTECTED US BY ABSORBING THE OTHER BOY'S ATTACK!
G- G- G- G- G- G-

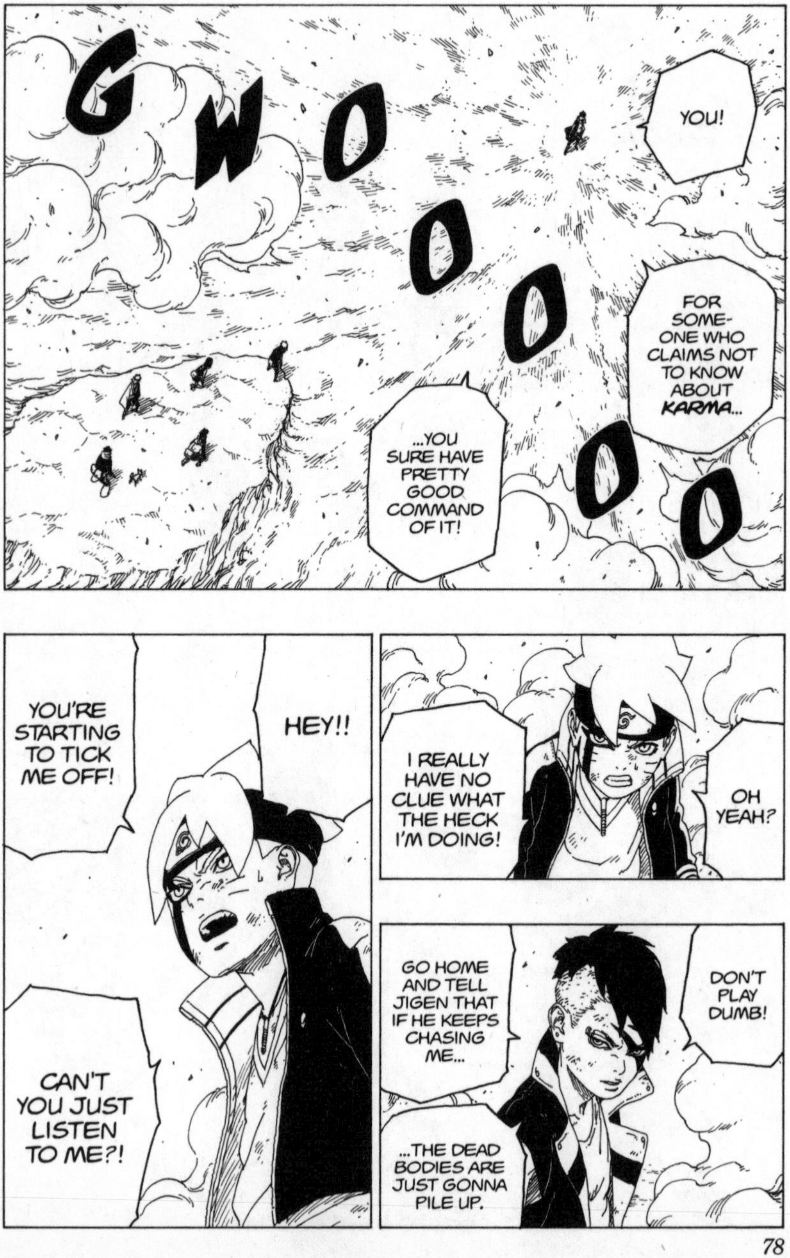
GWOOOOOO
YOU!
FOR SOMEONE WHO CLAIMS NOT TO KNOW ABOUT *KARMA*...
...YOU SURE HAVE PRETTY GOOD COMMAND OF IT!
I REALLY HAVE NO CLUE WHAT THE HECK I'M DOING!
OH YEAH?
DON'T PLAY DUMB!
GO HOME AND TELL JIGEN THAT IF HE KEEPS CHASING ME...
...THE DEAD BODIES ARE JUST GONNA PILE UP.
HEY!!
YOU'RE STARTING TO TICK ME OFF!
CAN'T YOU JUST LISTEN TO ME?!

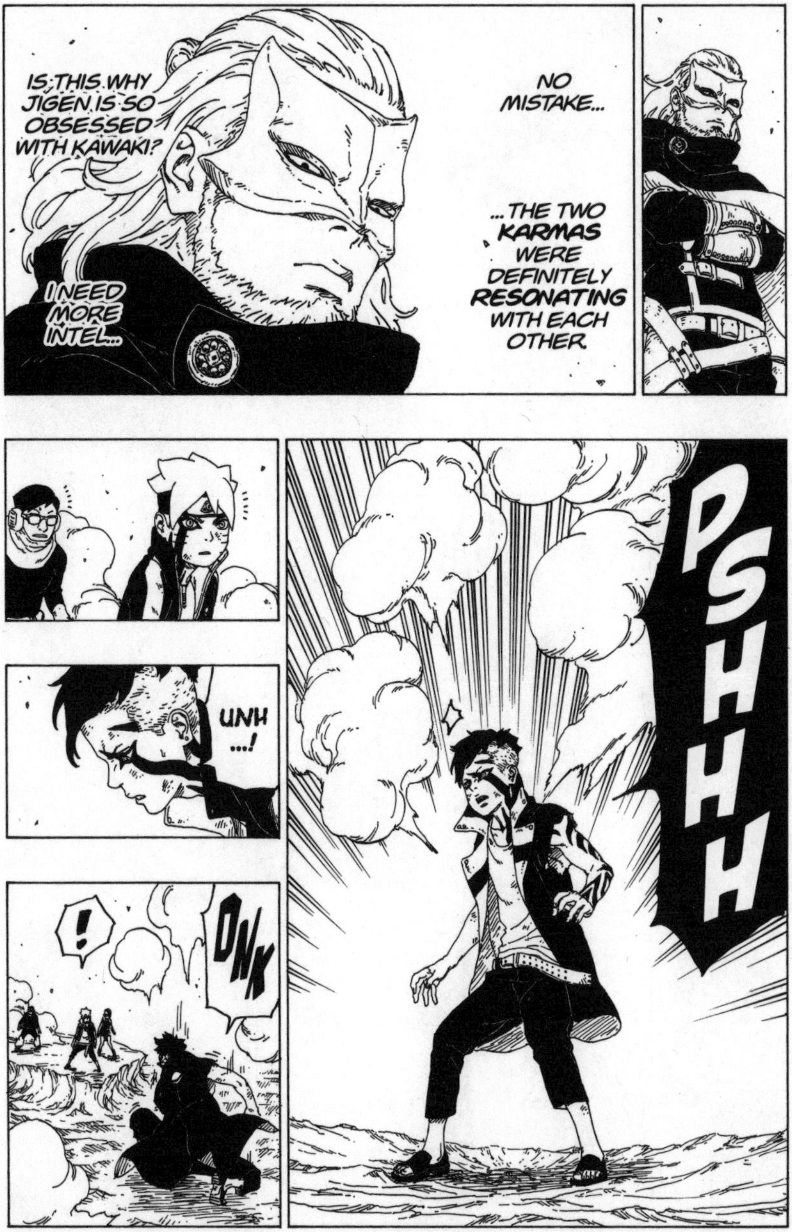
NO MISTAKE...
...THE TWO KARMAS WERE DEFINITELY RESONATING WITH EACH OTHER.
IS THIS WHY JIGEN IS SO OBSESSED WITH KAWAKI?
I NEED MORE INTEL...
PSHHH
UNH ...!
DNK
!

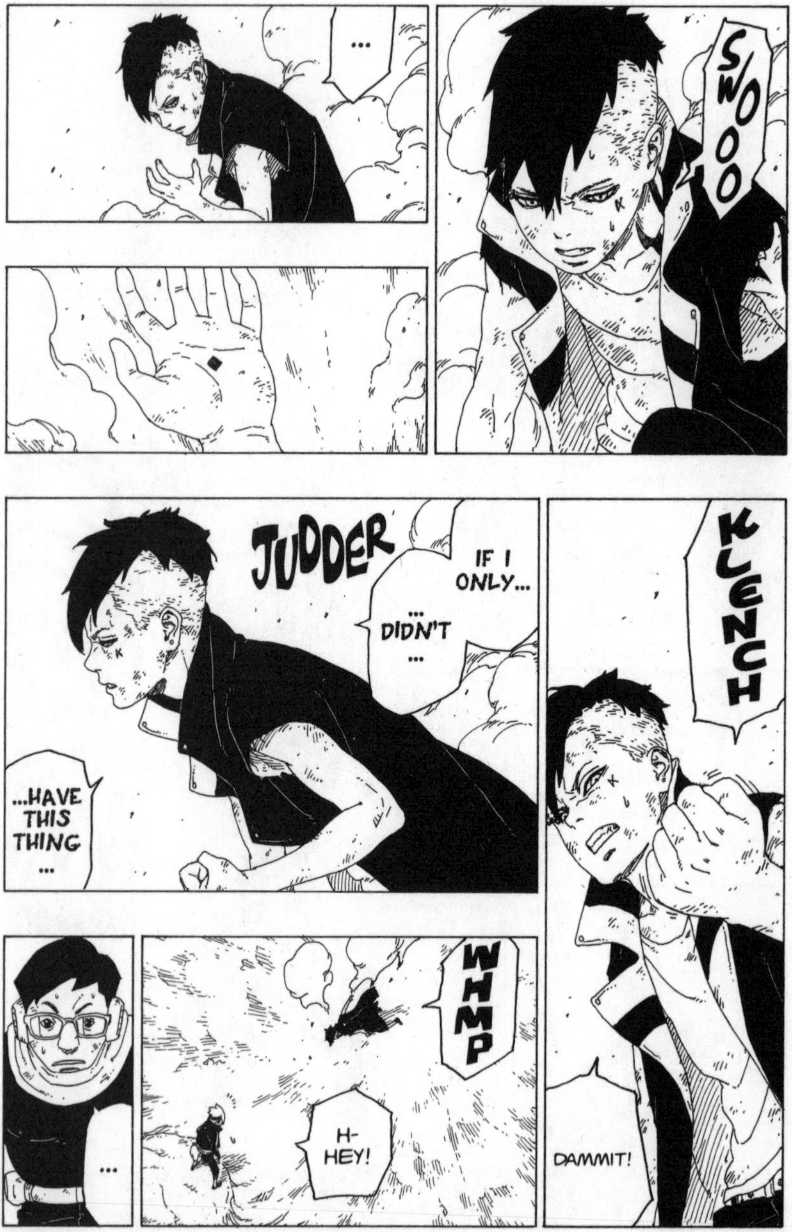
SWOOO
...
JUDDER
IF I ONLY...
...DIDN'T...
...HAVE THIS THING...
KLENCH
DAMMIT!
WHMP
H-HEY!
...

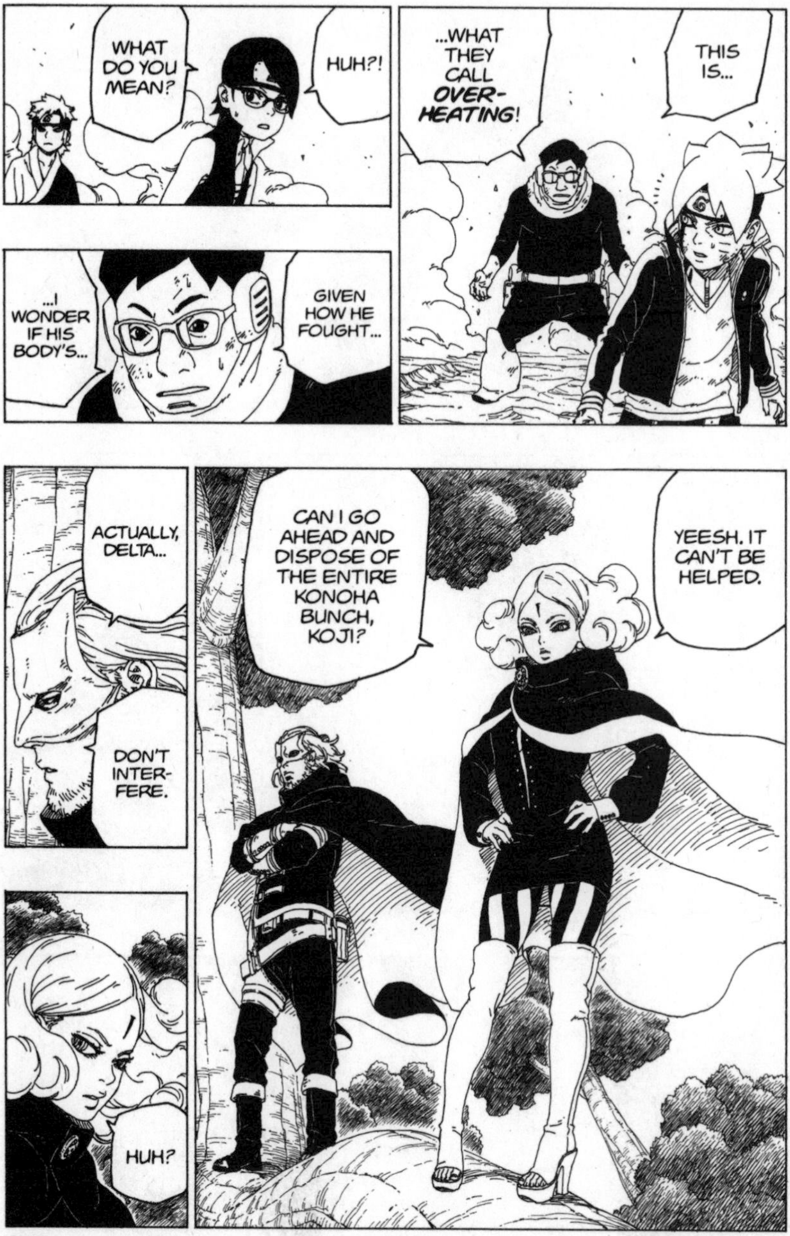
THIS IS...
...WHAT THEY CALL OVER-HEATING!
HUH?!
WHAT DO YOU MEAN?
GIVEN HOW HE FOUGHT...
...I WONDER IF HIS BODY'S...
YEESH. IT CAN'T BE HELPED.
CAN I GO AHEAD AND DISPOSE OF THE ENTIRE KONOHA BUNCH, KOJI?
ACTUALLY, DELTA...
DON'T INTER-FERE.
HUH?

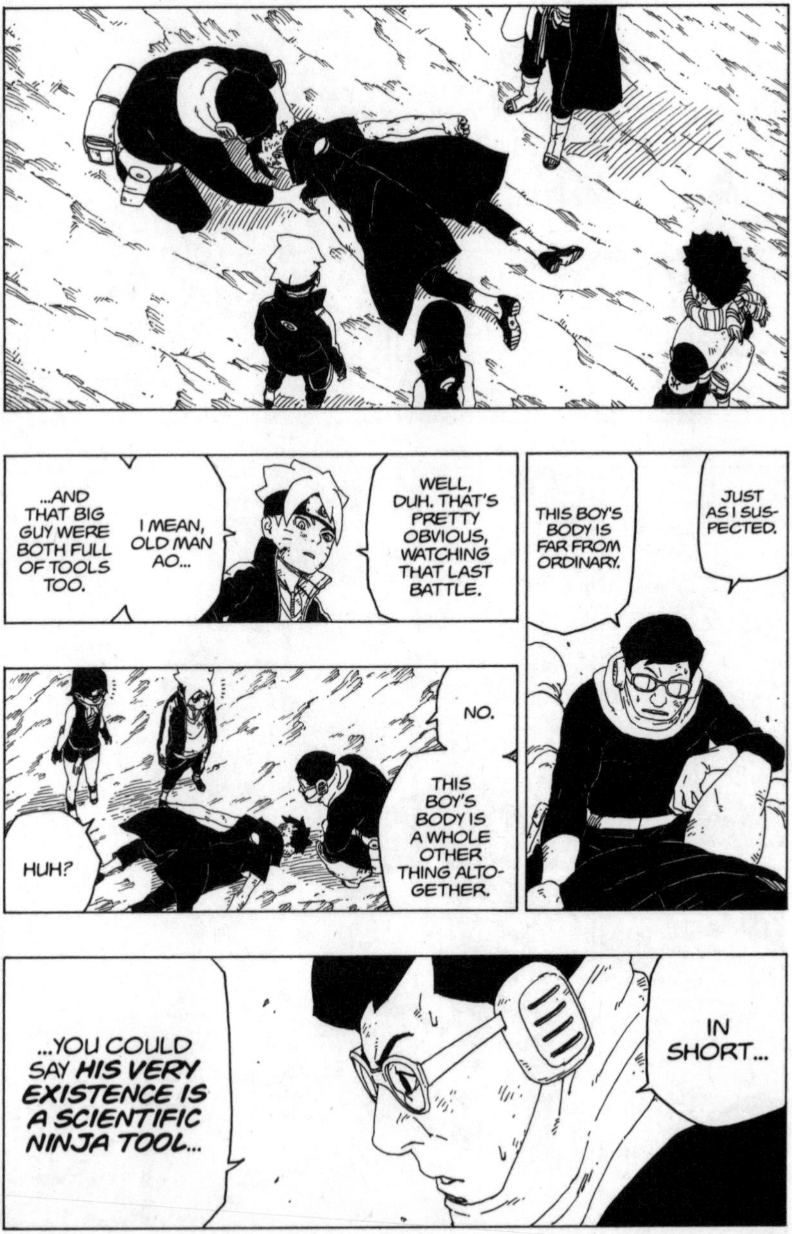
JUST AS I SUSPECTED.
THIS BOY'S BODY IS FAR FROM ORDINARY.
WELL, DUH. THAT'S PRETTY OBVIOUS, WATCHING THAT LAST BATTLE.
I MEAN, OLD MAN AO...
...AND THAT BIG GUY WERE BOTH FULL OF TOOLS TOO.
NO.
THIS BOY'S BODY IS A WHOLE OTHER THING ALTOGETHER.
HUH?
IN SHORT...
...YOU COULD SAY **HIS VERY EXISTENCE IS A SCIENTIFIC NINJA TOOL...**

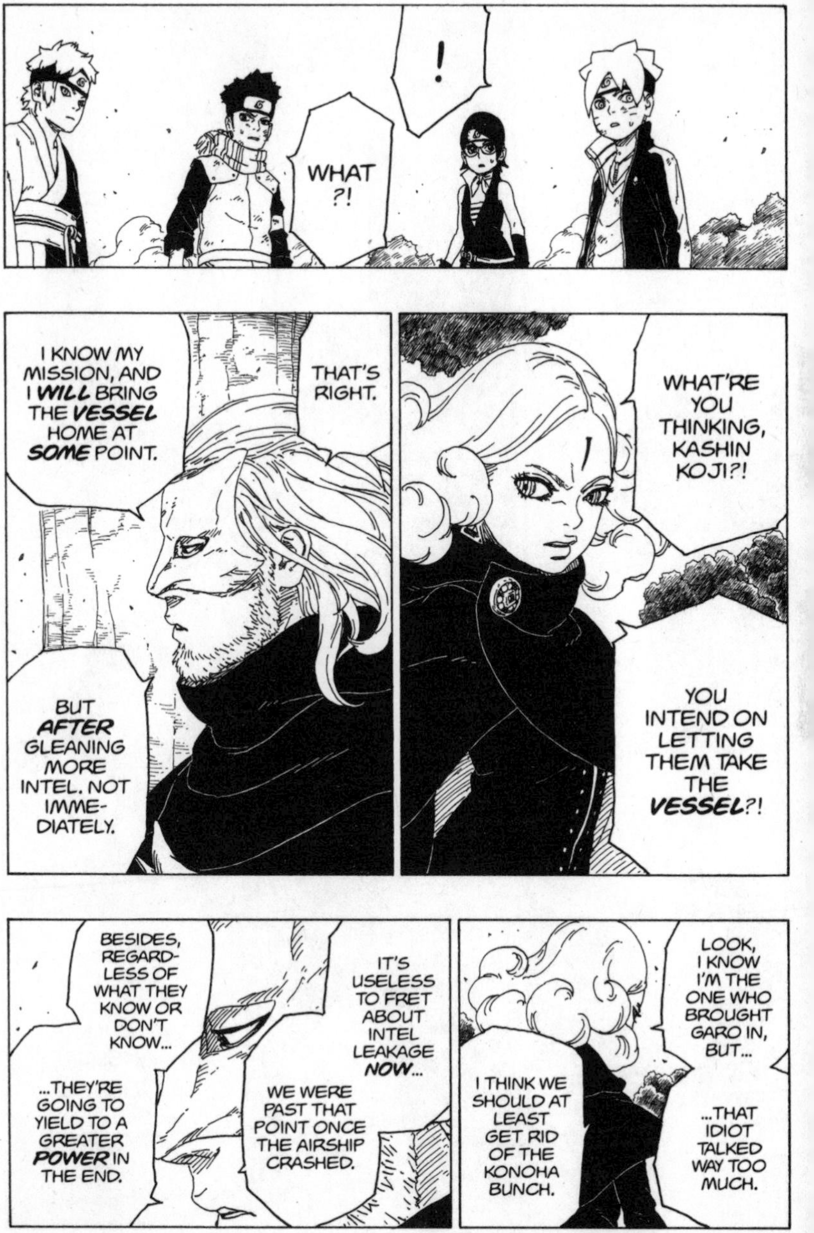
!
WHAT ?!
WHAT'RE YOU THINKING, KASHIN KOJI?!
YOU INTEND ON LETTING THEM TAKE THE VESSEL?!
THAT'S RIGHT.
I KNOW MY MISSION, AND I WILL BRING THE VESSEL HOME AT SOME POINT.
BUT AFTER GLEANING MORE INTEL. NOT IMME-DIATELY.
LOOK, I KNOW I'M THE ONE WHO BROUGHT GARO IN, BUT...
...THAT IDIOT TALKED WAY TOO MUCH.
I THINK WE SHOULD AT LEAST GET RID OF THE KONOHA BUNCH.
IT'S USELESS TO FRET ABOUT INTEL LEAKAGE NOW...
WE WERE PAST THAT POINT ONCE THE AIRSHIP CRASHED.
BESIDES, REGARDLESS OF WHAT THEY KNOW OR DON'T KNOW...
...THEY'RE GOING TO YIELD TO A GREATER POWER IN THE END.

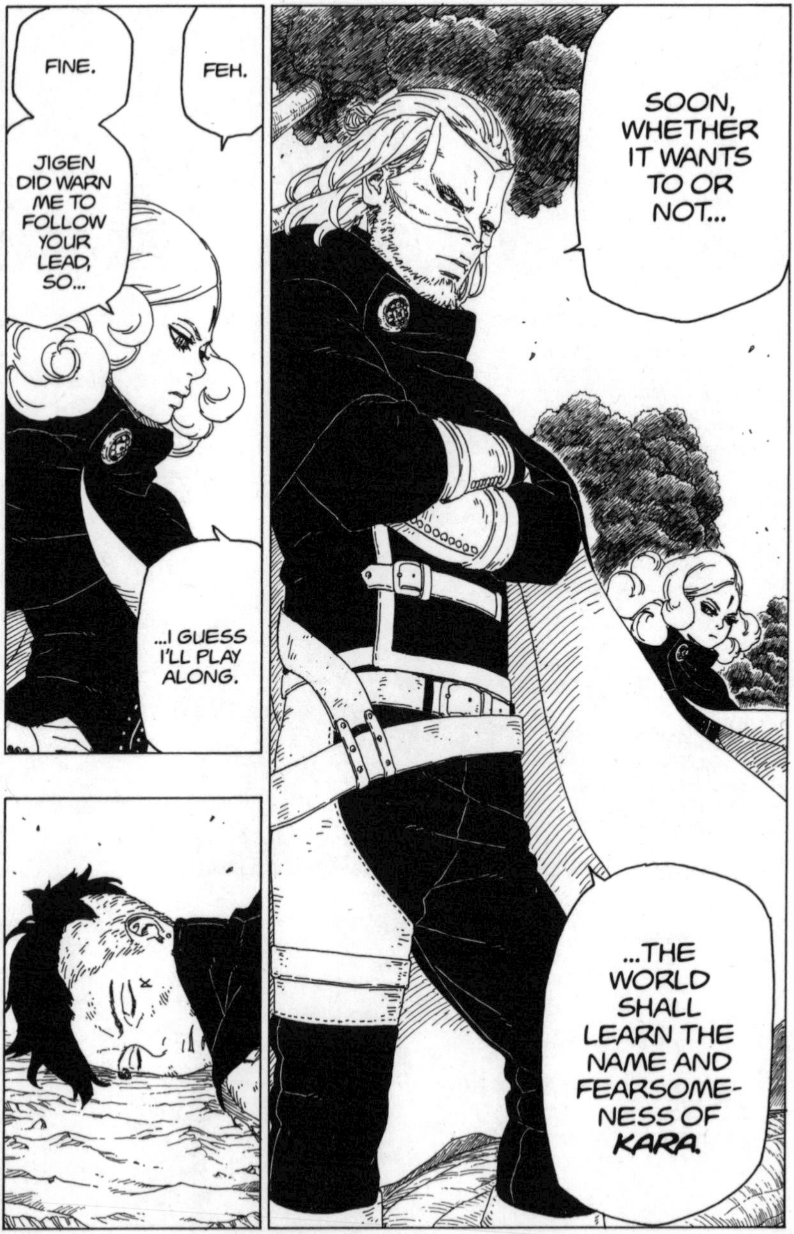
SOON, WHETHER IT WANTS TO OR NOT...
...THE WORLD SHALL LEARN THE NAME AND FEARSOME-NESS OF ***KARA***.
FEH.
FINE.
JIGEN DID WARN ME TO FOLLOW YOUR LEAD, SO...
...I GUESS I'LL PLAY ALONG.

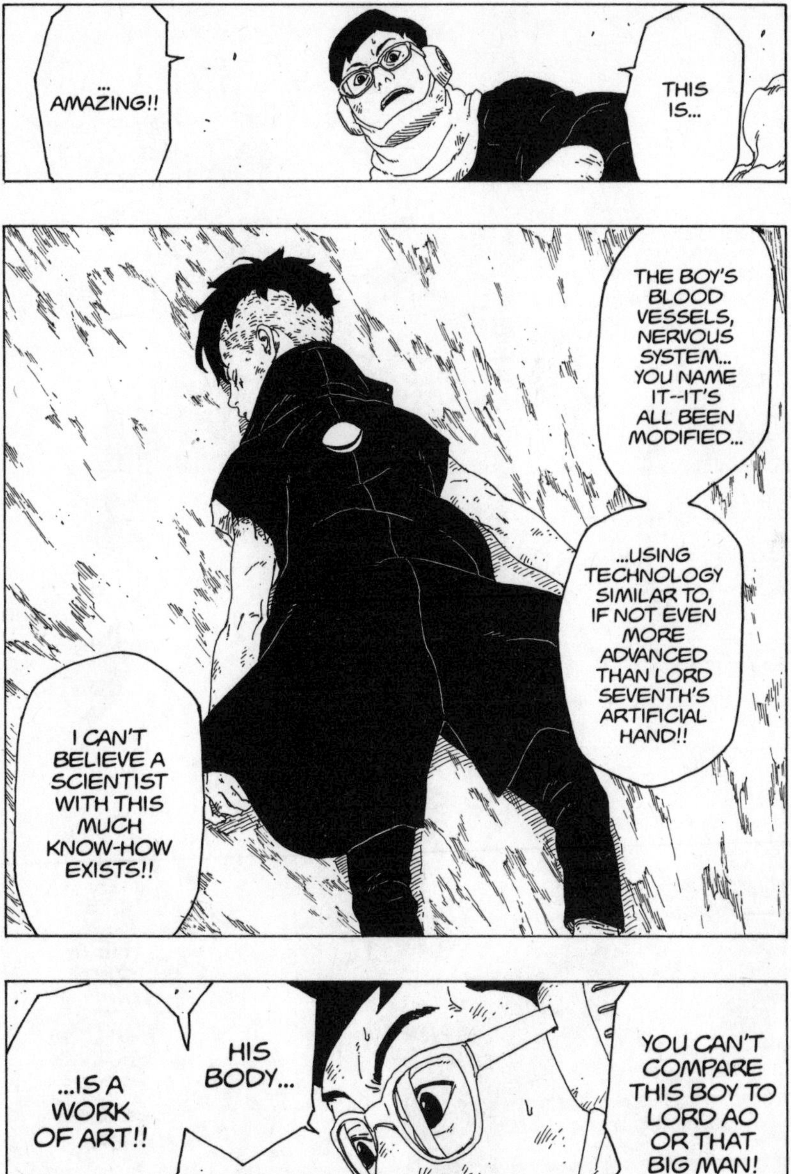
THIS IS...
... AMAZING!!
THE BOY'S BLOOD VESSELS, NERVOUS SYSTEM... YOU NAME IT--IT'S ALL BEEN MODIFIED...
...USING TECHNOLOGY SIMILAR TO, IF NOT EVEN MORE ADVANCED THAN LORD SEVENTH'S ARTIFICIAL HAND!!
I CAN'T BELIEVE A SCIENTIST WITH THIS MUCH KNOW-HOW EXISTS!!
YOU CAN'T COMPARE THIS BOY TO LORD AO OR THAT BIG MAN!
HIS BODY...
...IS A WORK OF ART!!

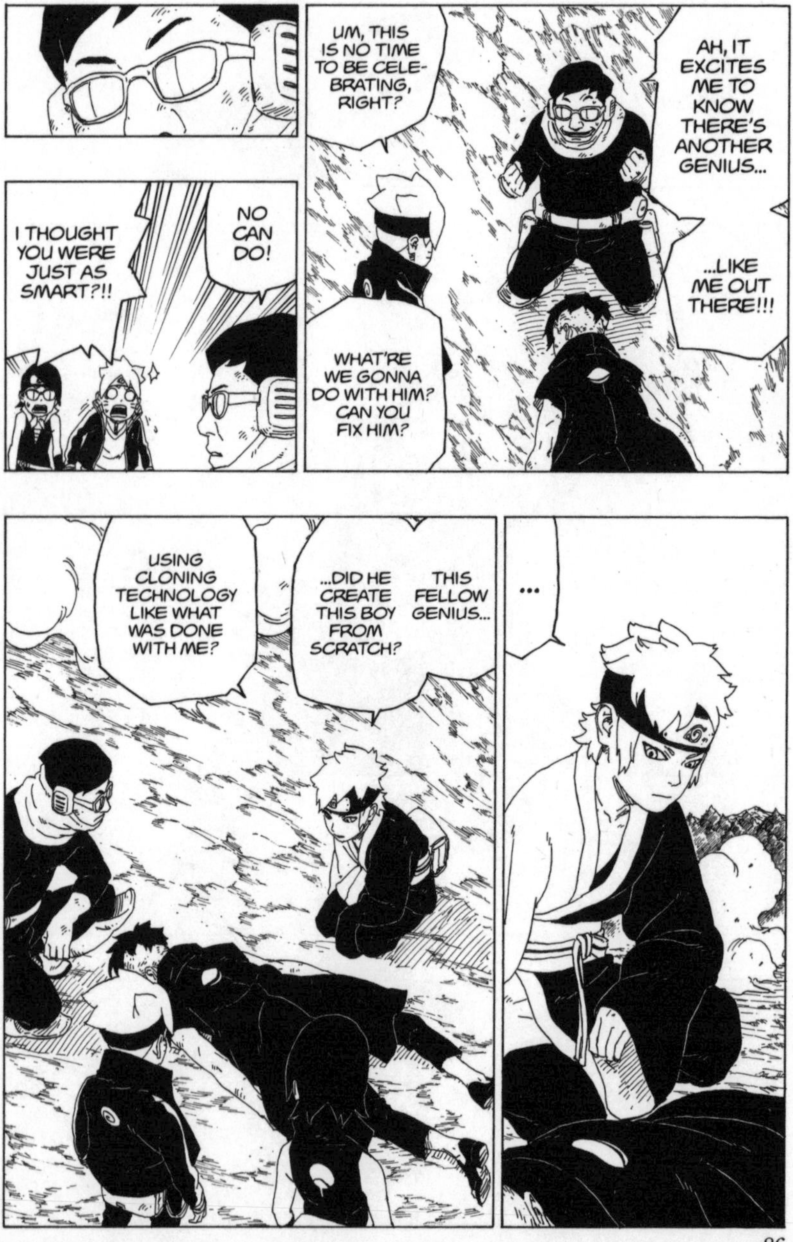
AH, IT EXCITES ME TO KNOW THERE'S ANOTHER GENIUS...
...LIKE ME OUT THERE!!!
UM, THIS IS NO TIME TO BE CELE-BRATING, RIGHT?
WHAT'RE WE GONNA DO WITH HIM? CAN YOU FIX HIM?
NO CAN DO!
I THOUGHT YOU WERE JUST AS SMART?!!
...
THIS FELLOW GENIUS...
...DID HE CREATE THIS BOY FROM SCRATCH?
USING CLONING TECHNOLOGY LIKE WHAT WAS DONE WITH ME?

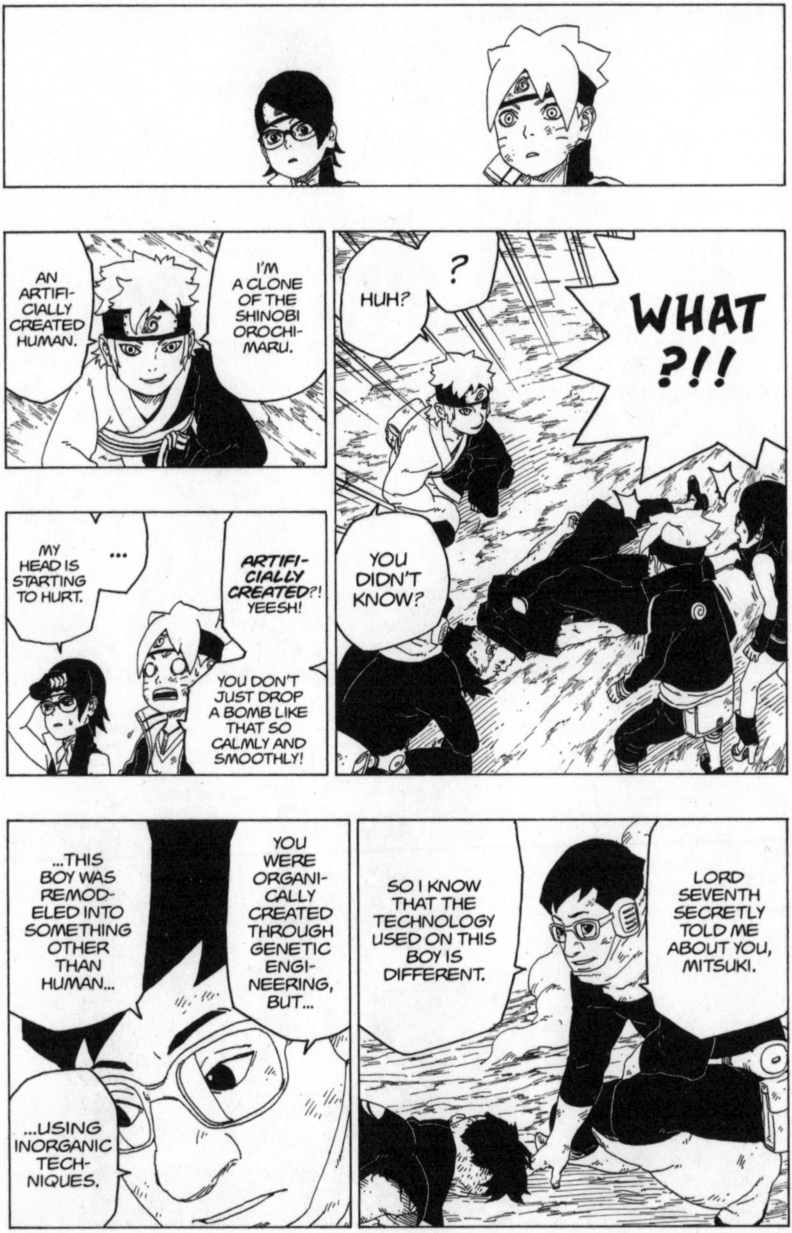
I'M A CLONE OF THE SHINOBI OROCHI-MARU.
AN ARTIFI-CIALLY CREATED HUMAN.
HUH?
?
WHAT ?!!
YOU DIDN'T KNOW?
ARTIFI-CIALLY CREATED?! YEESH!
YOU DON'T JUST DROP A BOMB LIKE THAT SO CALMLY AND SMOOTHLY!
...
MY HEAD IS STARTING TO HURT.
LORD SEVENTH SECRETLY TOLD ME ABOUT YOU, MITSUKI.
SO I KNOW THAT THE TECHNOLOGY USED ON THIS BOY IS DIFFERENT.
YOU WERE ORGANI-CALLY CREATED THROUGH GENETIC ENGI-NEERING, BUT...
...THIS BOY WAS REMOD-ELED INTO SOMETHING OTHER THAN HUMAN...
...USING INORGANIC TECH-NIQUES.

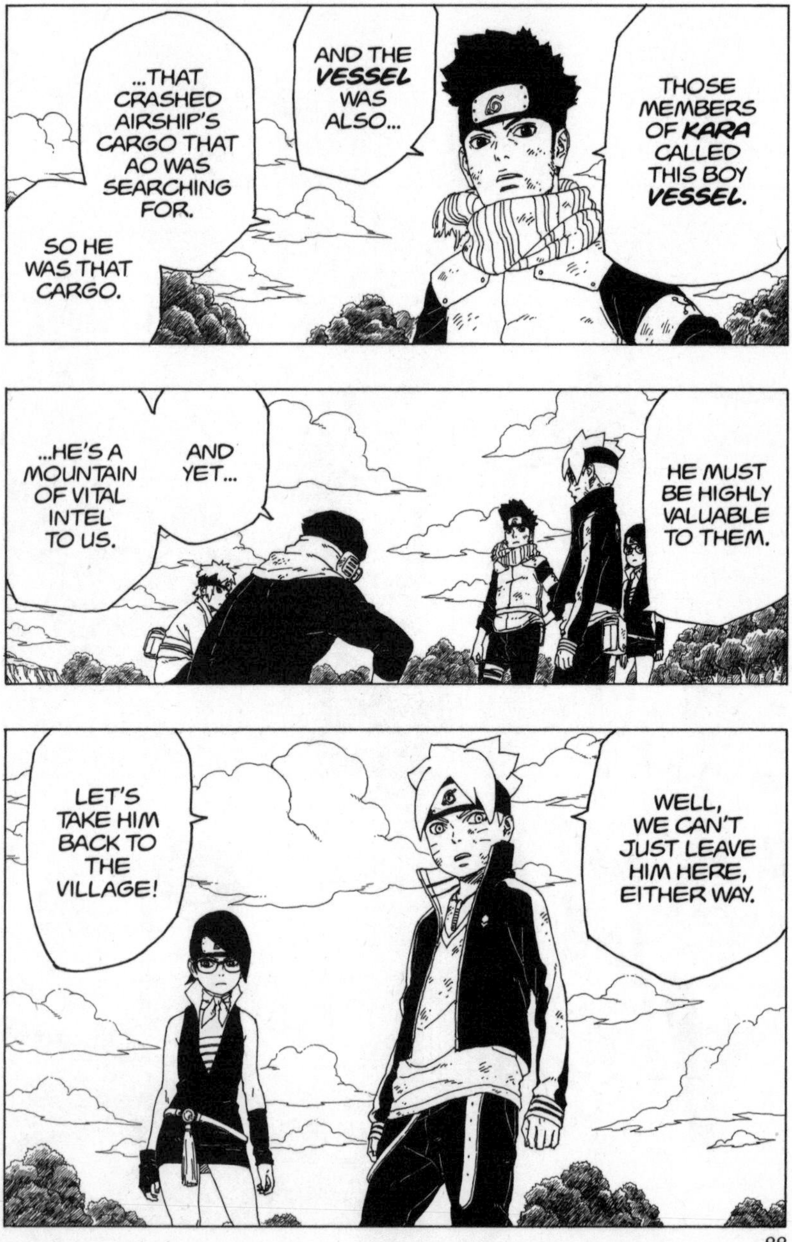
THOSE MEMBERS OF KARA CALLED THIS BOY VESSEL.
AND THE VESSEL WAS ALSO...
...THAT CRASHED AIRSHIP'S CARGO THAT AO WAS SEARCHING FOR.
SO HE WAS THAT CARGO.
HE MUST BE HIGHLY VALUABLE TO THEM.
AND YET...
...HE'S A MOUNTAIN OF VITAL INTEL TO US.
WELL, WE CAN'T JUST LEAVE HIM HERE, EITHER WAY.
LET'S TAKE HIM BACK TO THE VILLAGE!

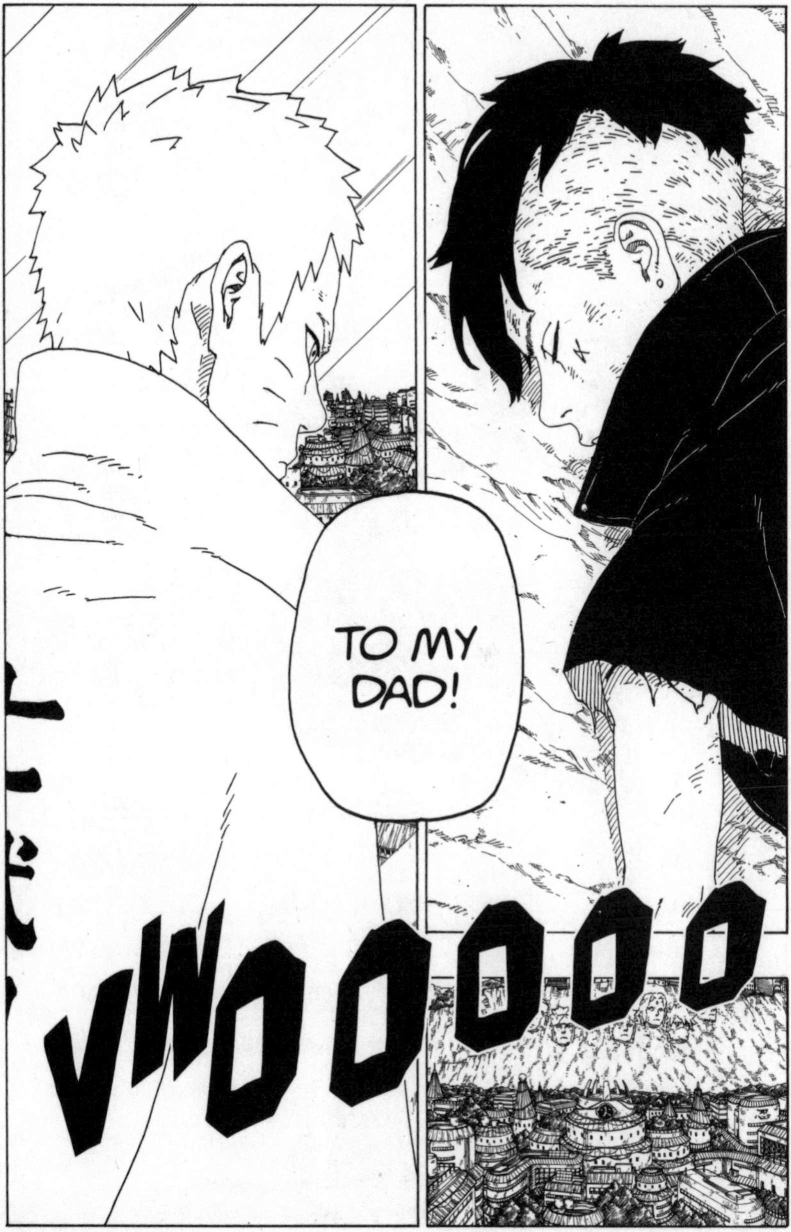
TO MY DAD!
VWOOOOO

NINJA ENCYCLOPEDIA · ENTRY 20

GARO

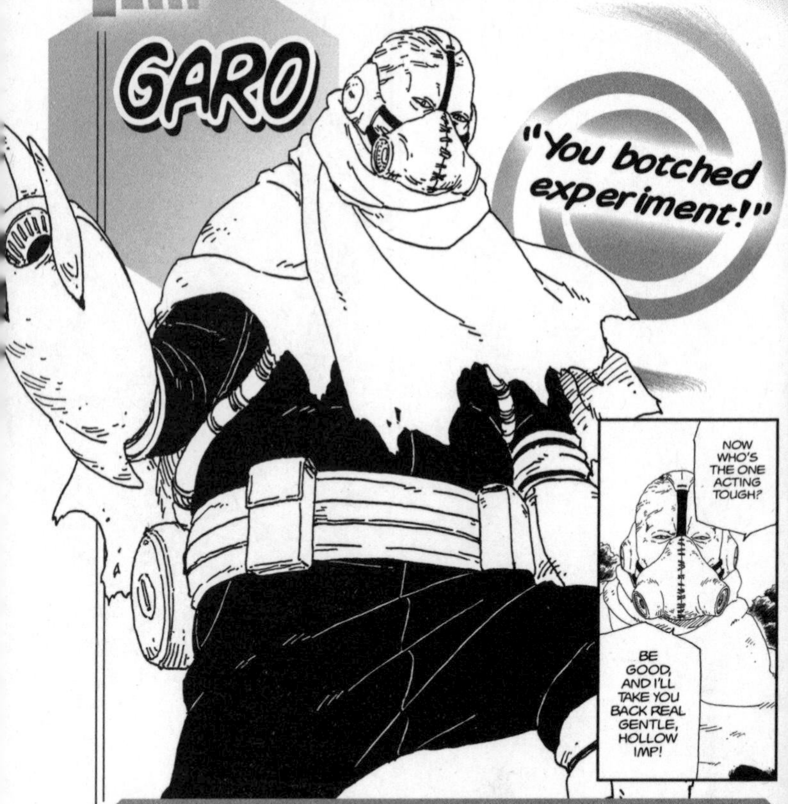
"You botched experiment!"
NOW WHO'S THE ONE ACTING TOUGH?
BE GOOD, AND I'LL TAKE YOU BACK REAL GENTLE, HOLLOW IMP!

Attributes

Strength	132 [192]	Dexterity	85 [125]
Intelligence	77	Chakra	96
Perception	100 [192]	Negotiation	64

Skills

Combat ☆☆☆☆ Coercion & Intimidation ☆☆☆ Interrogation & Torture ☆☆

Shinobi Tools

Muscle Bulking via Condensing, Mode 5 Shinobi Gauntlets, Argos Unit, etc.

*Average attribute value is 60 for ordinary people and 90 for genin. Skill values range from 1 to 5☆ with 5☆ signifying super top-notch.

Number 26: A Present

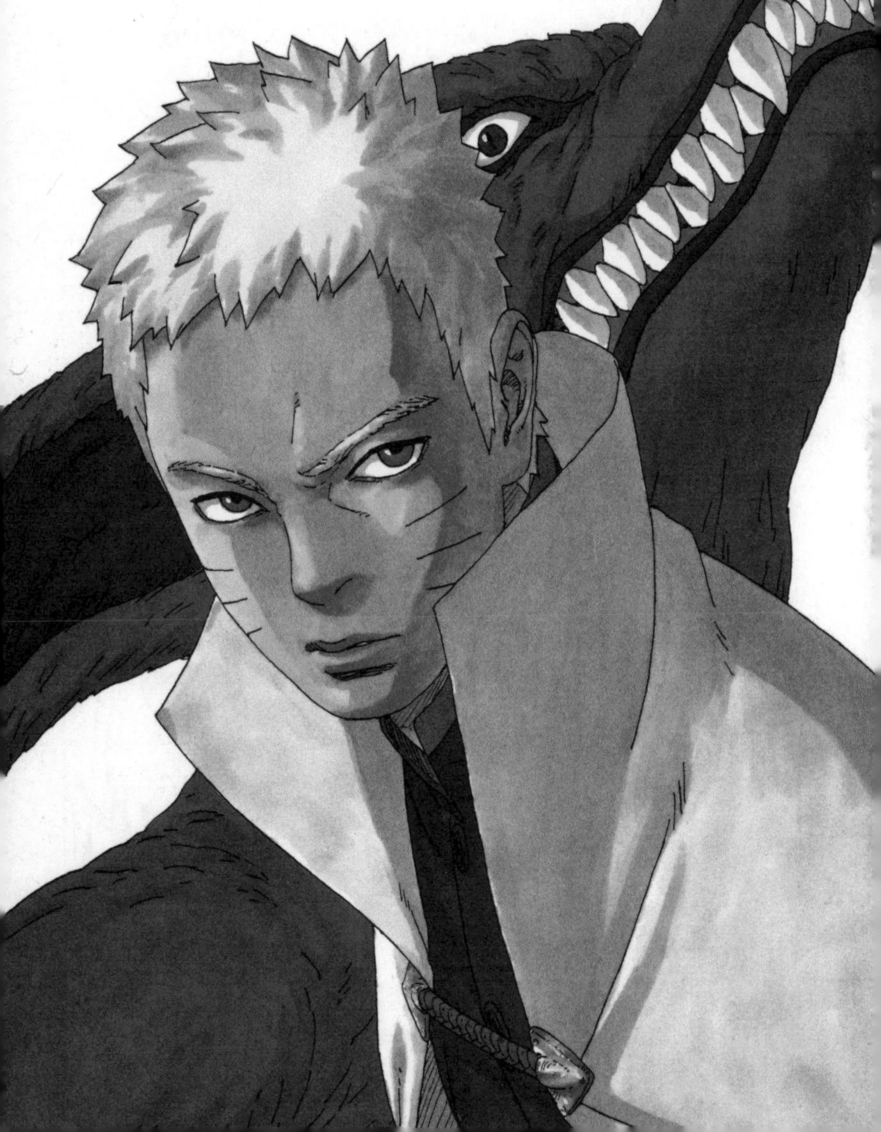

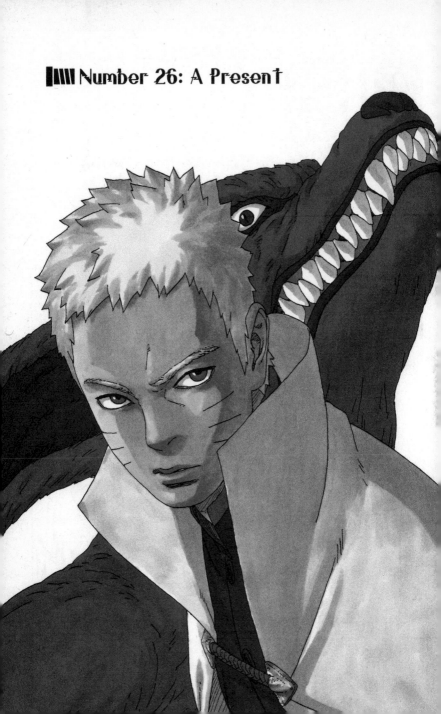

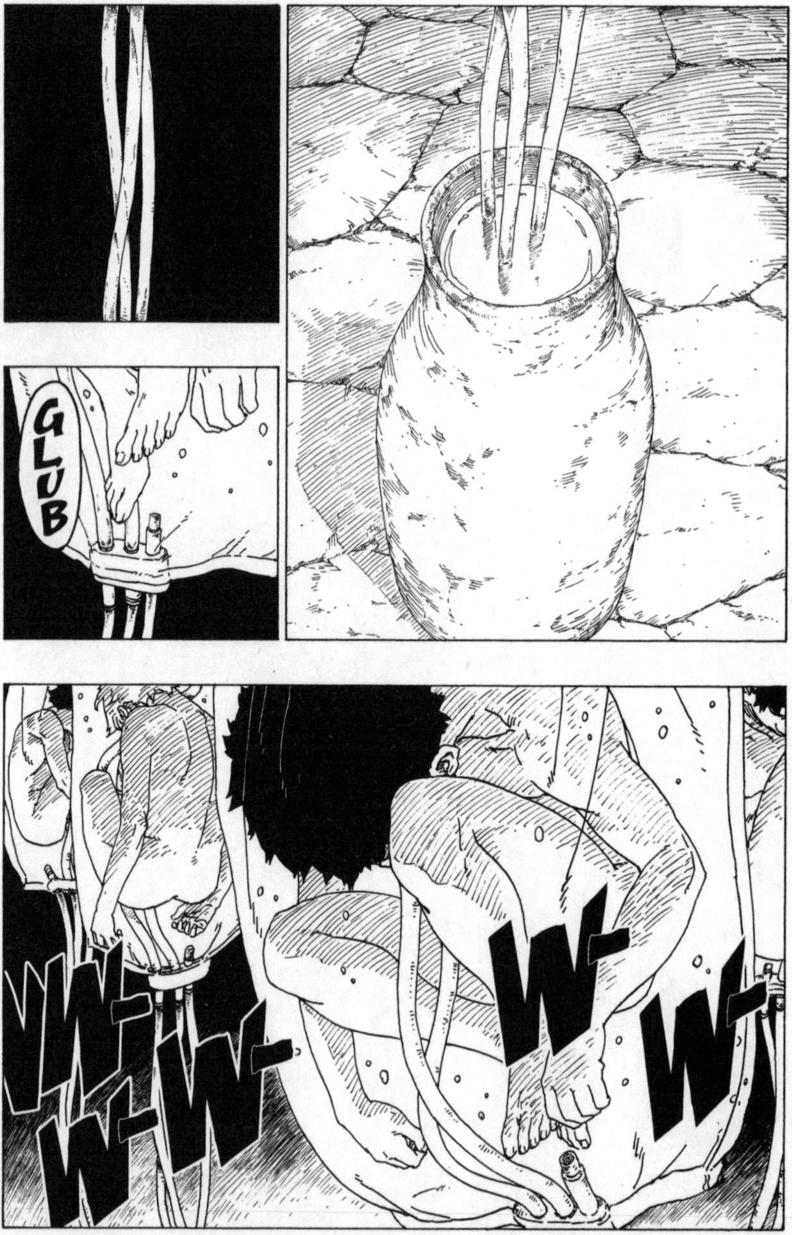
GLUB
W- W-
W-W- W-W-

VW-W- W- W- W- W- W-

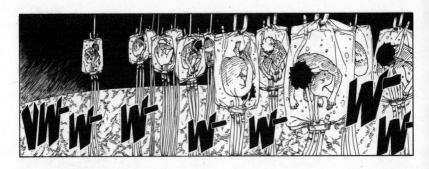

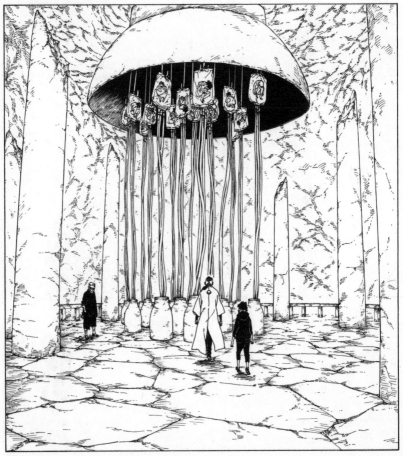

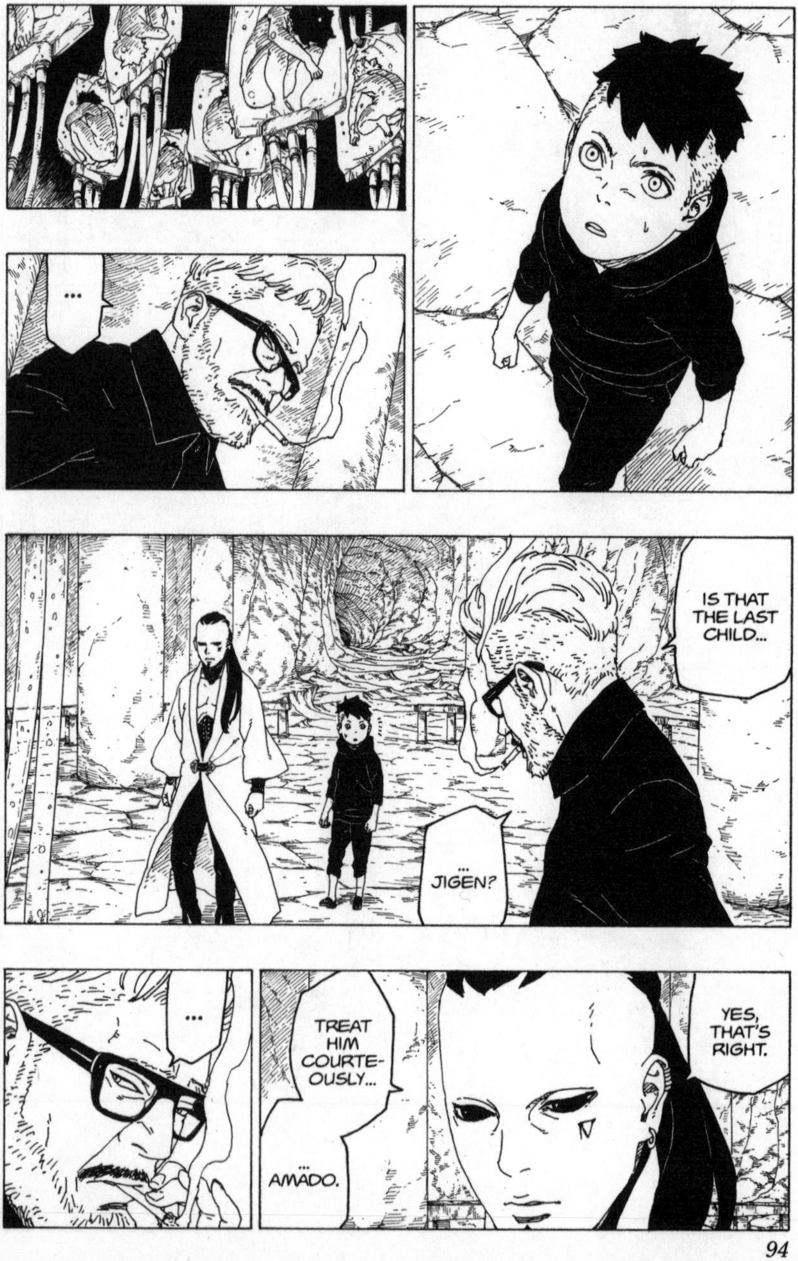
...
IS THAT THE LAST CHILD...
...JIGEN?
YES, THAT'S RIGHT.
TREAT HIM COURTEOUSLY...
...AMADO.
...

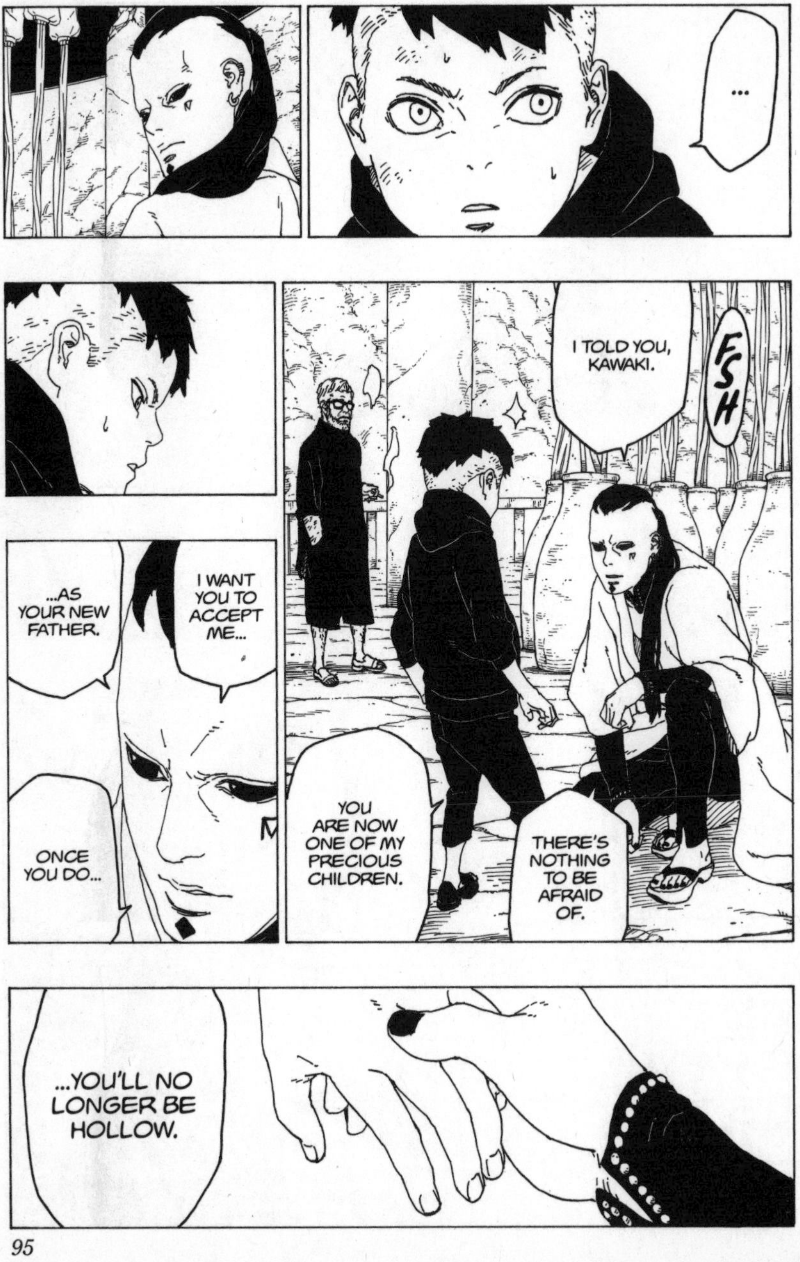
...
I TOLD YOU, KAWAKI.
FSH
THERE'S NOTHING TO BE AFRAID OF.
YOU ARE NOW ONE OF MY PRECIOUS CHILDREN.
I WANT YOU TO ACCEPT ME...
...AS YOUR NEW FATHER.
ONCE YOU DO...
...YOU'LL NO LONGER BE HOLLOW.

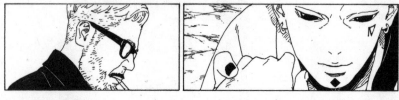

SPLICH

...BECOME PARENT AND CHILD FOR REAL...

WHEN YOU...

...AND I...

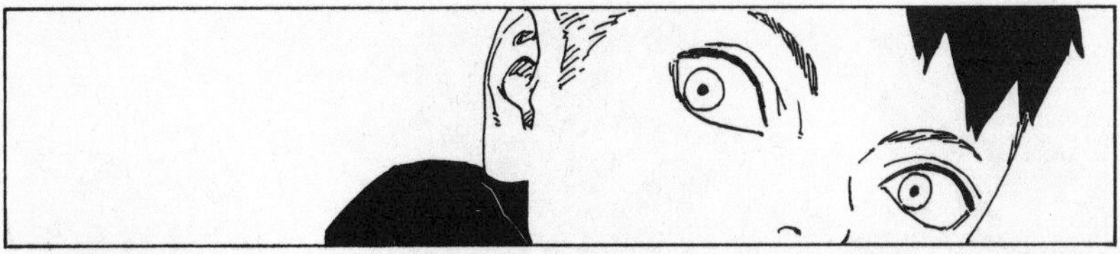
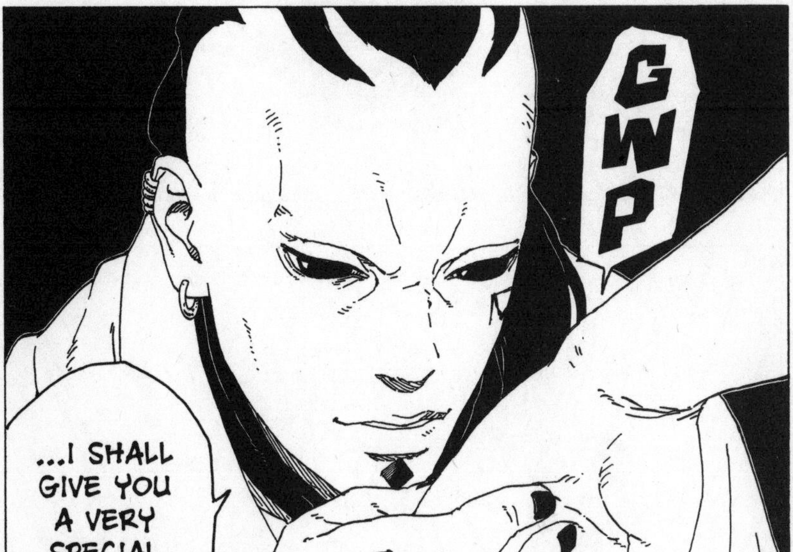
GWP
...I SHALL GIVE YOU A VERY SPECIAL PRESENT.
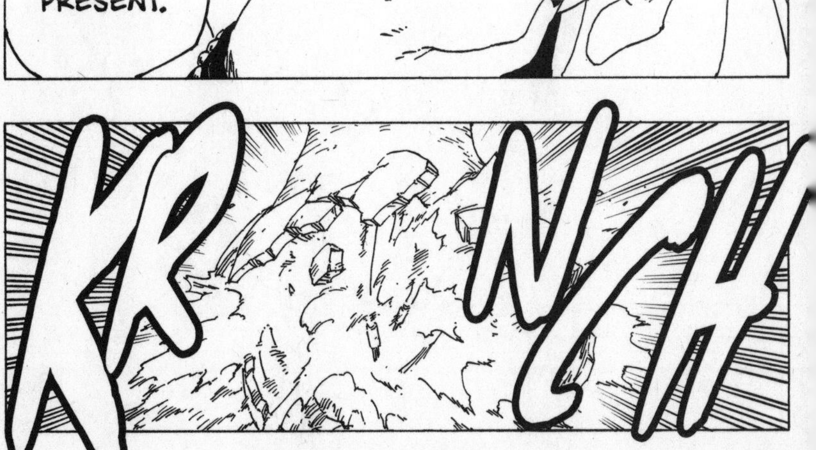
KRNCH

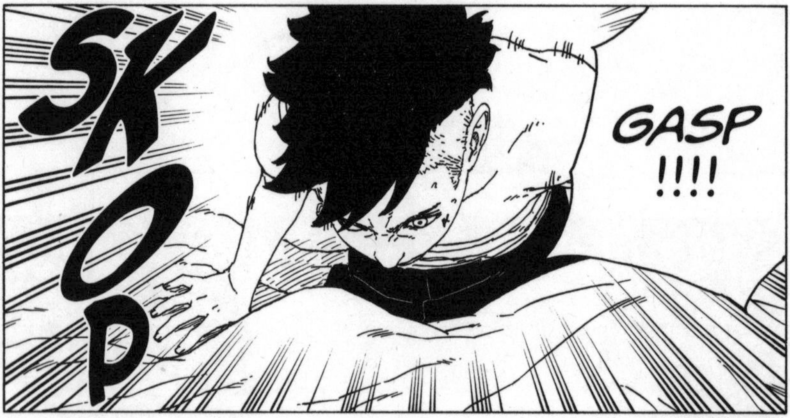
GASP
!!!!
SKOOP
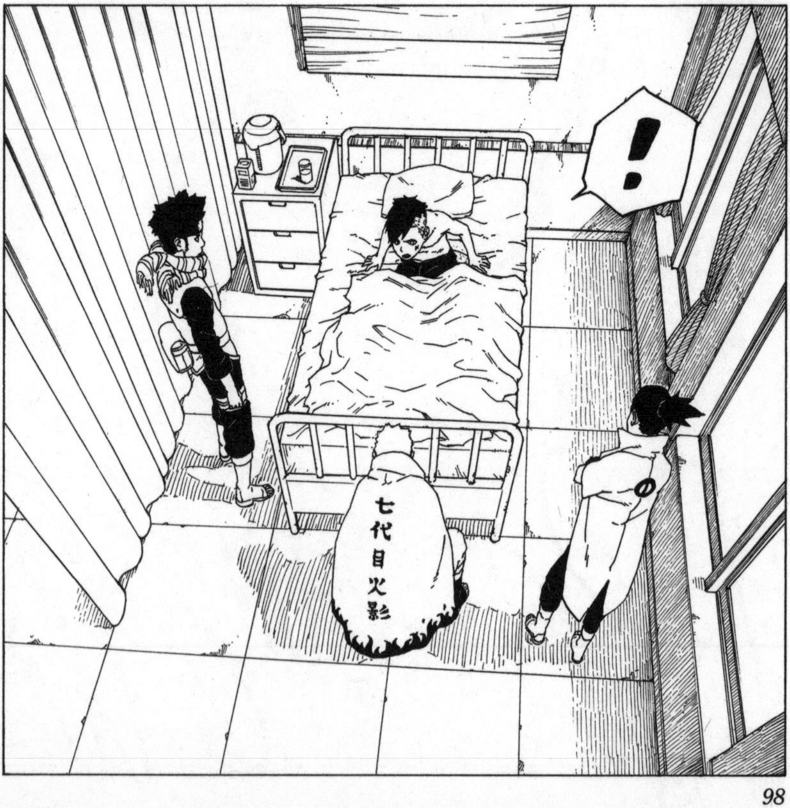
!
七代目火影

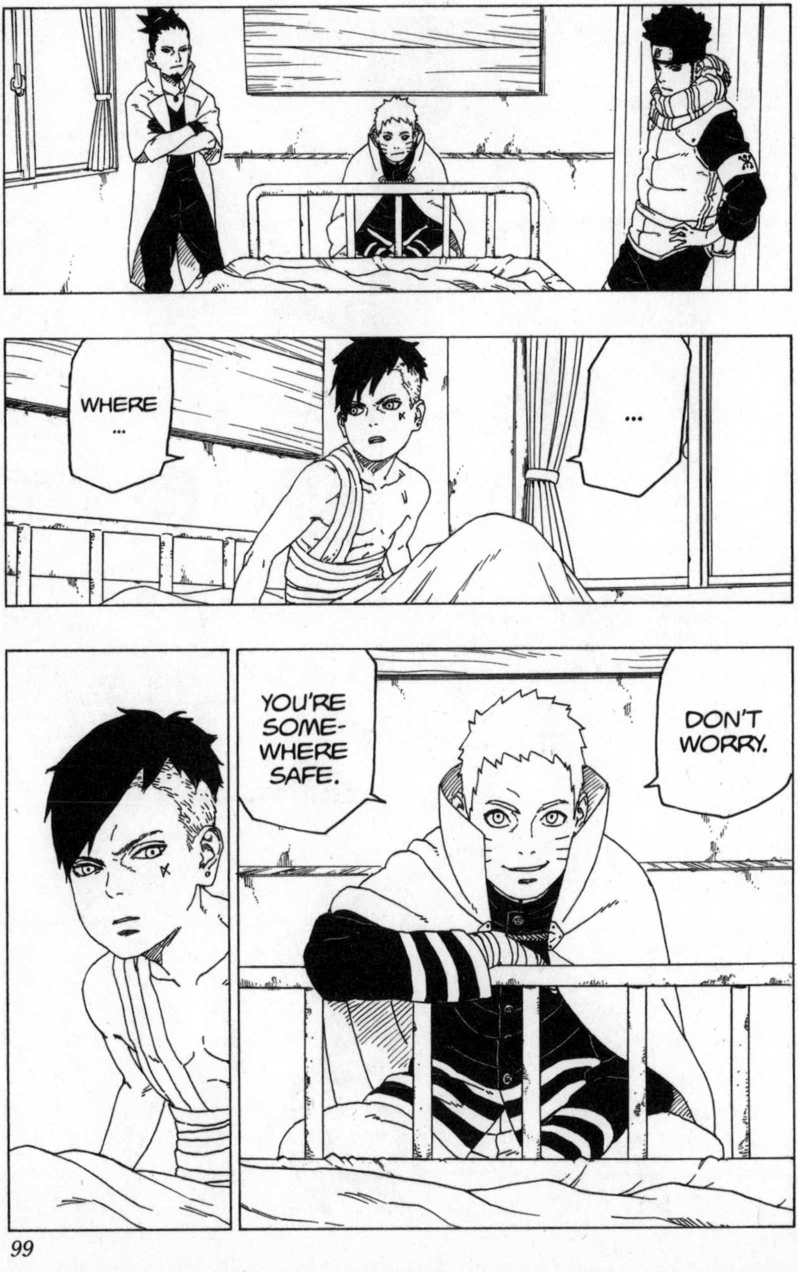
...
WHERE ...
DON'T WORRY.
YOU'RE SOME-WHERE SAFE.

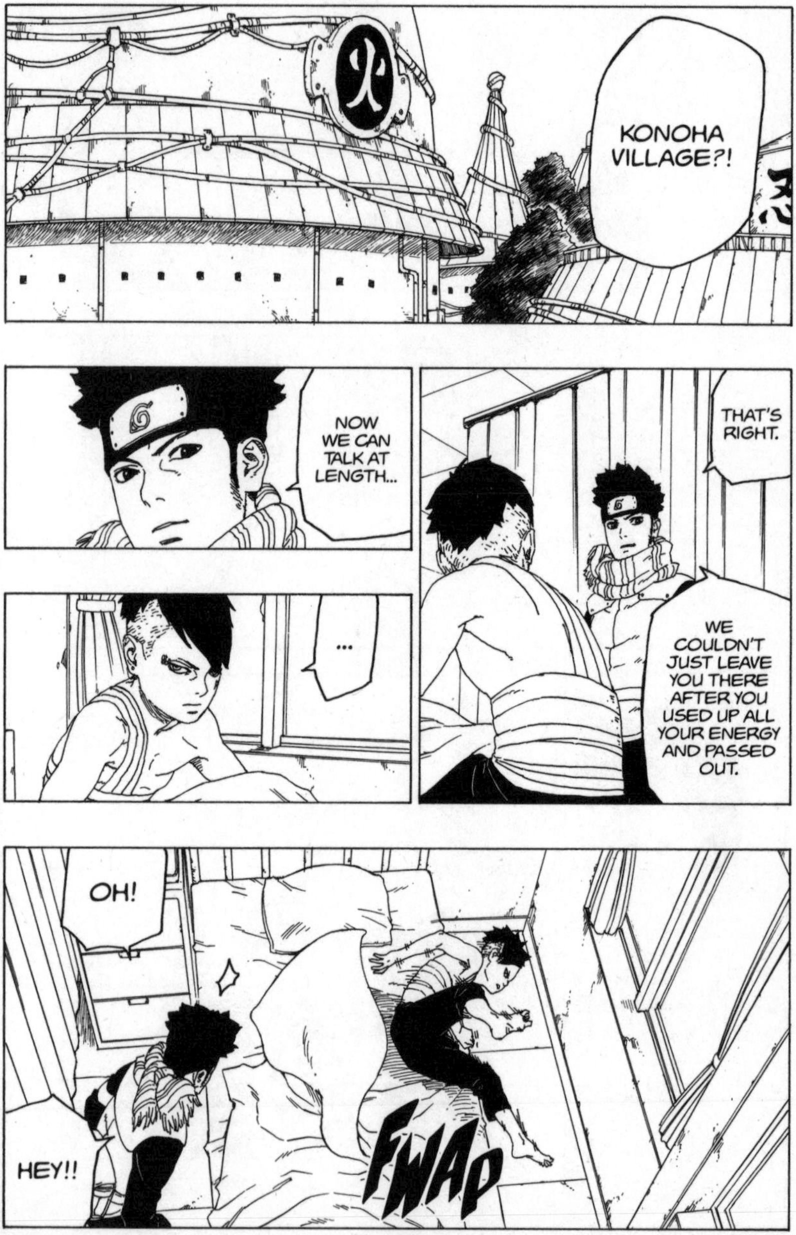
KONOHA VILLAGE?!
THAT'S RIGHT.
WE COULDN'T JUST LEAVE YOU THERE AFTER YOU USED UP ALL YOUR ENERGY AND PASSED OUT.
NOW WE CAN TALK AT LENGTH...
...
OH!
FWAP
HEY!!

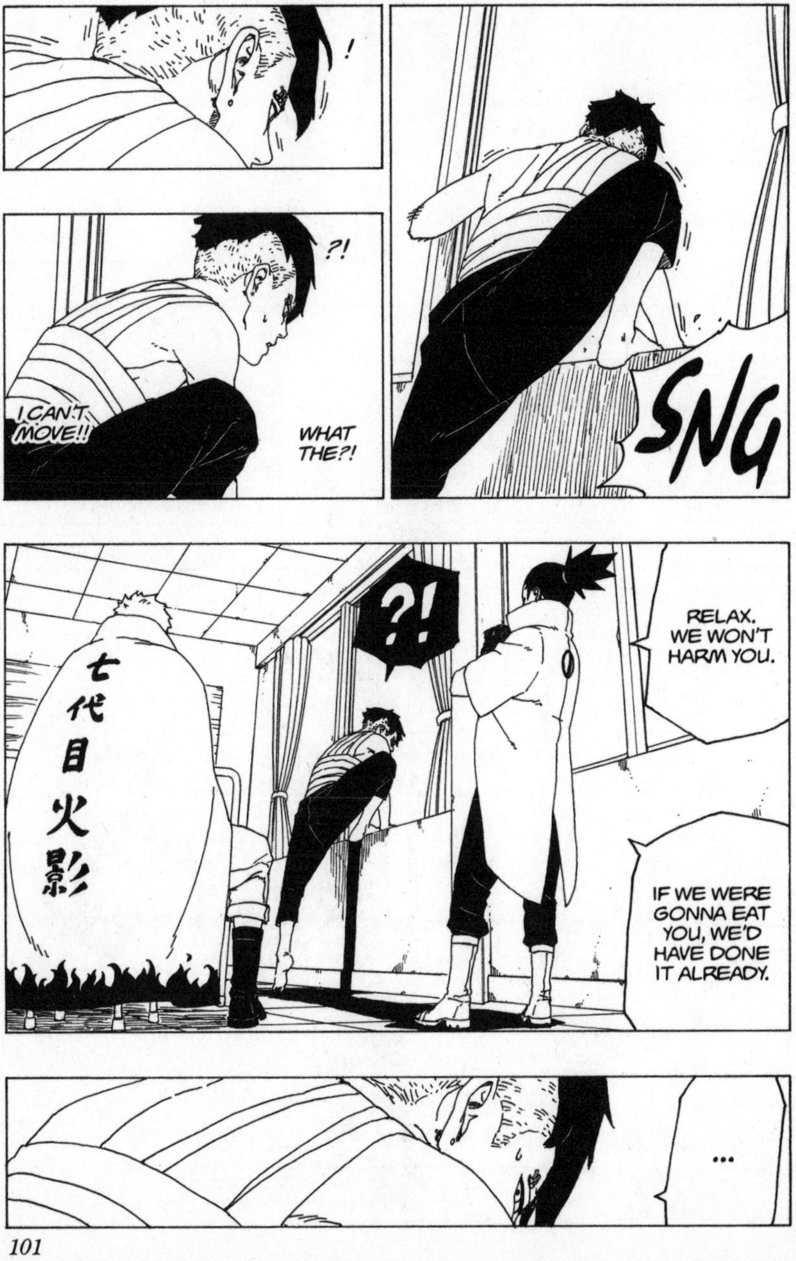
SNG
!
?!
WHAT THE?!
I CAN'T MOVE!!
RELAX. WE WON'T HARM YOU.
?!
七代目火影
IF WE WERE GONNA EAT YOU, WE'D HAVE DONE IT ALREADY.
...

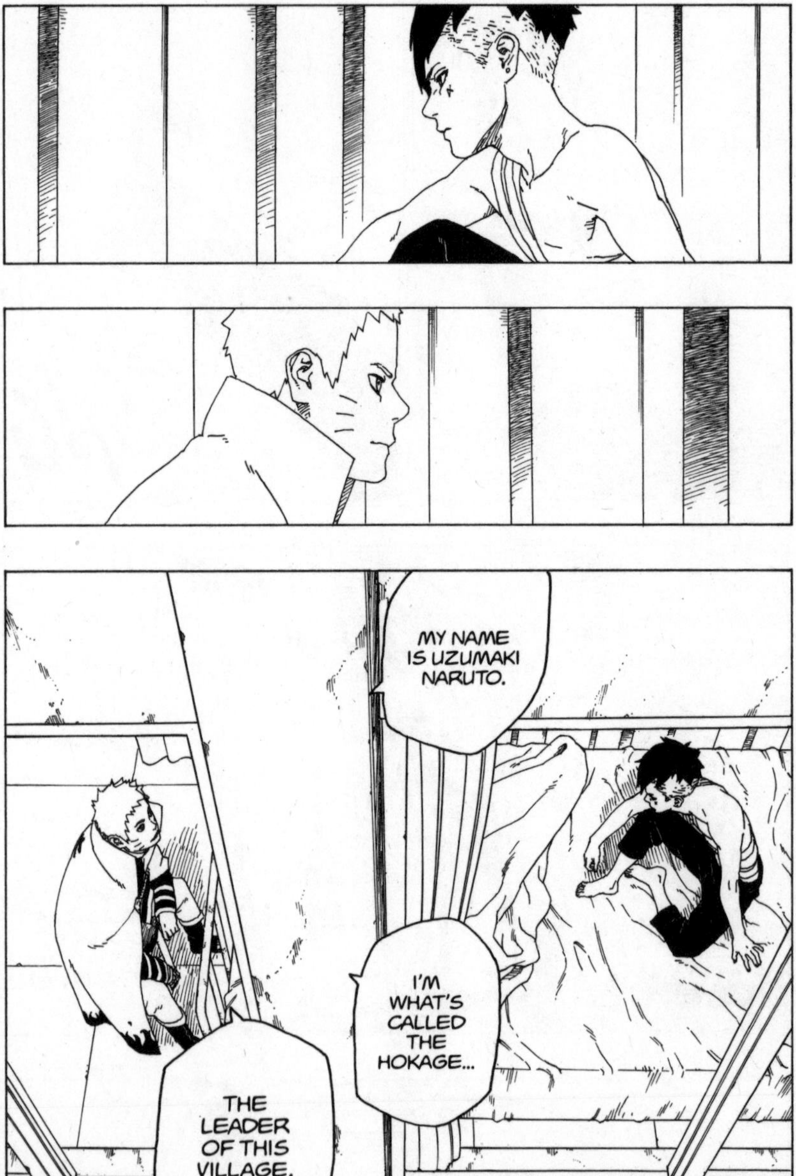
MY NAME IS UZUMAKI NARUTO.
I'M WHAT'S CALLED THE HOKAGE...
THE LEADER OF THIS VILLAGE.

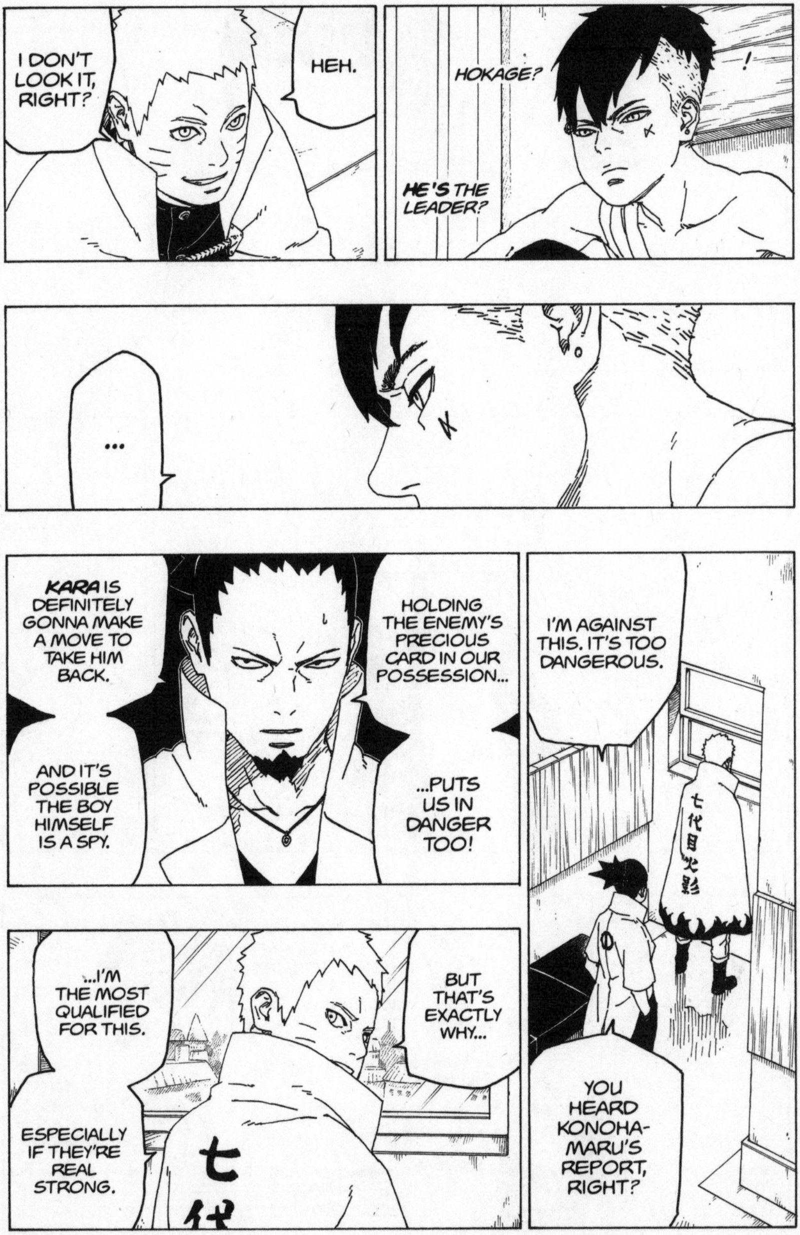
!
HOKAGE?
HE'S THE LEADER?
HEH.
I DON'T LOOK IT, RIGHT?
...
I'M AGAINST THIS. IT'S TOO DANGEROUS.
七代目火影
YOU HEARD KONOHAMARU'S REPORT, RIGHT?
HOLDING THE ENEMY'S PRECIOUS CARD IN OUR POSSESSION...
...PUTS US IN DANGER TOO!
KARA IS DEFINITELY GONNA MAKE A MOVE TO TAKE HIM BACK.
AND IT'S POSSIBLE THE BOY HIMSELF IS A SPY.
BUT THAT'S EXACTLY WHY...
...I'M THE MOST QUALIFIED FOR THIS.
ESPECIALLY IF THEY'RE REAL STRONG.
七代

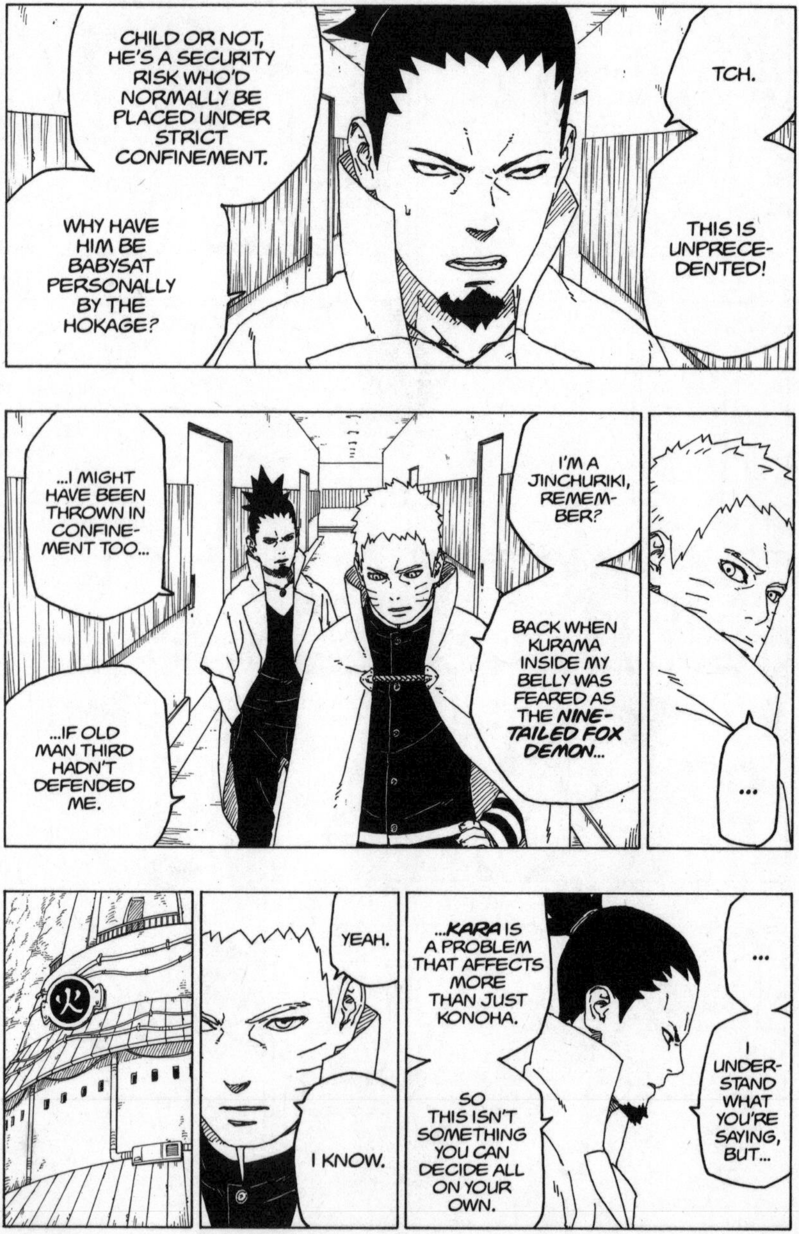
TCH.
THIS IS UNPRECEDENTED!
CHILD OR NOT, HE'S A SECURITY RISK WHO'D NORMALLY BE PLACED UNDER STRICT CONFINEMENT.
WHY HAVE HIM BE BABYSAT PERSONALLY BY THE HOKAGE?
...
I'M A JINCHURIKI, REMEMBER?
BACK WHEN KURAMA INSIDE MY BELLY WAS FEARED AS THE ***NINE-TAILED FOX DEMON***...
...I MIGHT HAVE BEEN THROWN IN CONFINEMENT TOO...
...IF OLD MAN THIRD HADN'T DEFENDED ME.
...
I UNDERSTAND WHAT YOU'RE SAYING, BUT...
...***KARA*** IS A PROBLEM THAT AFFECTS MORE THAN JUST KONOHA.
SO THIS ISN'T SOMETHING YOU CAN DECIDE ALL ON YOUR OWN.
YEAH.
I KNOW.

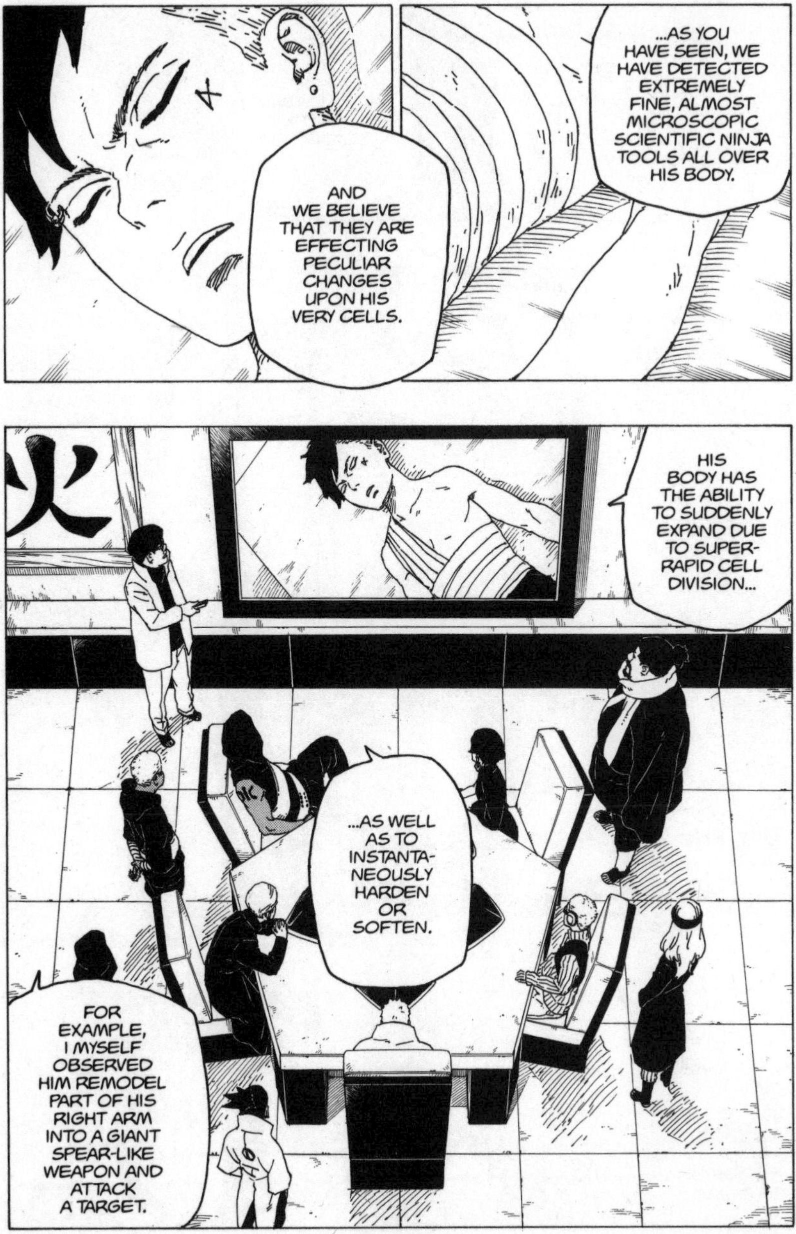
...AS YOU HAVE SEEN, WE HAVE DETECTED EXTREMELY FINE, ALMOST MICROSCOPIC SCIENTIFIC NINJA TOOLS ALL OVER HIS BODY.
AND WE BELIEVE THAT THEY ARE EFFECTING PECULIAR CHANGES UPON HIS VERY CELLS.
火
HIS BODY HAS THE ABILITY TO SUDDENLY EXPAND DUE TO SUPER-RAPID CELL DIVISION...
...AS WELL AS TO INSTANTA-NEOUSLY HARDEN OR SOFTEN.
FOR EXAMPLE, I MYSELF OBSERVED HIM REMODEL PART OF HIS RIGHT ARM INTO A GIANT SPEAR-LIKE WEAPON AND ATTACK A TARGET.

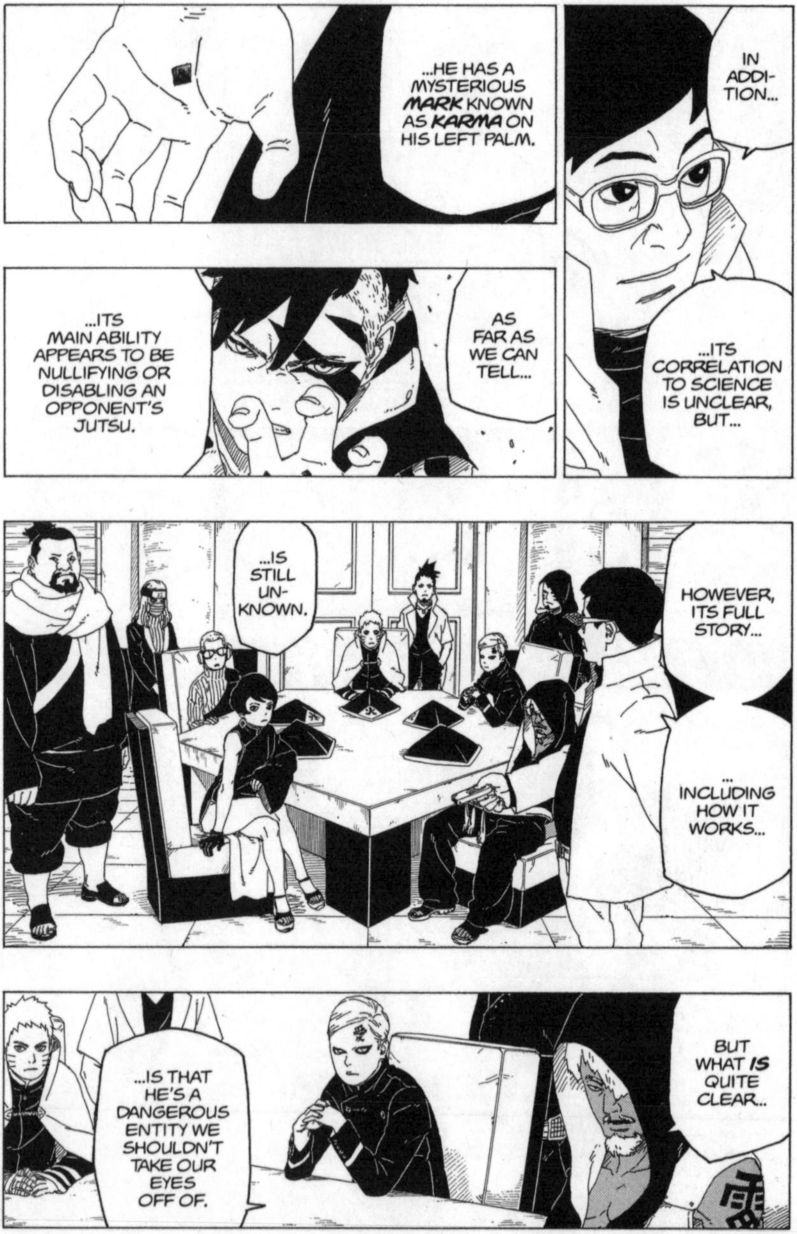
IN ADDITION...
...HE HAS A MYSTERIOUS **MARK** KNOWN AS ***KARMA*** ON HIS LEFT PALM.
...ITS CORRELATION TO SCIENCE IS UNCLEAR, BUT...
AS FAR AS WE CAN TELL...
...ITS MAIN ABILITY APPEARS TO BE NULLIFYING OR DISABLING AN OPPONENT'S JUTSU.
HOWEVER, ITS FULL STORY...
...INCLUDING HOW IT WORKS...
...IS STILL UNKNOWN.
BUT WHAT ***IS*** QUITE CLEAR...
...IS THAT HE'S A DANGEROUS ENTITY WE SHOULDN'T TAKE OUR EYES OFF OF.

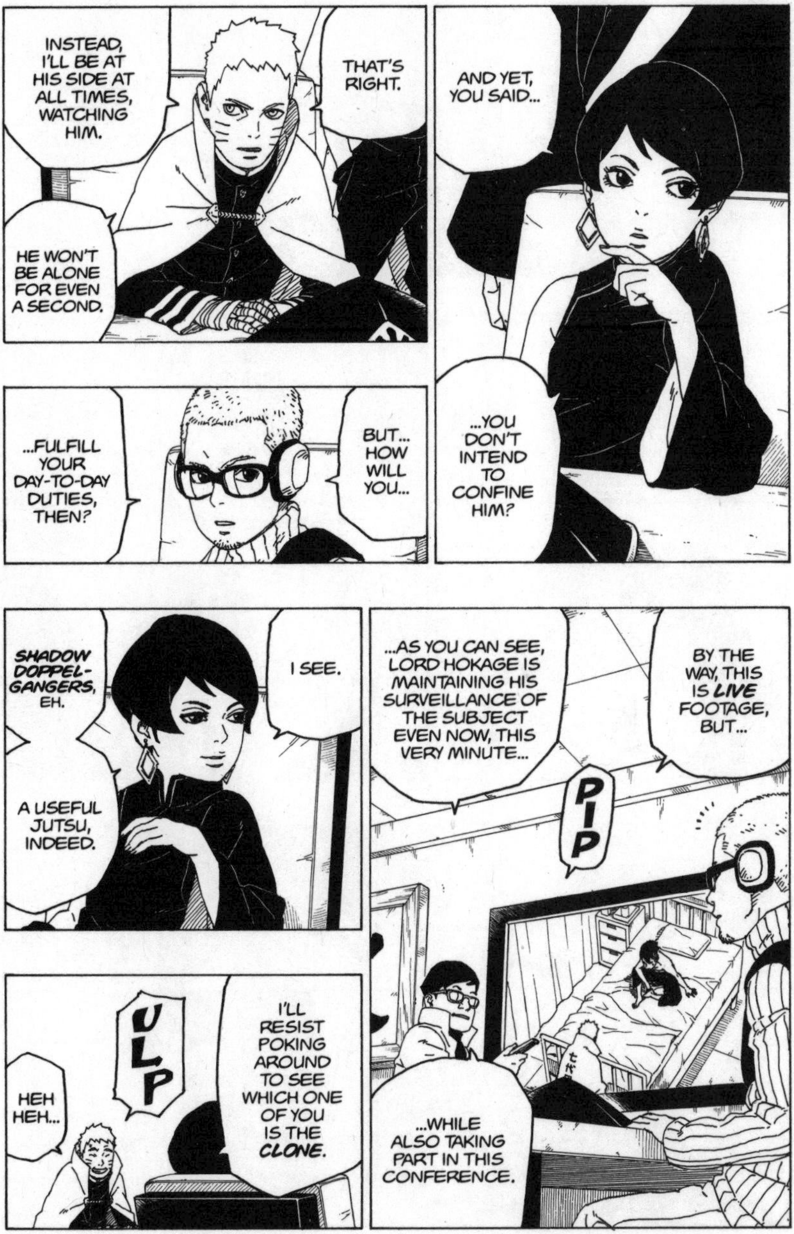
AND YET, YOU SAID...
...YOU DON'T INTEND TO CONFINE HIM?
THAT'S RIGHT.
INSTEAD, I'LL BE AT HIS SIDE AT ALL TIMES, WATCHING HIM.
HE WON'T BE ALONE FOR EVEN A SECOND.
BUT... HOW WILL YOU...
...FULFILL YOUR DAY-TO-DAY DUTIES, THEN?
BY THE WAY, THIS IS *LIVE* FOOTAGE, BUT...
...AS YOU CAN SEE, LORD HOKAGE IS MAINTAINING HIS SURVEILLANCE OF THE SUBJECT EVEN NOW, THIS VERY MINUTE...
PIP
...WHILE ALSO TAKING PART IN THIS CONFERENCE.
I SEE.
SHADOW DOPPEL-GANGERS, EH.
A USEFUL JUTSU, INDEED.
I'LL RESIST POKING AROUND TO SEE WHICH ONE OF YOU IS THE *CLONE*.
ULP
HEH HEH...

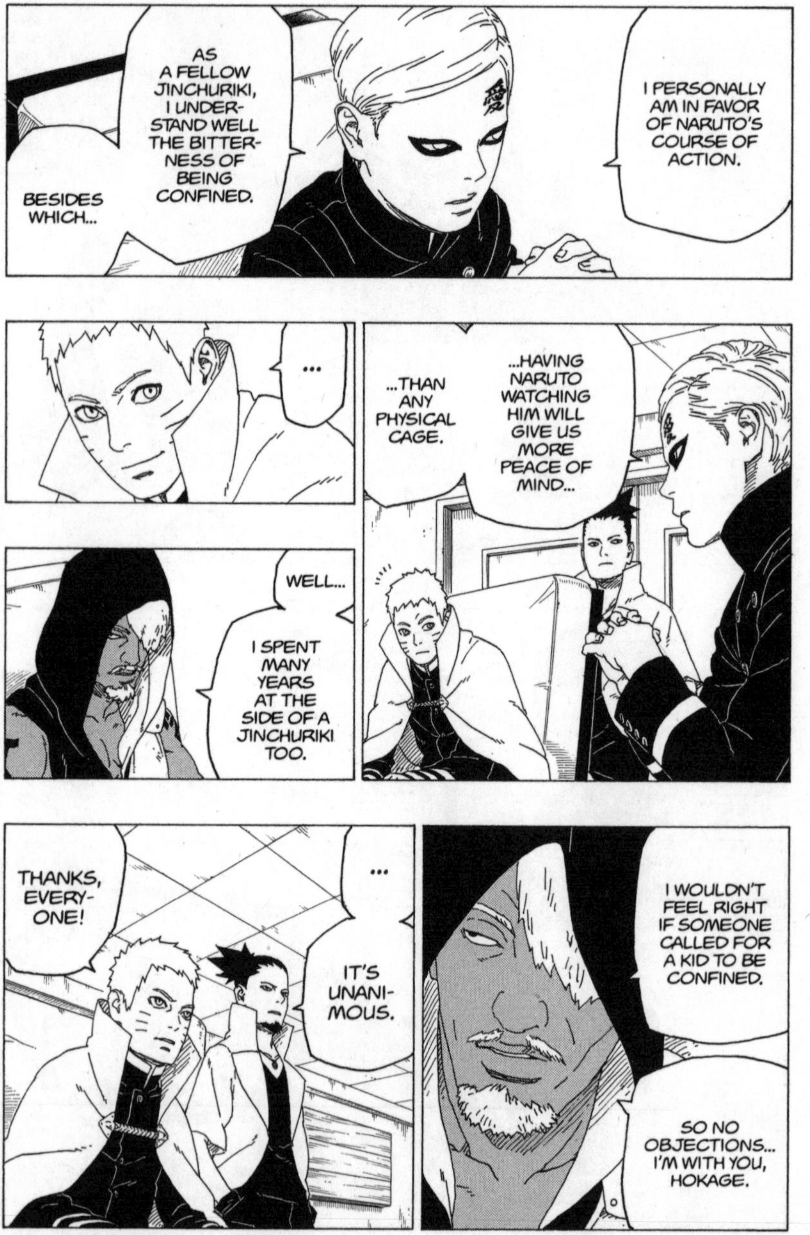
I PERSONALLY AM IN FAVOR OF NARUTO'S COURSE OF ACTION.
AS A FELLOW JINCHURIKI, I UNDERSTAND WELL THE BITTERNESS OF BEING CONFINED.
BESIDES WHICH...
...HAVING NARUTO WATCHING HIM WILL GIVE US MORE PEACE OF MIND...
...THAN ANY PHYSICAL CAGE.
...
WELL...
I SPENT MANY YEARS AT THE SIDE OF A JINCHURIKI TOO.
I WOULDN'T FEEL RIGHT IF SOMEONE CALLED FOR A KID TO BE CONFINED.
SO NO OBJECTIONS... I'M WITH YOU, HOKAGE.
...
IT'S UNANIMOUS.
THANKS, EVERYONE!

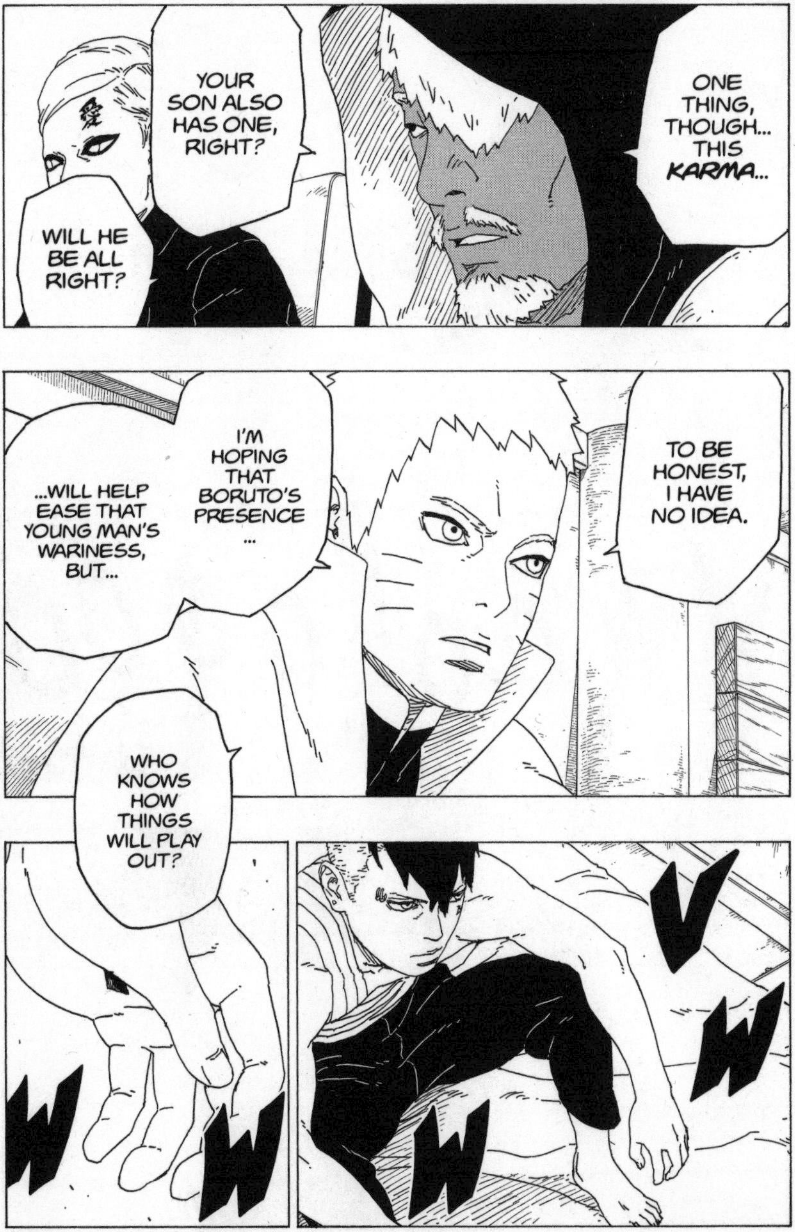
ONE THING, THOUGH... THIS *KARMA*...
YOUR SON ALSO HAS ONE, RIGHT?
WILL HE BE ALL RIGHT?
TO BE HONEST, I HAVE NO IDEA.
I'M HOPING THAT BORUTO'S PRESENCE ...
...WILL HELP EASE THAT YOUNG MAN'S WARINESS, BUT...
WHO KNOWS HOW THINGS WILL PLAY OUT?
VWW
W
WW

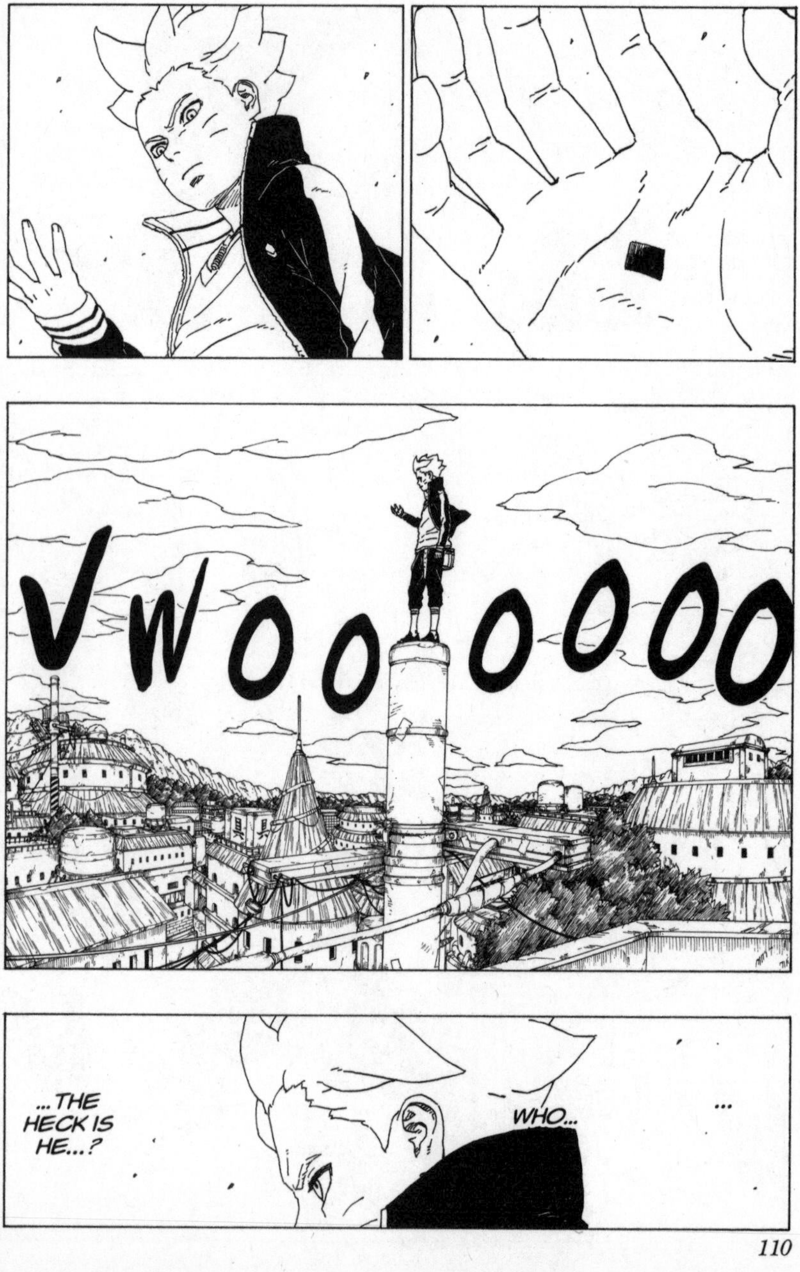
VWOOOOOO
...
WHO...
...THE HECK IS HE...?

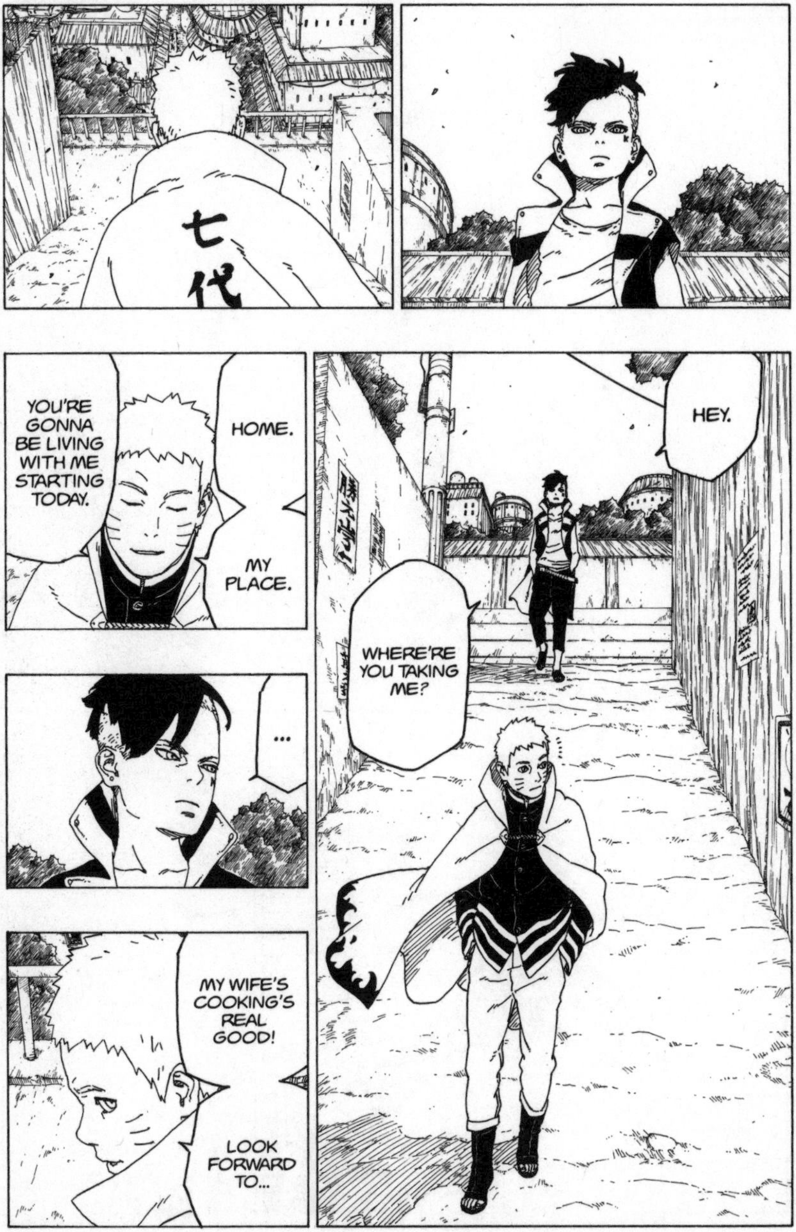
七代
HEY.
WHERE'RE YOU TAKING ME?
HOME.
MY PLACE.
YOU'RE GONNA BE LIVING WITH ME STARTING TODAY.
...
MY WIFE'S COOKING'S REAL GOOD!
LOOK FORWARD TO...

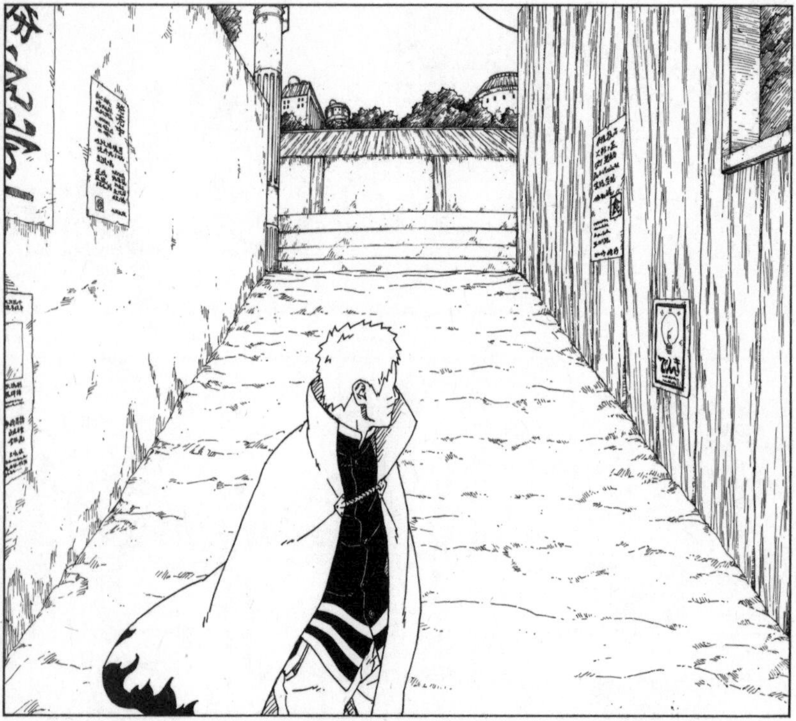

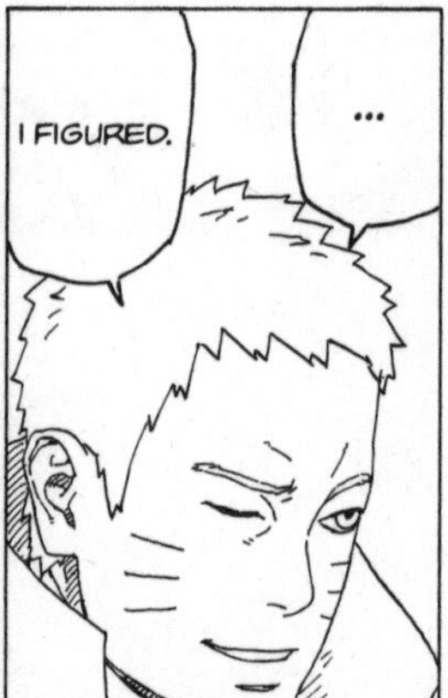
...
I FIGURED.

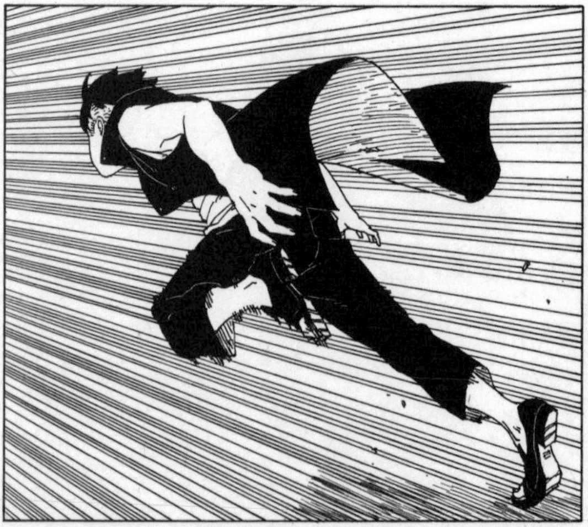

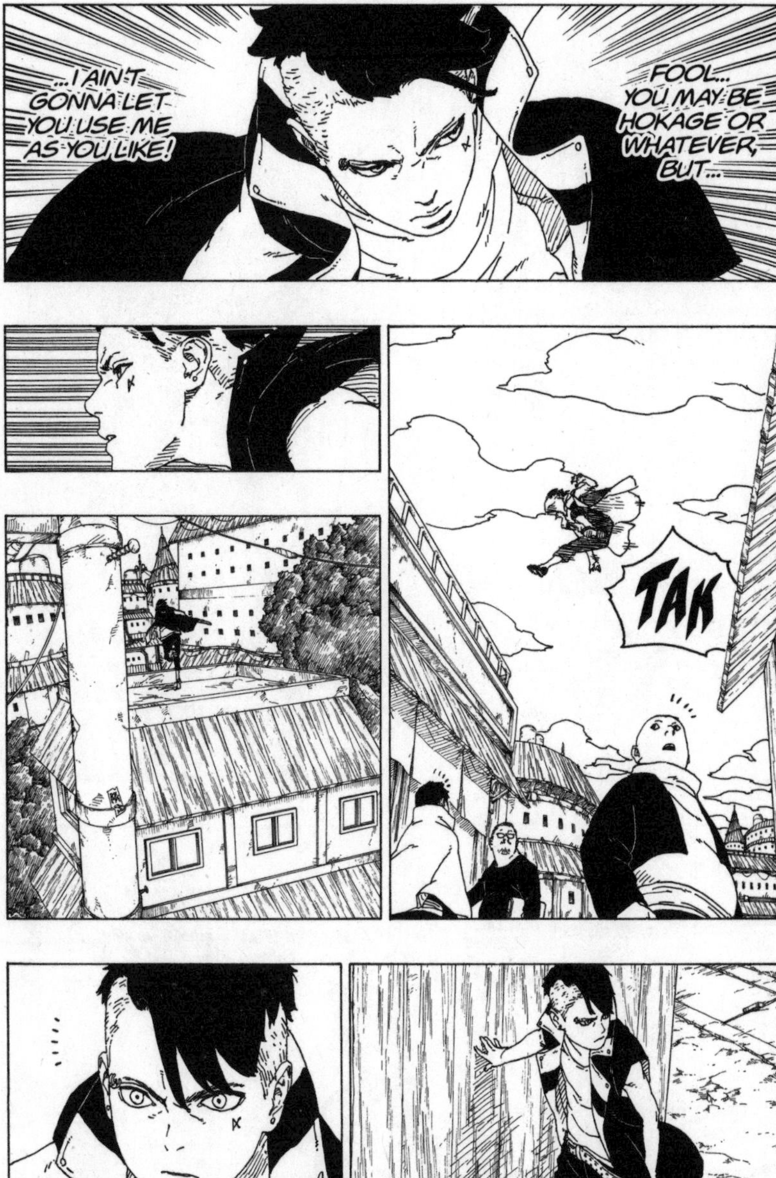
FOOL... YOU MAY BE HOKAGE OR WHATEVER, BUT...
...I AIN'T GONNA LET YOU USE ME AS YOU LIKE!
TAK

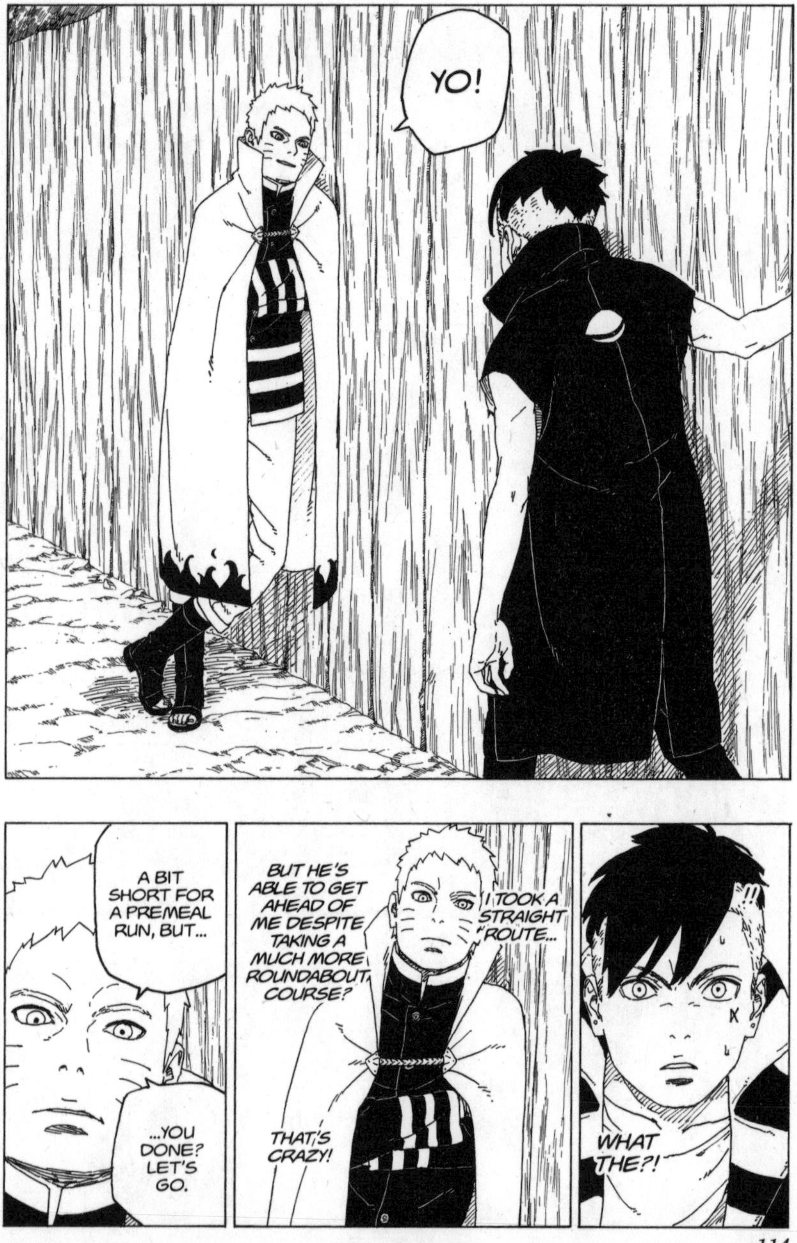
YO!
WHAT THE?!
I TOOK A STRAIGHT ROUTE...
BUT HE'S ABLE TO GET AHEAD OF ME DESPITE TAKING A MUCH MORE ROUNDABOUT COURSE?
THAT'S CRAZY!
A BIT SHORT FOR A PREMEAL RUN, BUT...
...YOU DONE? LET'S GO.

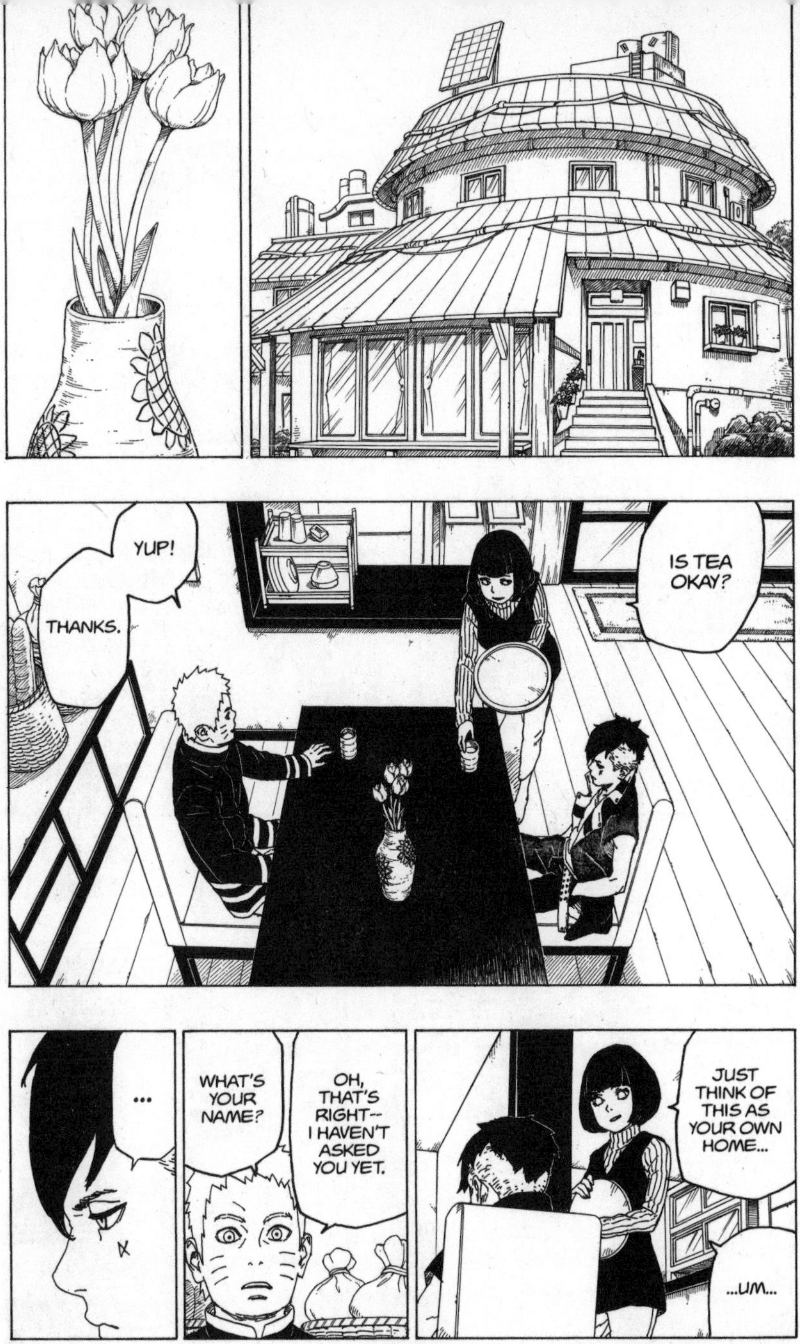
IS TEA OKAY?
YUP!
THANKS.
JUST THINK OF THIS AS YOUR OWN HOME...
...UM...
OH, THAT'S RIGHT-- I HAVEN'T ASKED YOU YET.
WHAT'S YOUR NAME?
...

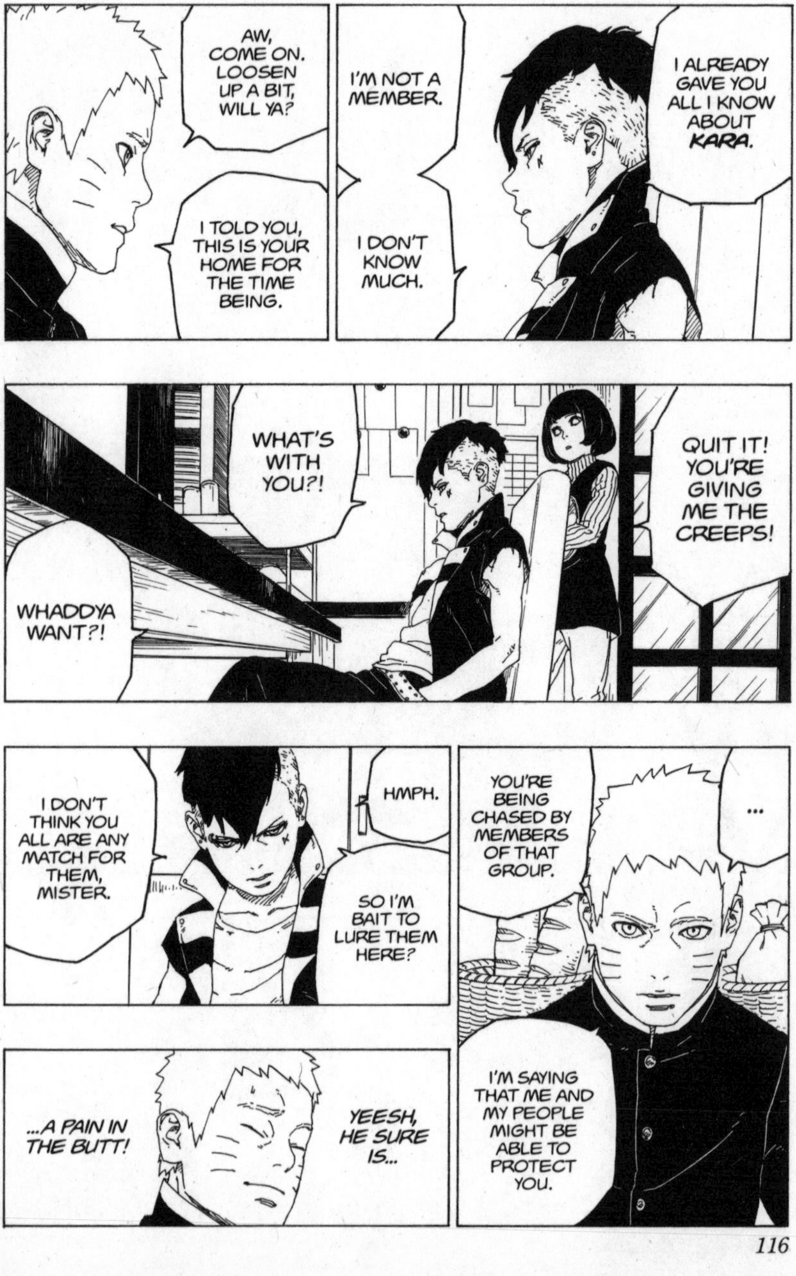
I ALREADY GAVE YOU ALL I KNOW ABOUT KARA.
I'M NOT A MEMBER.
I DON'T KNOW MUCH.
AW, COME ON. LOOSEN UP A BIT, WILL YA?
I TOLD YOU, THIS IS YOUR HOME FOR THE TIME BEING.
QUIT IT! YOU'RE GIVING ME THE CREEPS!
WHAT'S WITH YOU?!
WHADDYA WANT?!
...
YOU'RE BEING CHASED BY MEMBERS OF THAT GROUP.
I'M SAYING THAT ME AND MY PEOPLE MIGHT BE ABLE TO PROTECT YOU.
HMPH.
SO I'M BAIT TO LURE THEM HERE?
I DON'T THINK YOU ALL ARE ANY MATCH FOR THEM, MISTER.
YEESH, HE SURE IS...
...A PAIN IN THE BUTT!

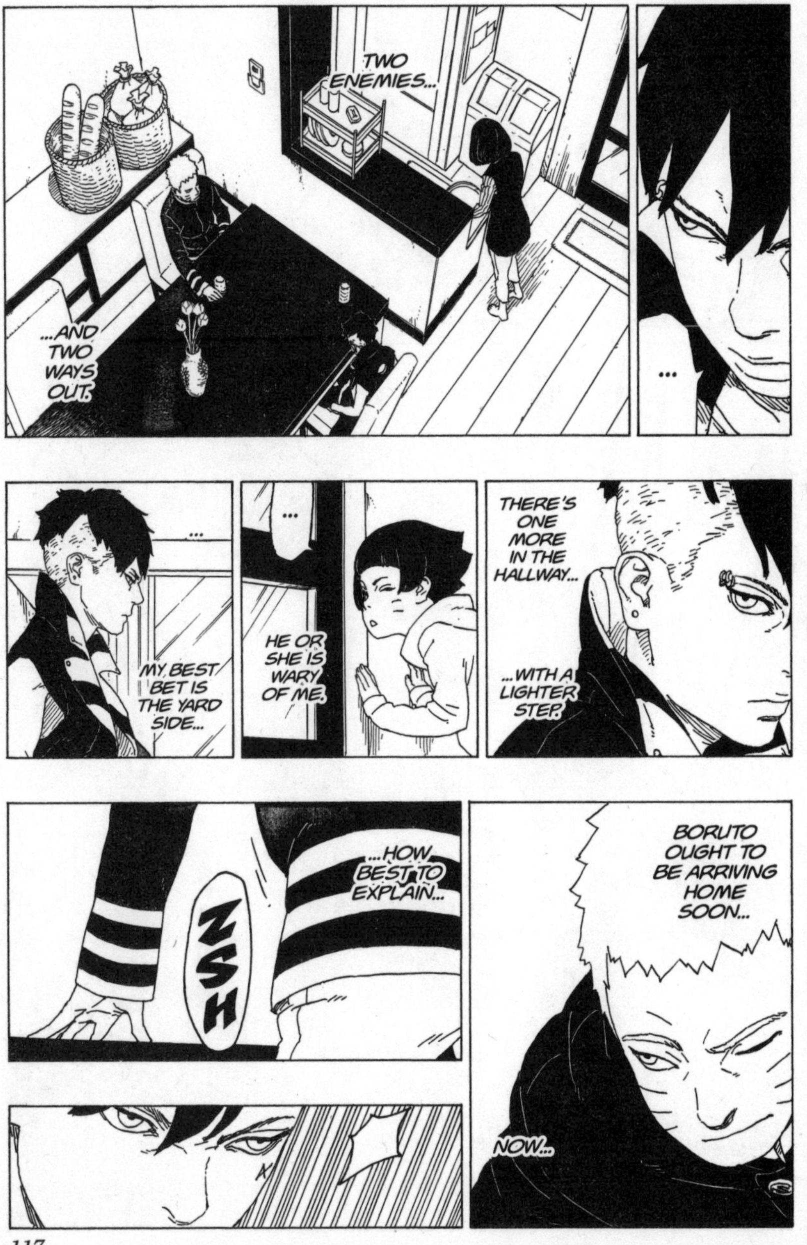
...
TWO ENEMIES...
...AND TWO WAYS OUT.
THERE'S ONE MORE IN THE HALLWAY...
...WITH A LIGHTER STEP.
...
HE OR SHE IS WARY OF ME.
...
MY BEST BET IS THE YARD SIDE...
BORUTO OUGHT TO BE ARRIVING HOME SOON...
NOW...
...HOW BEST TO EXPLAIN...
ZSH

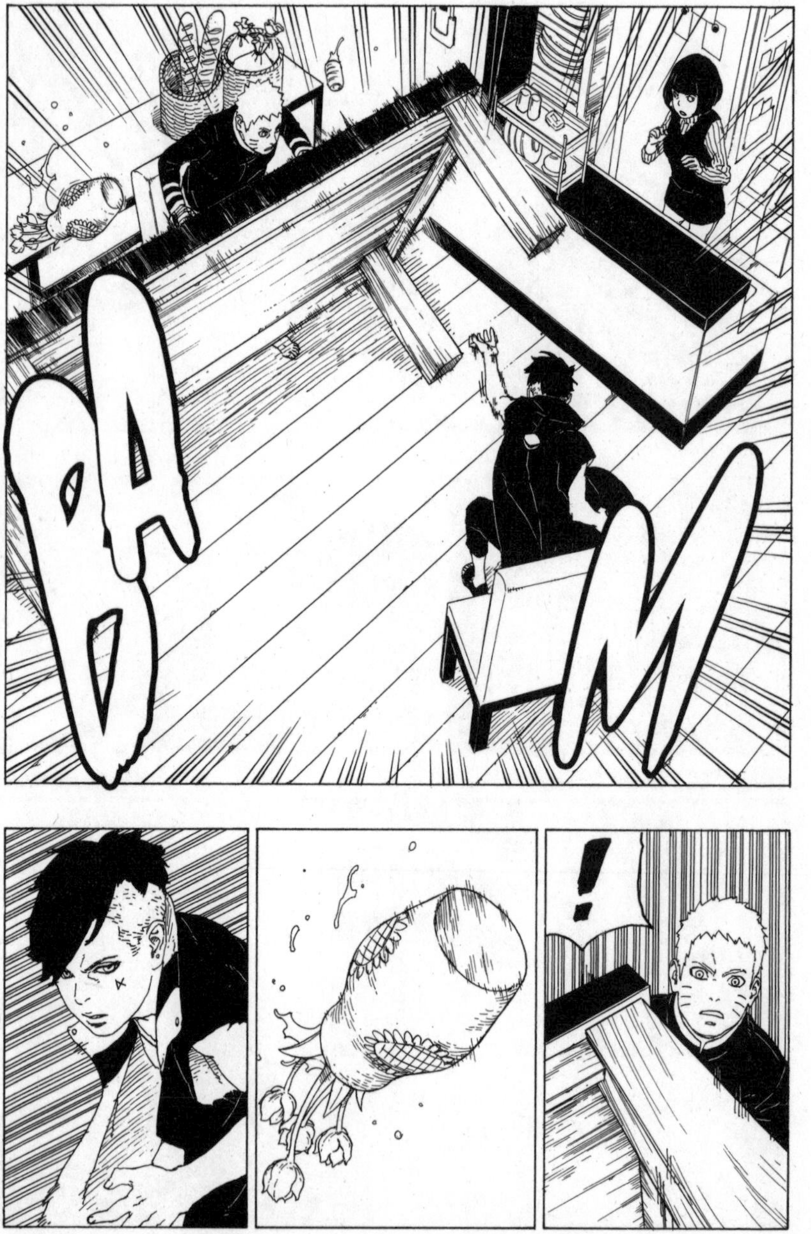
BAM
!

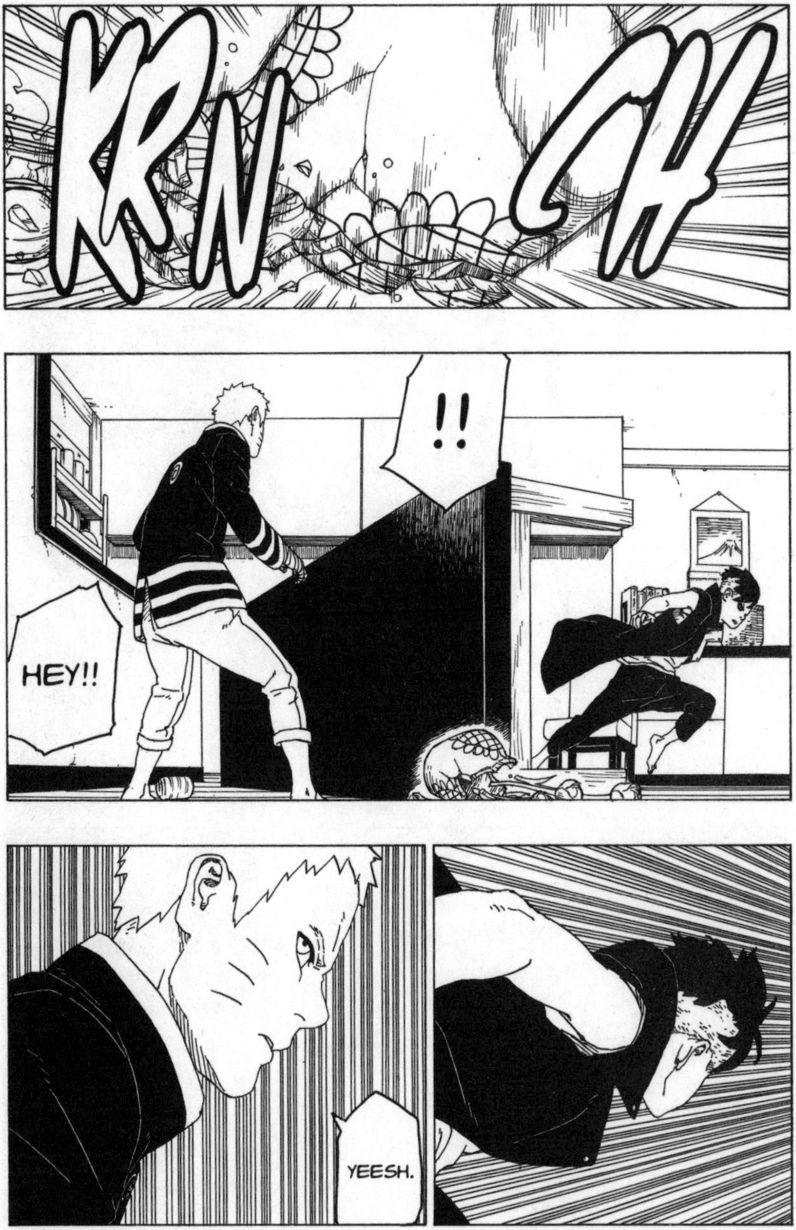
KRNCH
!!
HEY!!
YEESH.

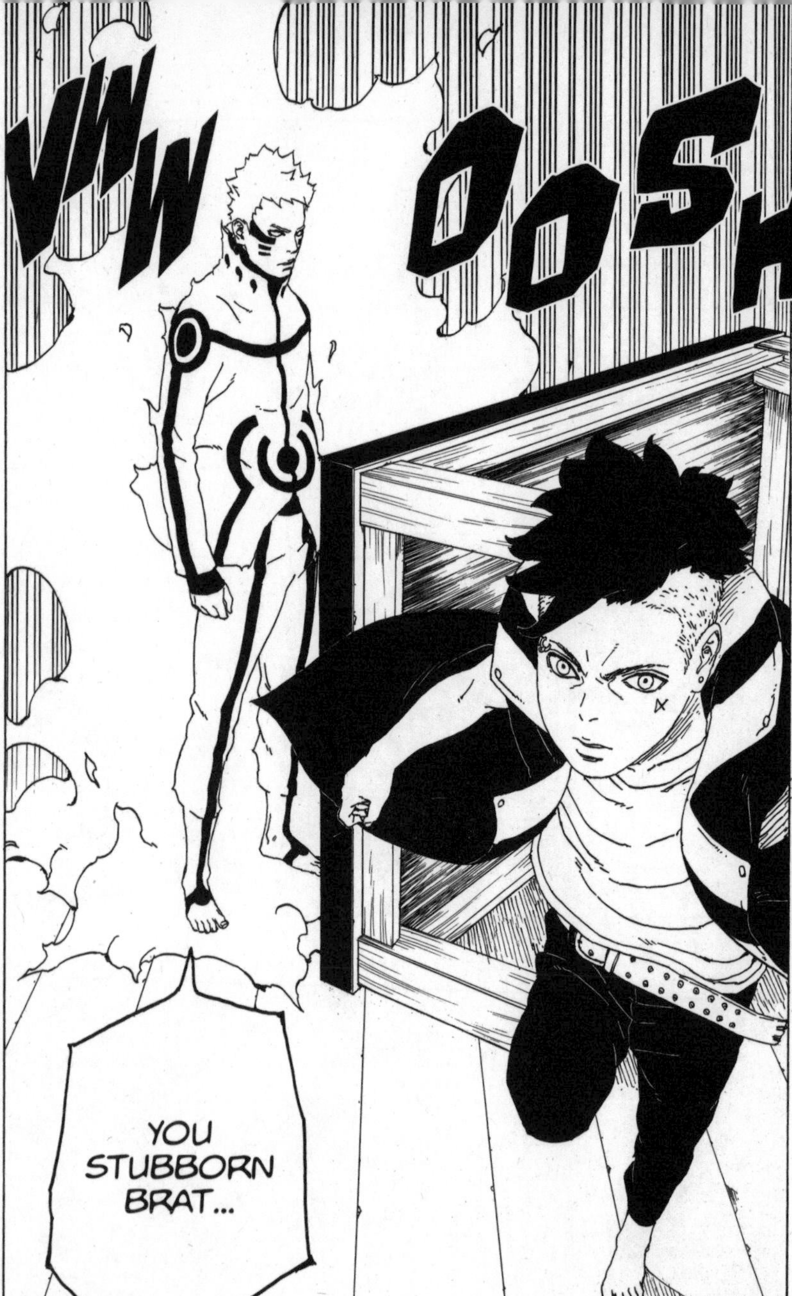
VWWOOSH
YOU STUBBORN BRAT...

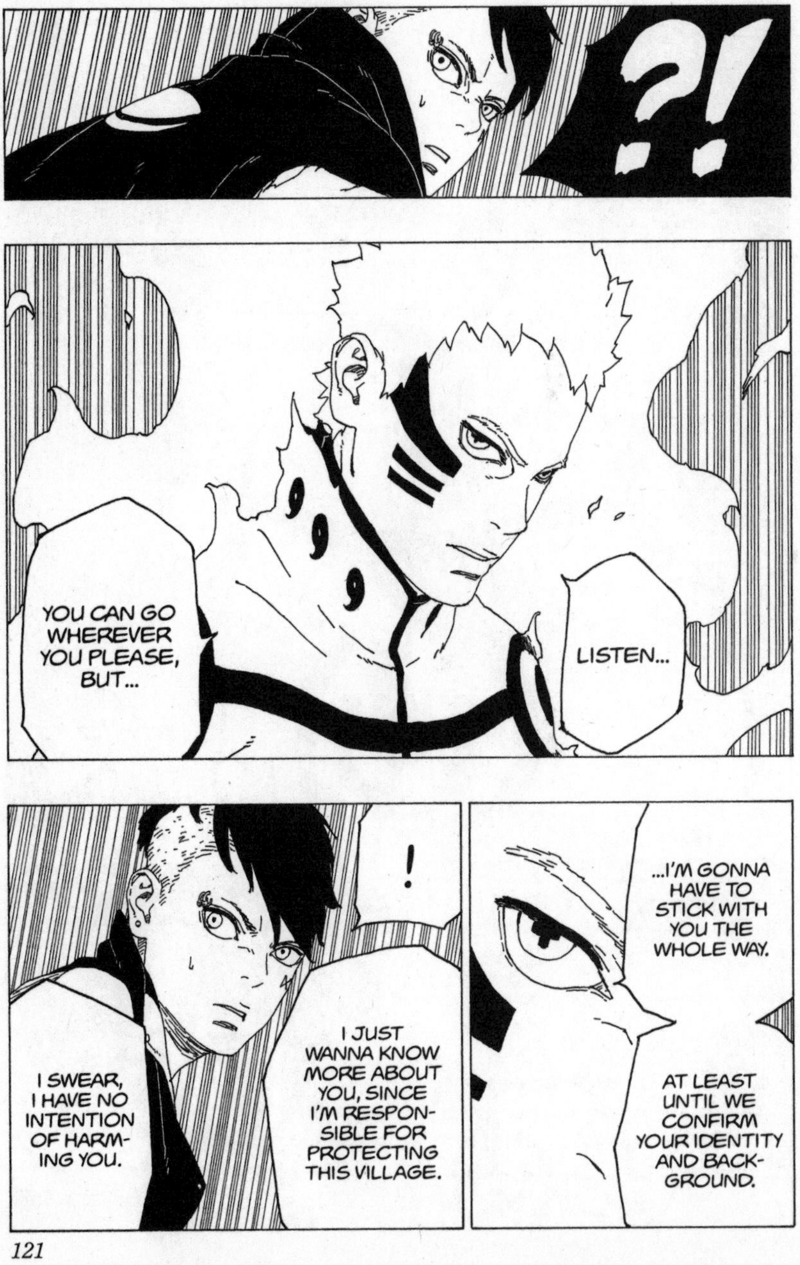
?!
LISTEN...
YOU CAN GO WHEREVER YOU PLEASE, BUT...
...I'M GONNA HAVE TO STICK WITH YOU THE WHOLE WAY.
AT LEAST UNTIL WE CONFIRM YOUR IDENTITY AND BACK-GROUND.
!
I JUST WANNA KNOW MORE ABOUT YOU, SINCE I'M RESPON-SIBLE FOR PROTECTING THIS VILLAGE.
I SWEAR, I HAVE NO INTENTION OF HARM-ING YOU.

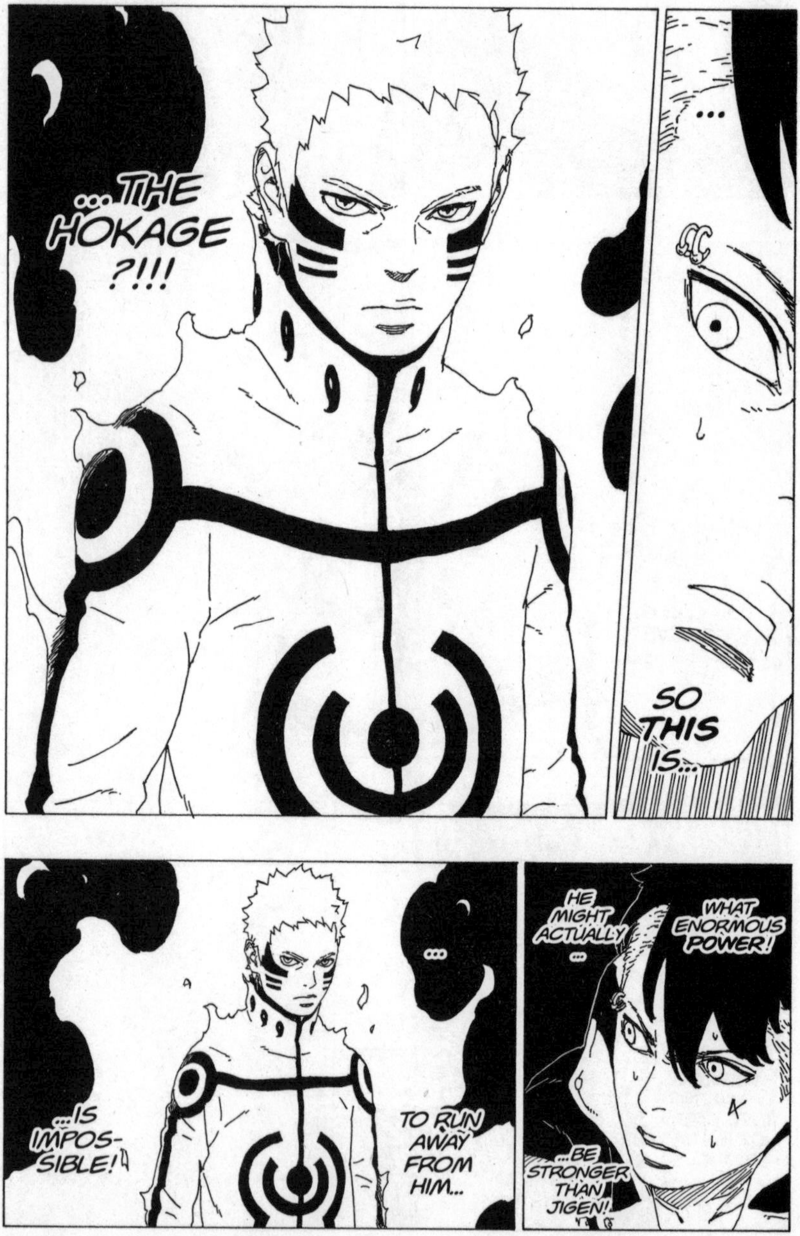
...
SO THIS IS...
...THE HOKAGE ?!!!
WHAT ENORMOUS POWER!
HE MIGHT ACTUALLY ...
...BE STRONGER THAN JIGEN!
...
TO RUN AWAY FROM HIM...
...IS IMPOSSIBLE!

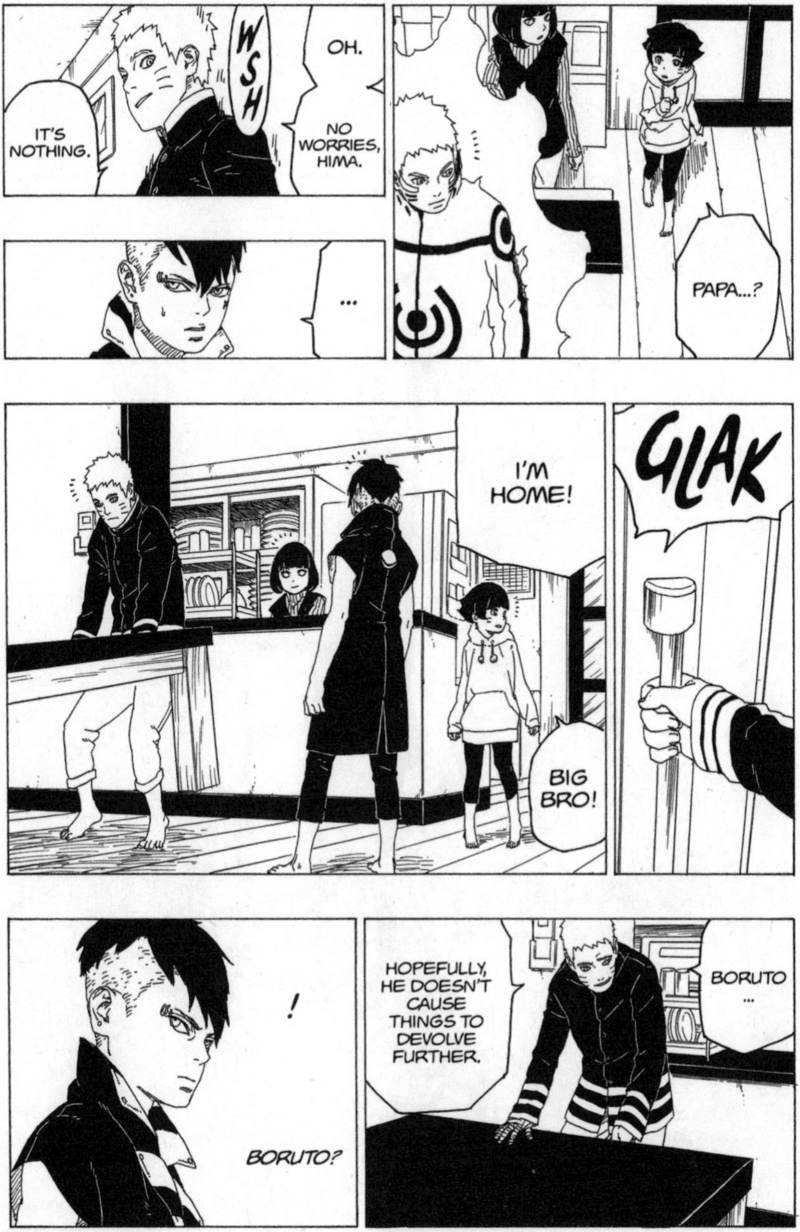
PAPA...?
OH.
NO WORRIES, HIMA.
WSH
IT'S NOTHING.
...
GLAK
I'M HOME!
BIG BRO!
BORUTO ...
HOPEFULLY, HE DOESN'T CAUSE THINGS TO DEVOLVE FURTHER.
!
BORUTO?

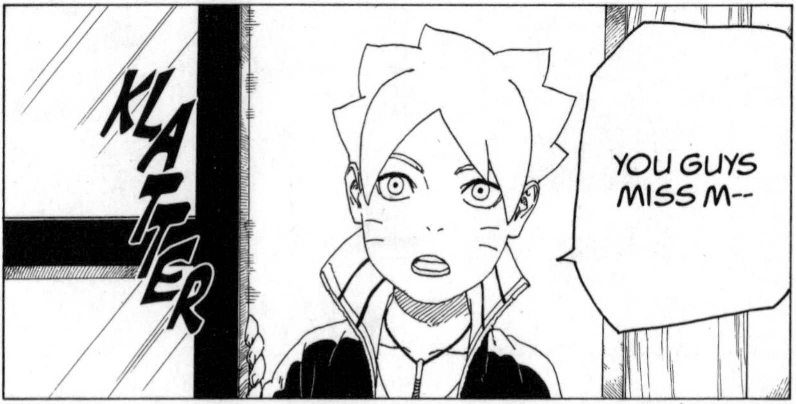
YOU GUYS MISS M--
KLATTER

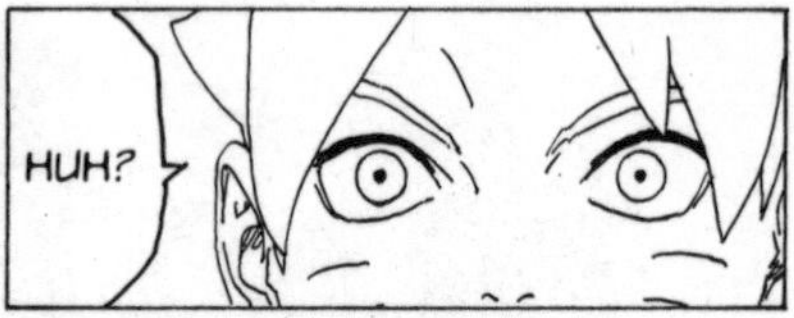
HUH?

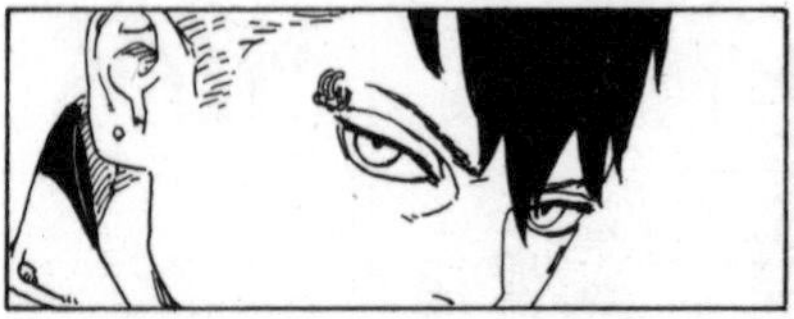

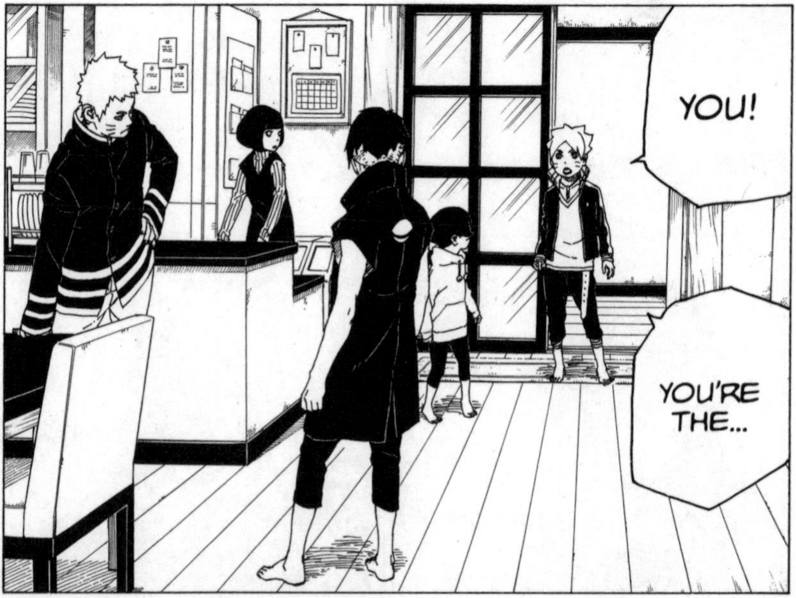
YOU!
YOU'RE THE...

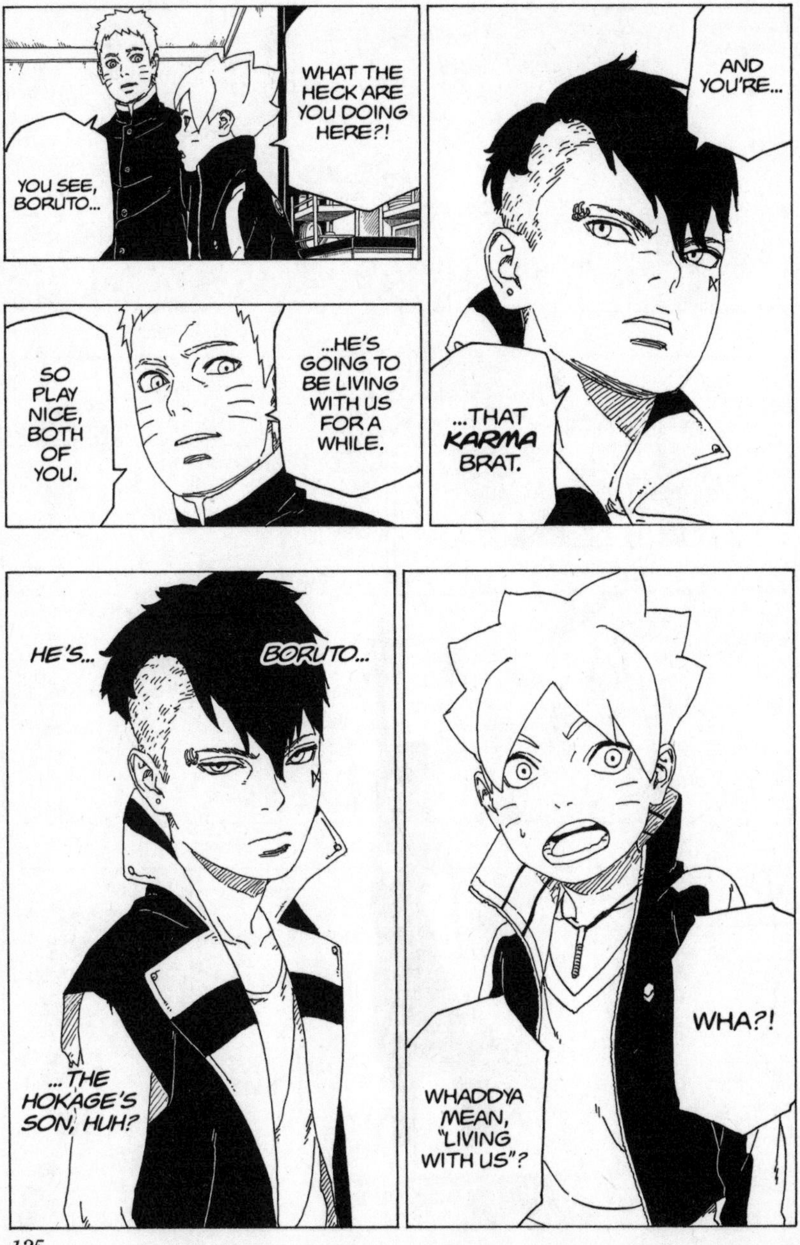
AND YOU'RE...
...THAT KARMA BRAT.
WHAT THE HECK ARE YOU DOING HERE?!
YOU SEE, BORUTO...
...HE'S GOING TO BE LIVING WITH US FOR A WHILE.
SO PLAY NICE, BOTH OF YOU.
WHA?!
WHADDYA MEAN, "LIVING WITH US"?
HE'S...
BORUTO...
...THE HOKAGE'S SON, HUH?

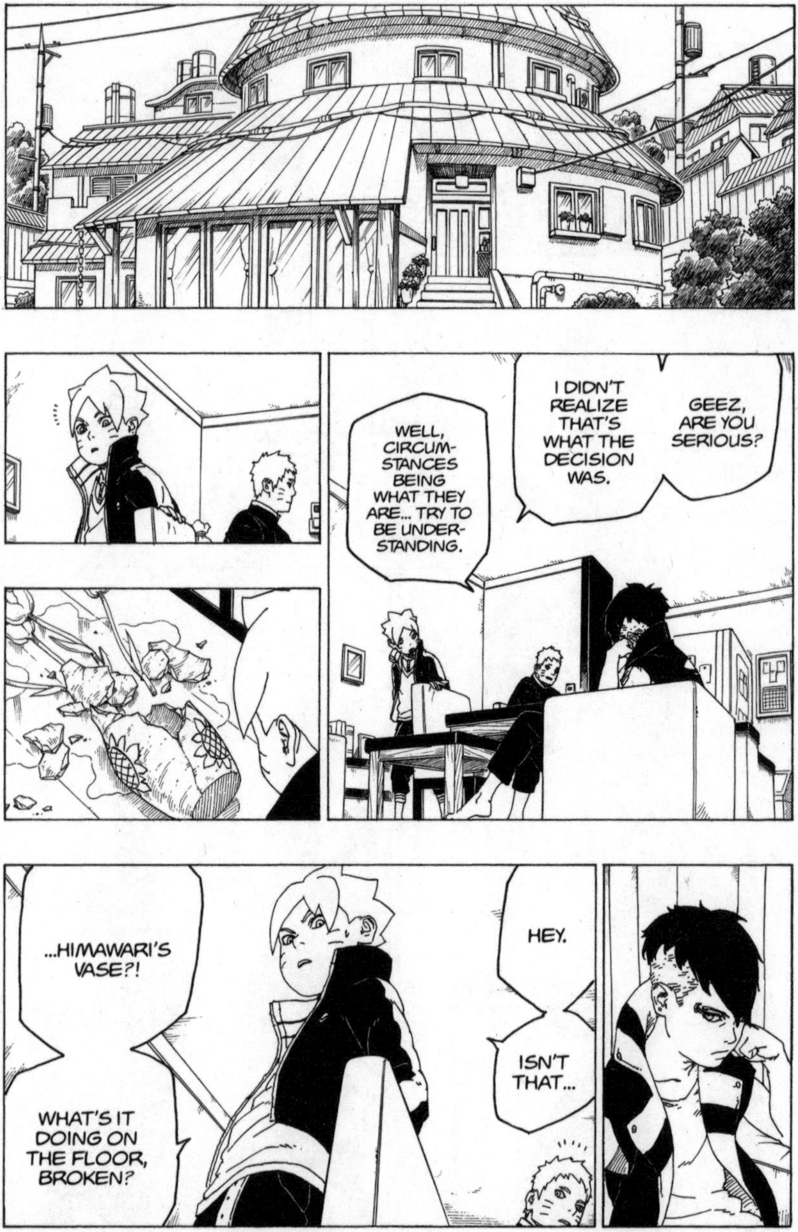
GEEZ, ARE YOU SERIOUS?
I DIDN'T REALIZE THAT'S WHAT THE DECISION WAS.
WELL, CIRCUM-STANCES BEING WHAT THEY ARE... TRY TO BE UNDER-STANDING.
HEY.
ISN'T THAT...
...HIMAWARI'S VASE?!
WHAT'S IT DOING ON THE FLOOR, BROKEN?

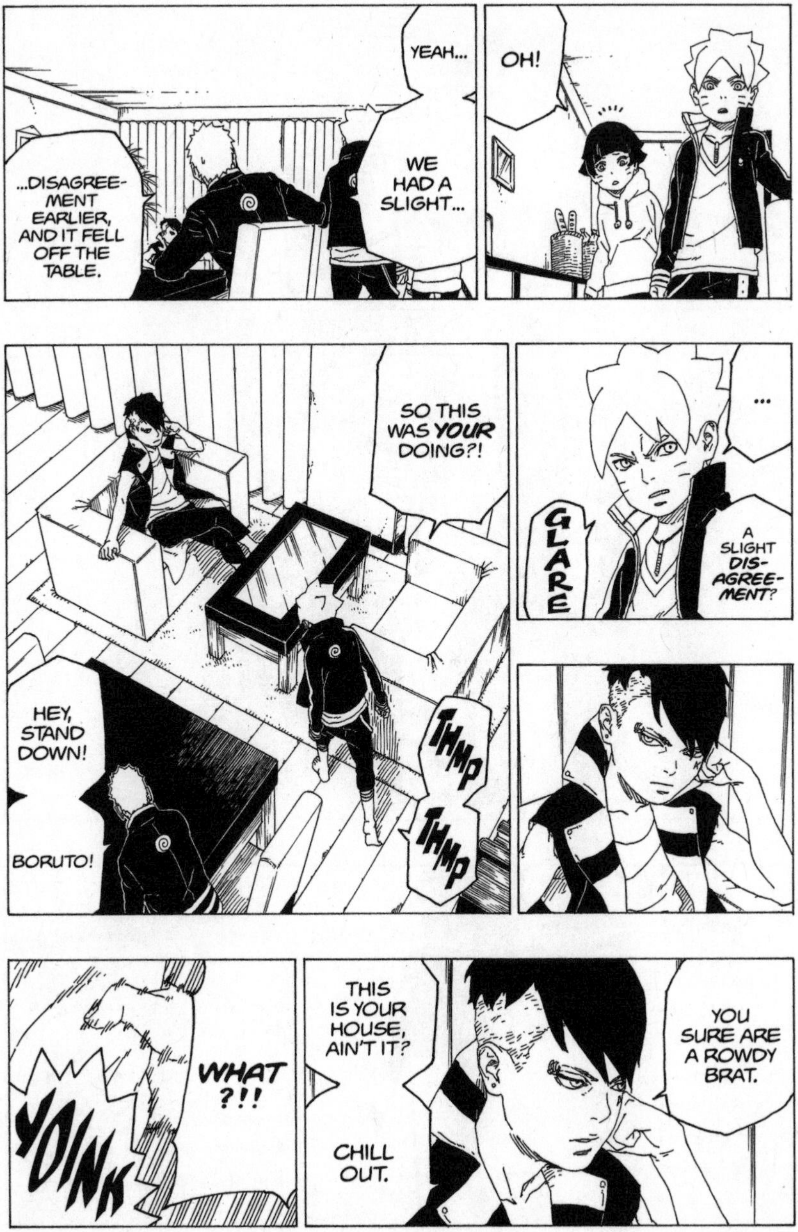
OH!
YEAH...
WE HAD A SLIGHT...
...DISAGREEMENT EARLIER, AND IT FELL OFF THE TABLE.
...
GLARE
A SLIGHT *DISAGREEMENT*?
SO THIS WAS *YOUR* DOING?!
THMP
THMP
HEY, STAND DOWN!
BORUTO!
YOU SURE ARE A ROWDY BRAT.
THIS IS YOUR HOUSE, AIN'T IT?
CHILL OUT.
YOINK
WHAT ?!!

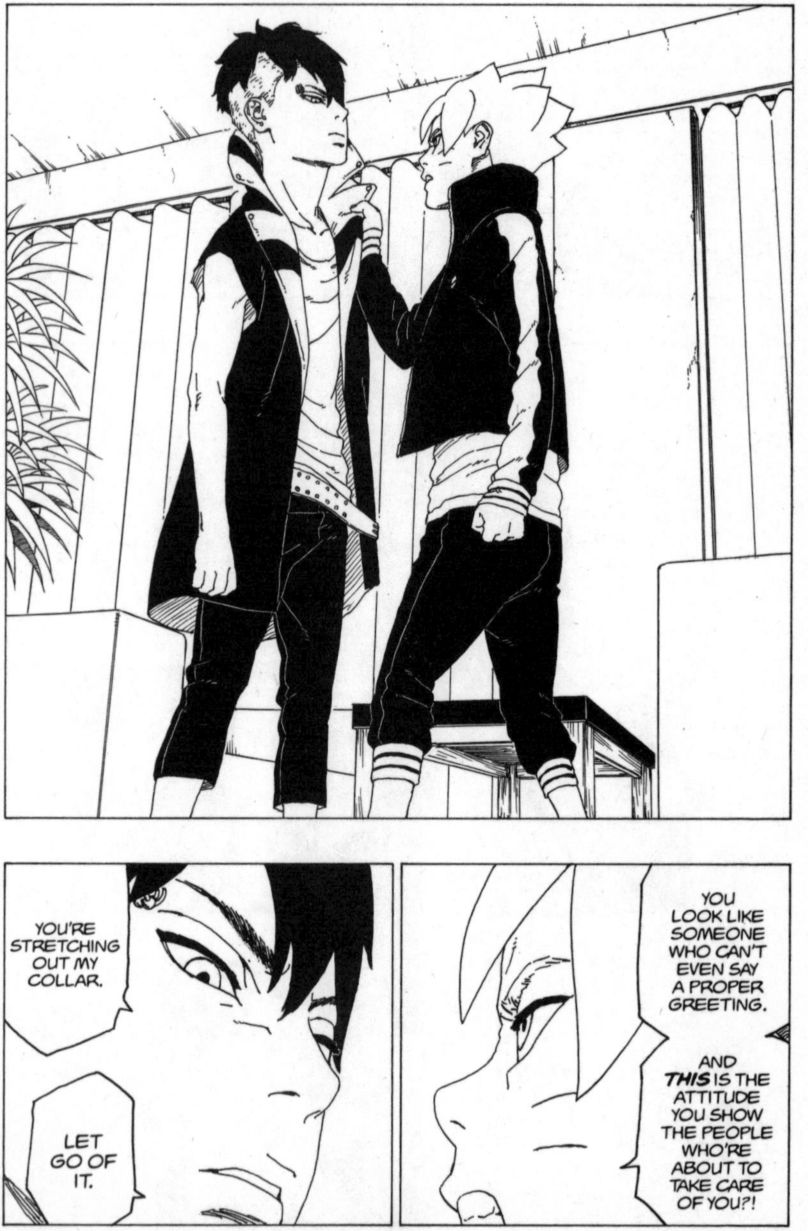
YOU LOOK LIKE SOMEONE WHO CAN'T EVEN SAY A PROPER GREETING.
AND **THIS** IS THE ATTITUDE YOU SHOW THE PEOPLE WHO'RE ABOUT TO TAKE CARE OF YOU?!
YOU'RE STRETCHING OUT MY COLLAR.
LET GO OF IT.

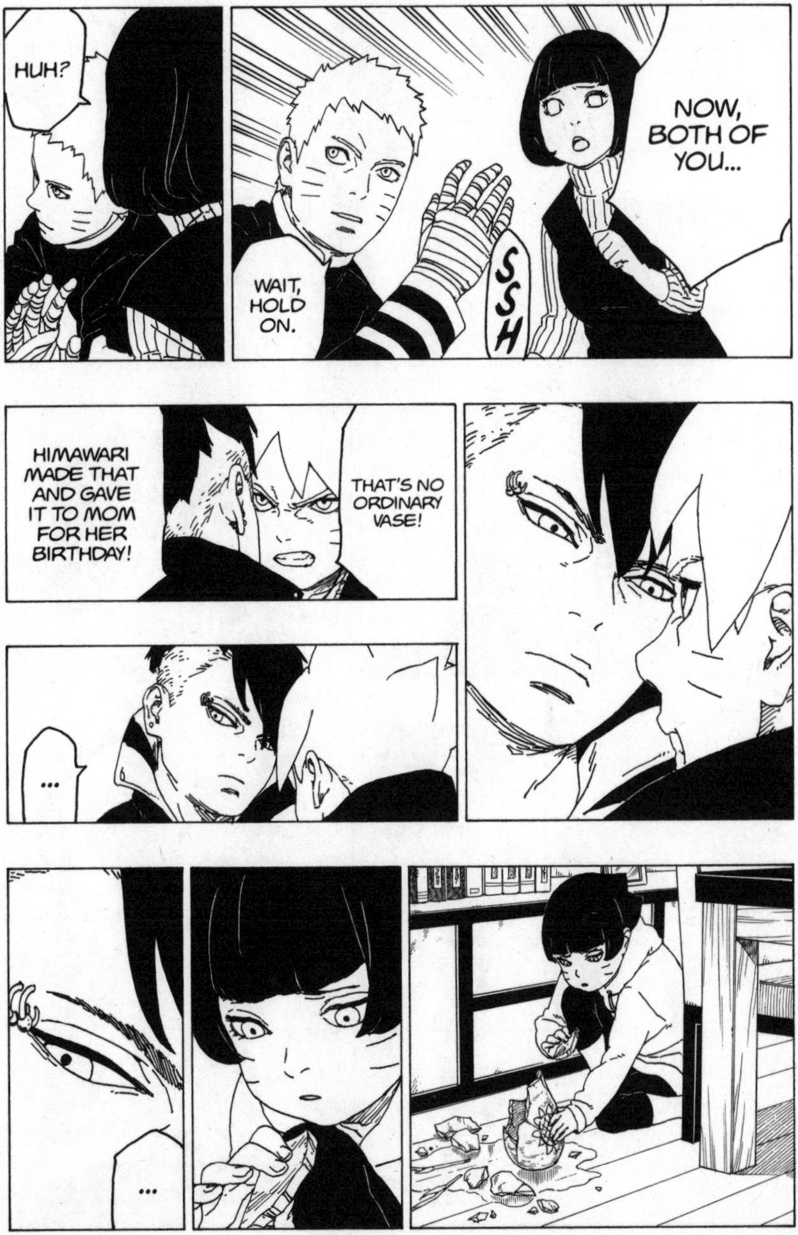
NOW, BOTH OF YOU...
SSH
WAIT, HOLD ON.
HUH?
THAT'S NO ORDINARY VASE!
HIMAWARI MADE THAT AND GAVE IT TO MOM FOR HER BIRTHDAY!
...
...

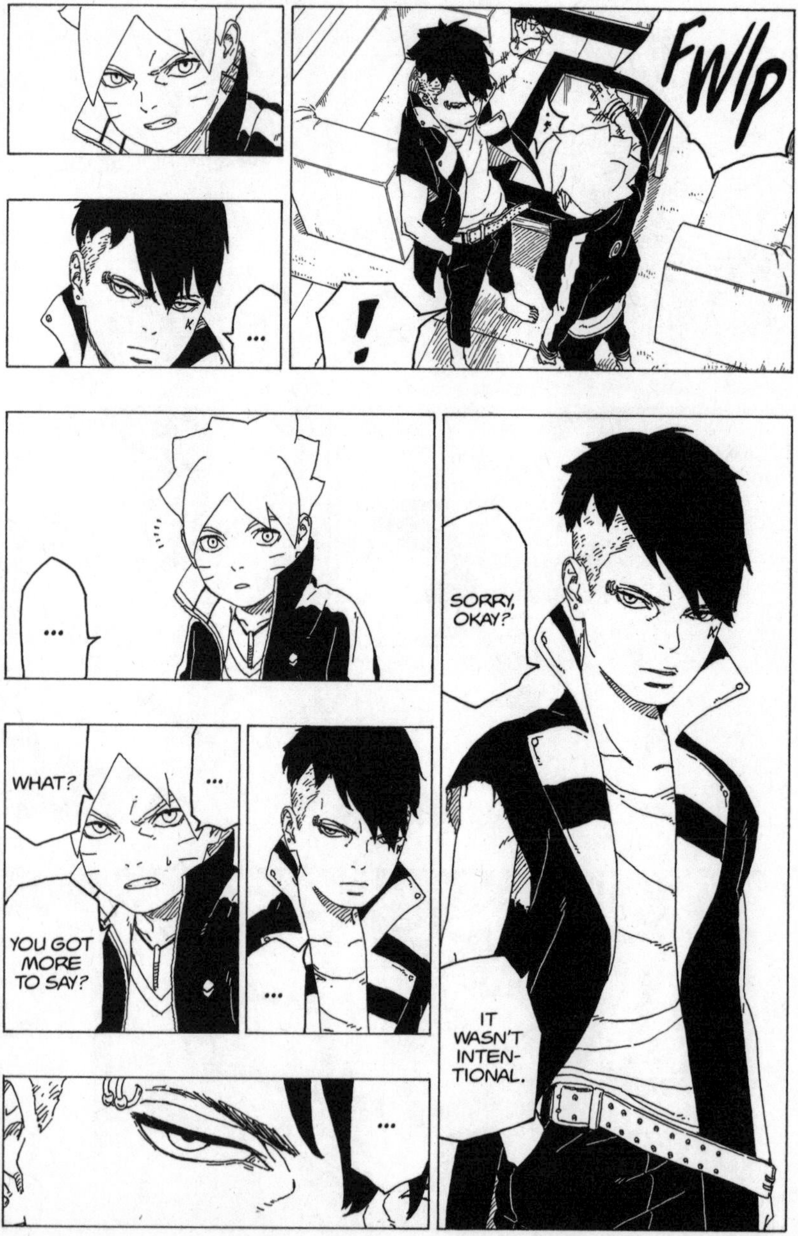
FWLP
!
...
SORRY, OKAY?
IT WASN'T INTEN-TIONAL.
...
...
WHAT?
...
YOU GOT MORE TO SAY?
...

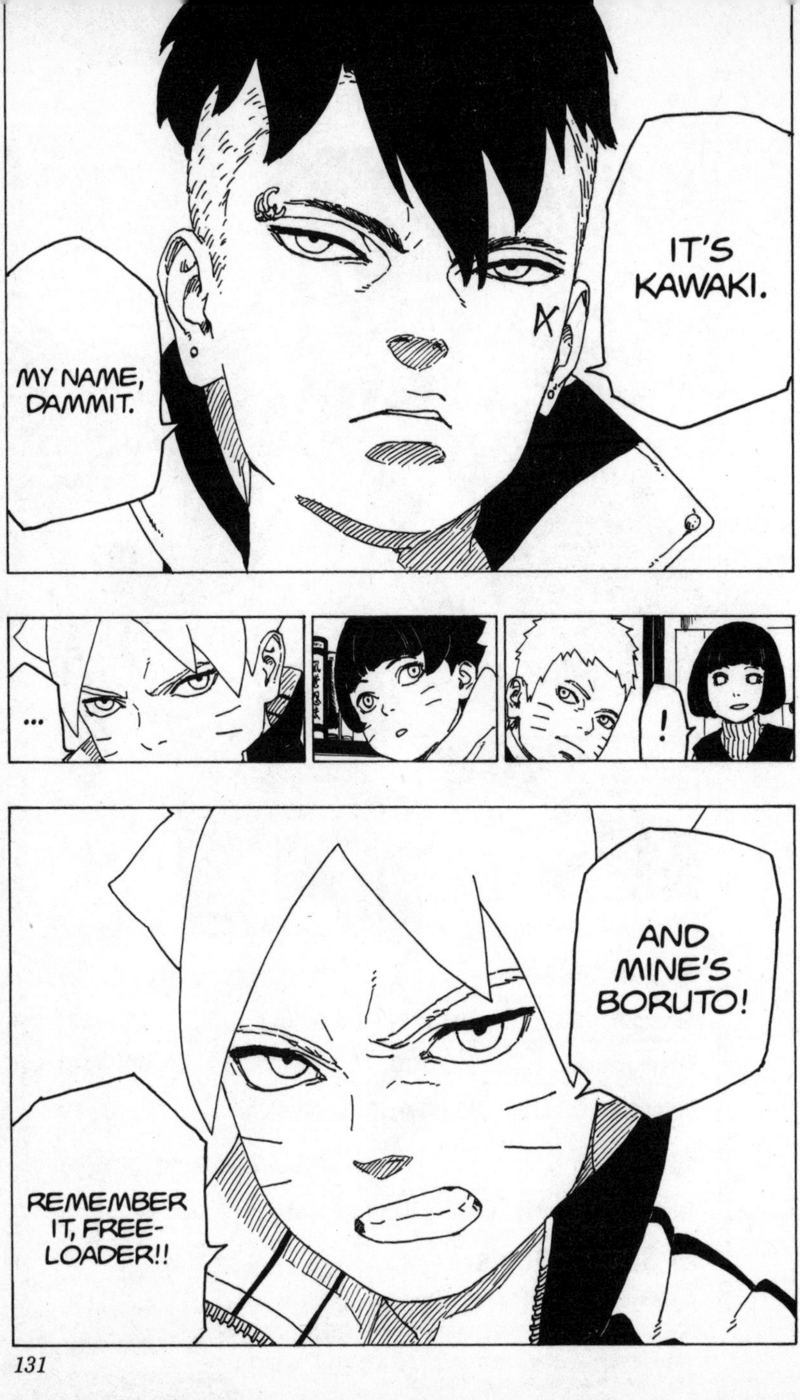
IT'S KAWAKI.
MY NAME, DAMMIT.
!
...
AND MINE'S BORUTO!
REMEMBER IT, FREE-LOADER!!

NINJA ENCYCLOPEDIA · ENTRY 21

KAWAKI

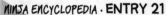

"What do Konoha shinobi want with me...?"

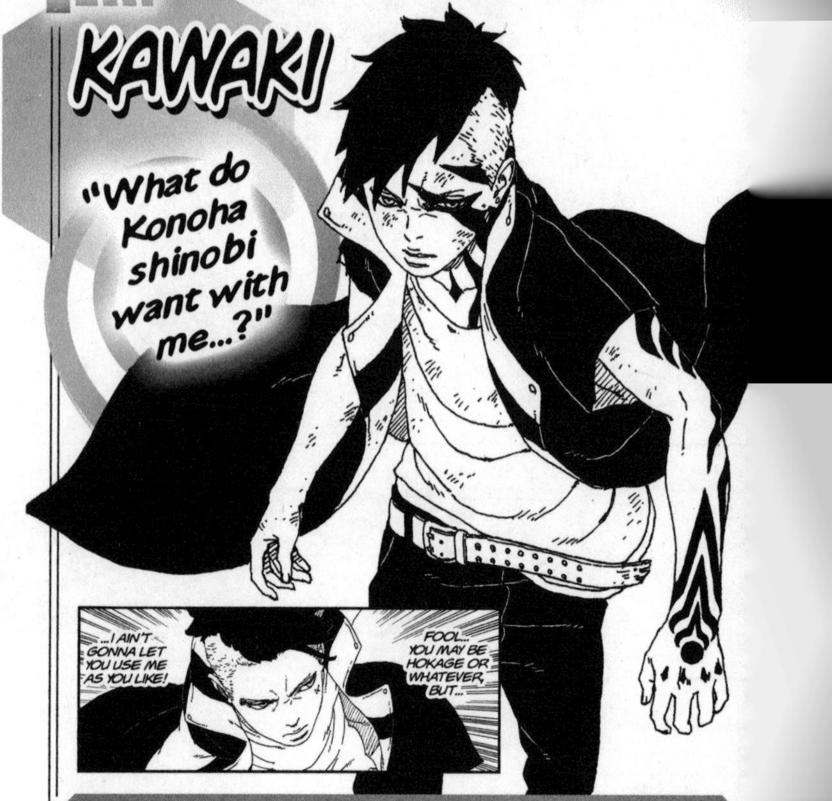
FOOL... YOU MAY BE HOKAGE OR WHATEVER, BUT...
...I AIN'T GONNA LET YOU USE ME AS YOU LIKE!

Attributes

Strength......................80 [170]	Dexterity......................66 [156]
Intelligence......................130	Chakra......................30 [120]
Perception..................60 [120]	Negotiation..........................70

Skills

Hand-to-hand Combat ☆☆☆☆ Machine Operation ☆☆ Sabotage ☆☆☆

Shinobi Tools

Disclosure of information about the **Vessel** is prohibited.

*Average attribute value is 60 for ordinary people and 90 for genin. Skill values range from 1 to 5☆ with 5☆ signifying super top-notch.

Number 27: Breakdown in Negotiations!!

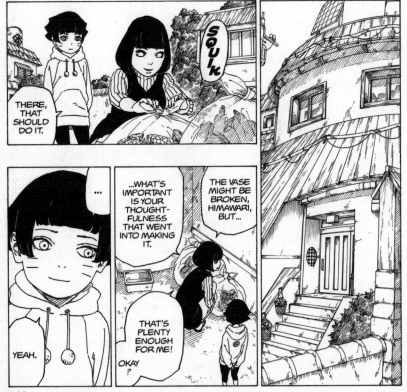

SQUIK
THERE, THAT SHOULD DO IT.
THE VASE MIGHT BE BROKEN, HIMAWARI, BUT...
...WHAT'S IMPORTANT IS YOUR THOUGHTFULNESS THAT WENT INTO MAKING IT.
THAT'S PLENTY ENOUGH FOR ME!
OKAY?
...
YEAH.

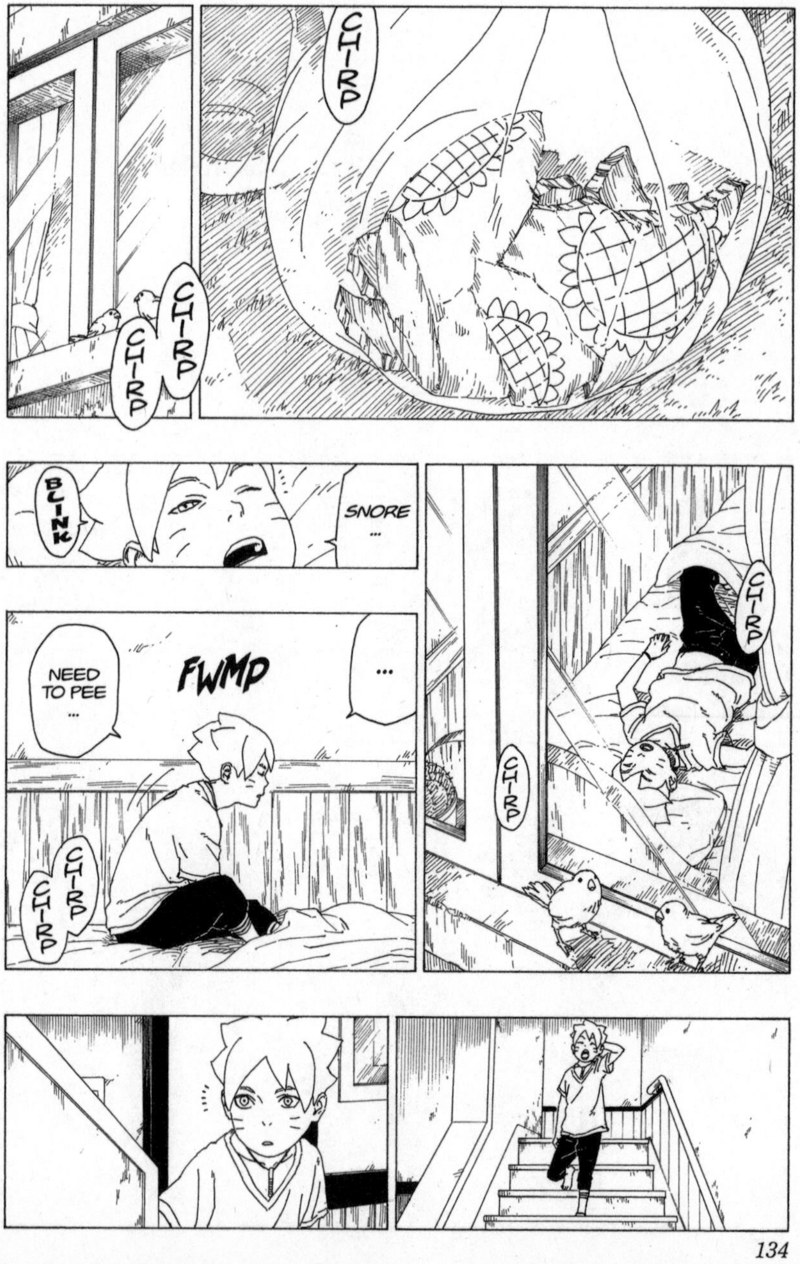
CHIRP
CHIRP
CHIRP
CHIRP
CHIRP
SNORE ...
BLINK
...
FWMP
NEED TO PEE ...
CHIRP
CHIRP

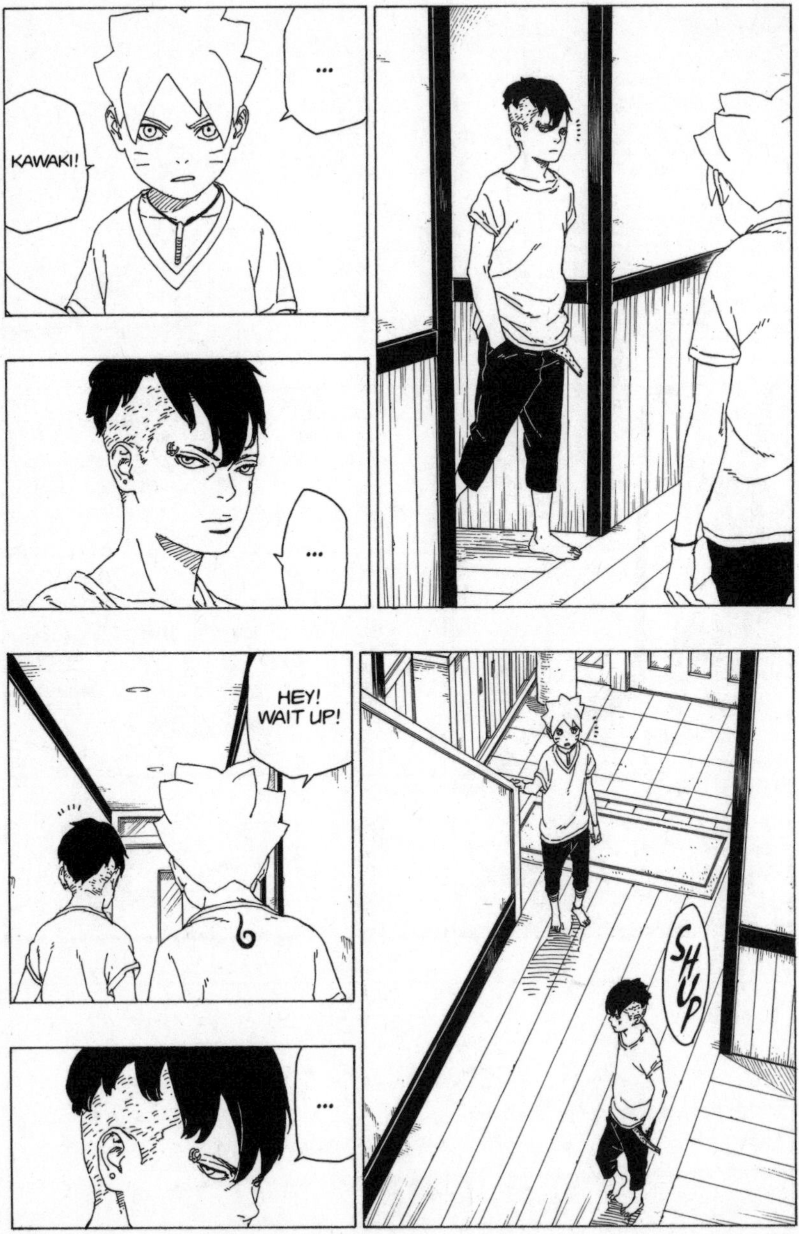
...
KAWAKI!
...
SHUP
HEY! WAIT UP!
...

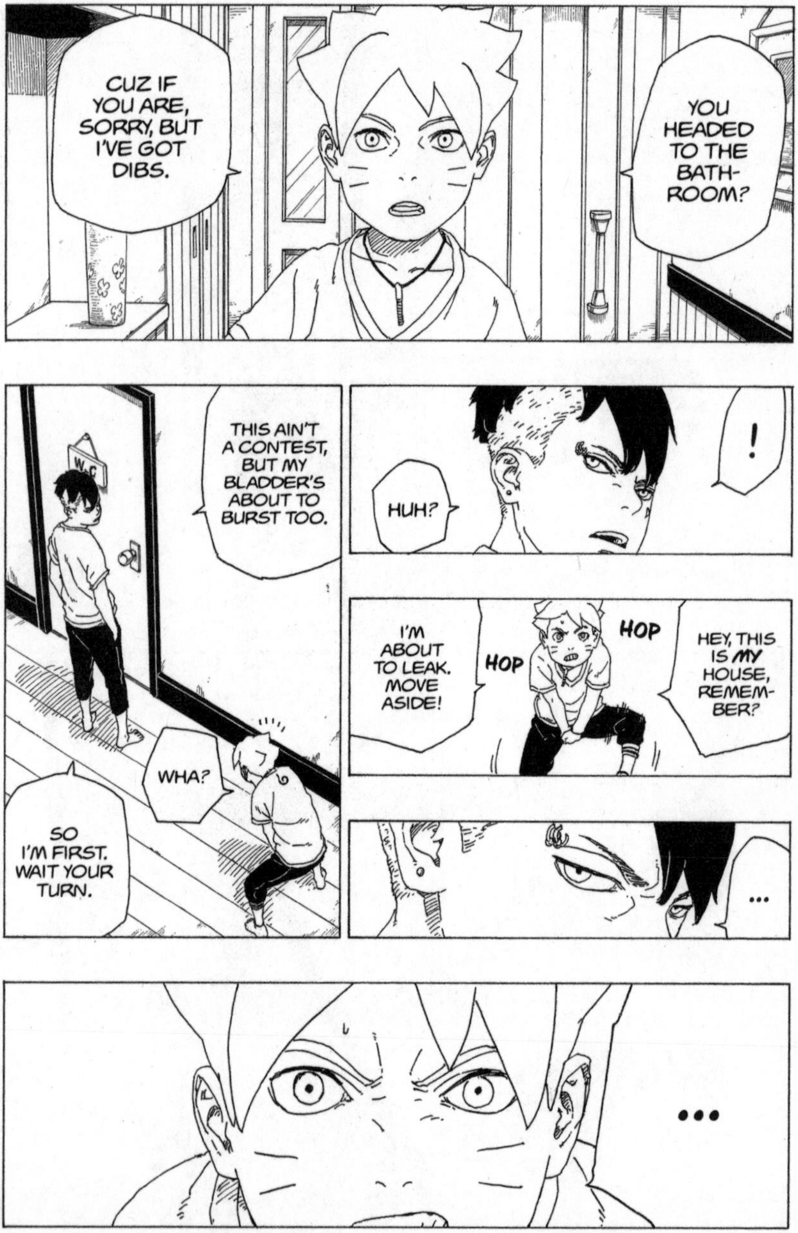
YOU HEADED TO THE BATH-ROOM?
CUZ IF YOU ARE, SORRY, BUT I'VE GOT DIBS.
!
HUH?
HEY, THIS IS MY HOUSE, REMEM-BER?
HOP
HOP
I'M ABOUT TO LEAK. MOVE ASIDE!
...
THIS AIN'T A CONTEST, BUT MY BLADDER'S ABOUT TO BURST TOO.
W.C
WHA?
SO I'M FIRST. WAIT YOUR TURN.
...

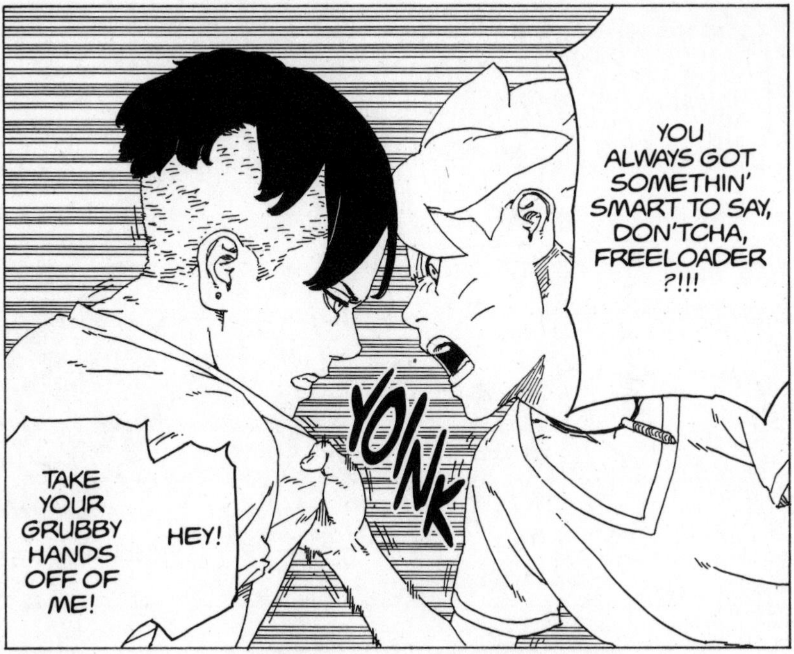
YOU ALWAYS GOT SOMETHIN' SMART TO SAY, DON'TCHA, FREELOADER ?!!!
YOINK
HEY!
TAKE YOUR GRUBBY HANDS OFF OF ME!

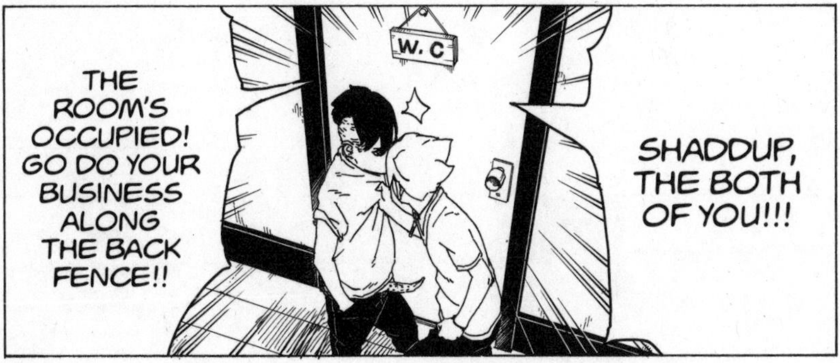
W.C
SHADDUP, THE BOTH OF YOU!!!
THE ROOM'S OCCUPIED! GO DO YOUR BUSINESS ALONG THE BACK FENCE!!

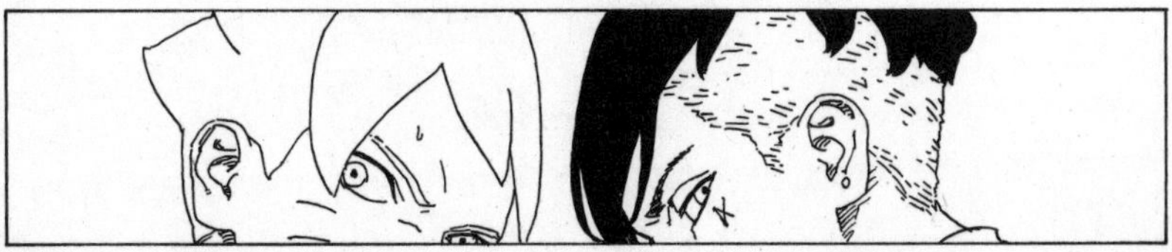

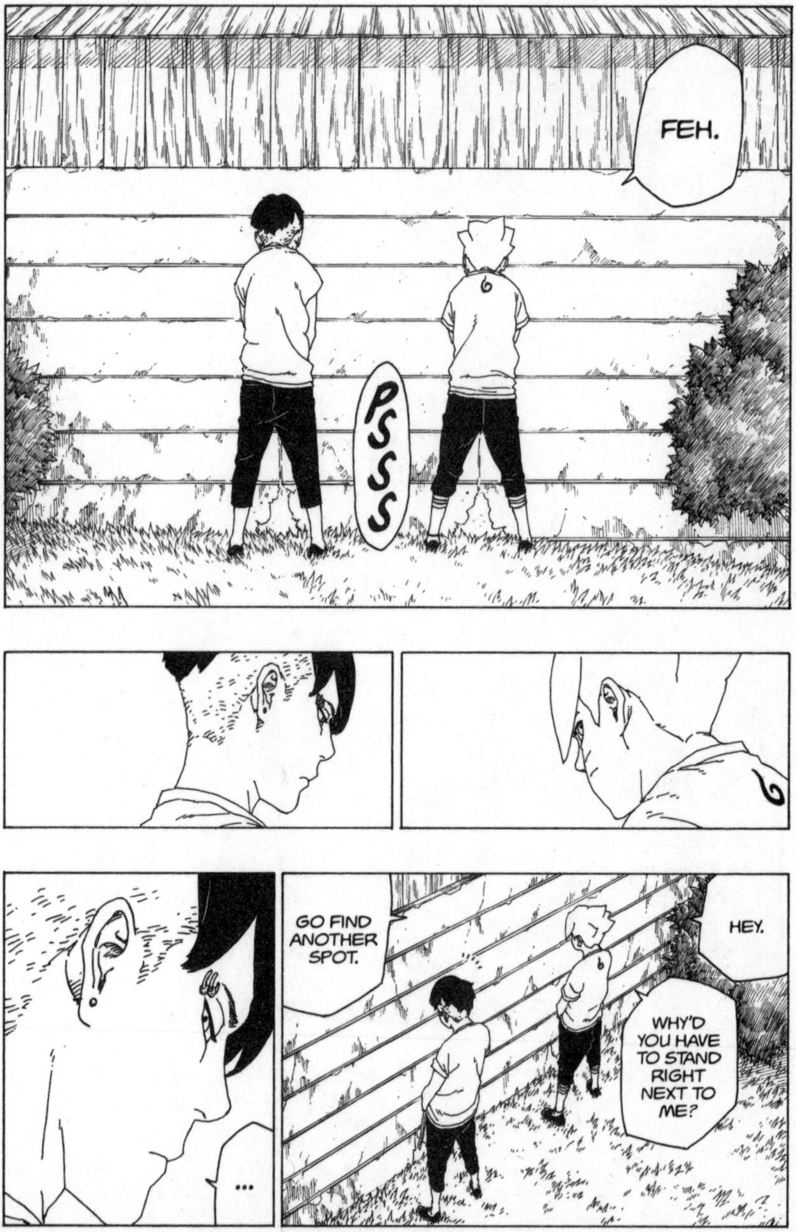
FEH.
PSSS
HEY.
WHY'D YOU HAVE TO STAND RIGHT NEXT TO ME?
GO FIND ANOTHER SPOT.
...

YOU SQUIRT.

QUIT ORDERIN' ME AROUND.

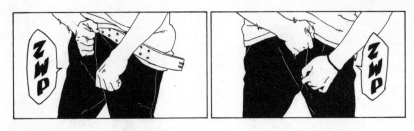

ZWP

ZWP

...

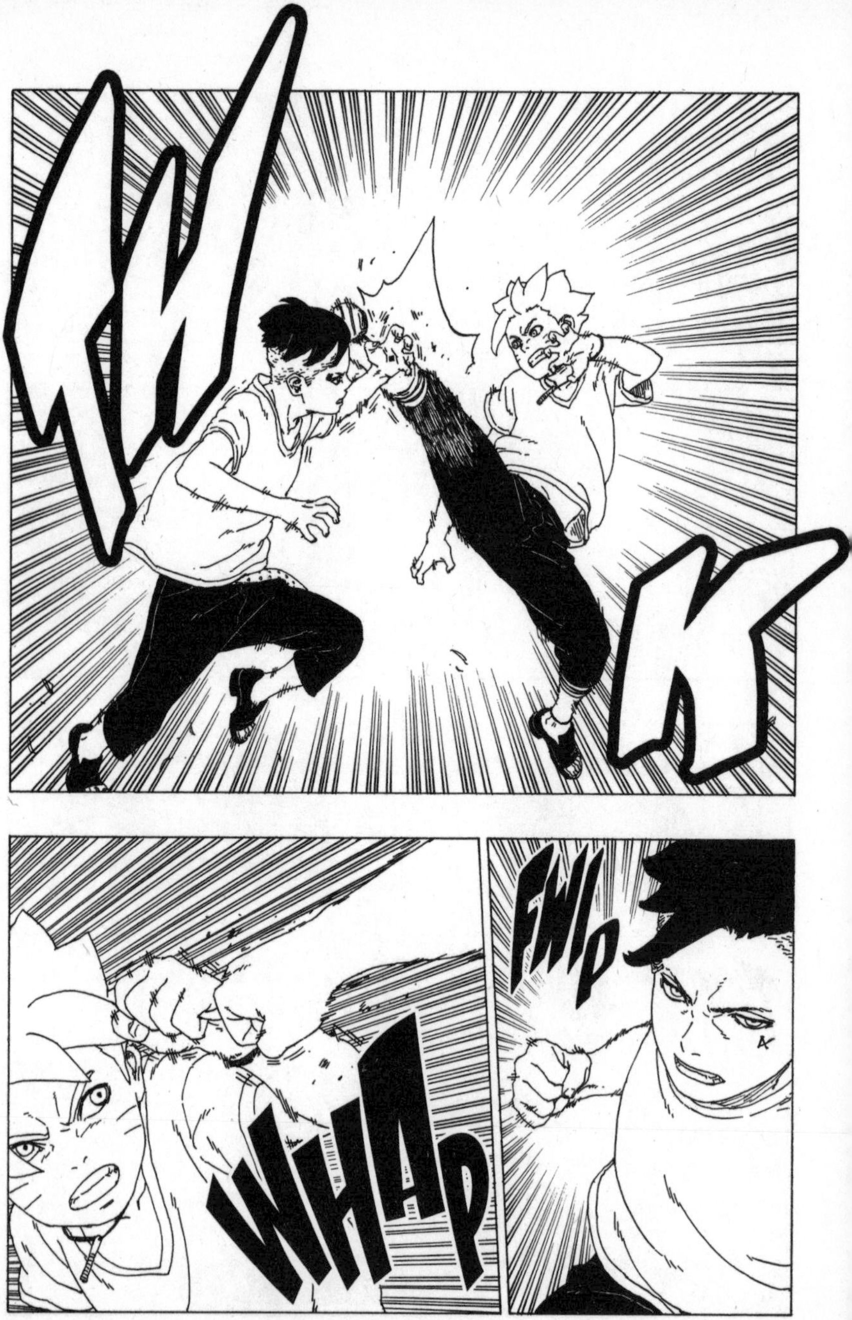
FWIP
WHAP

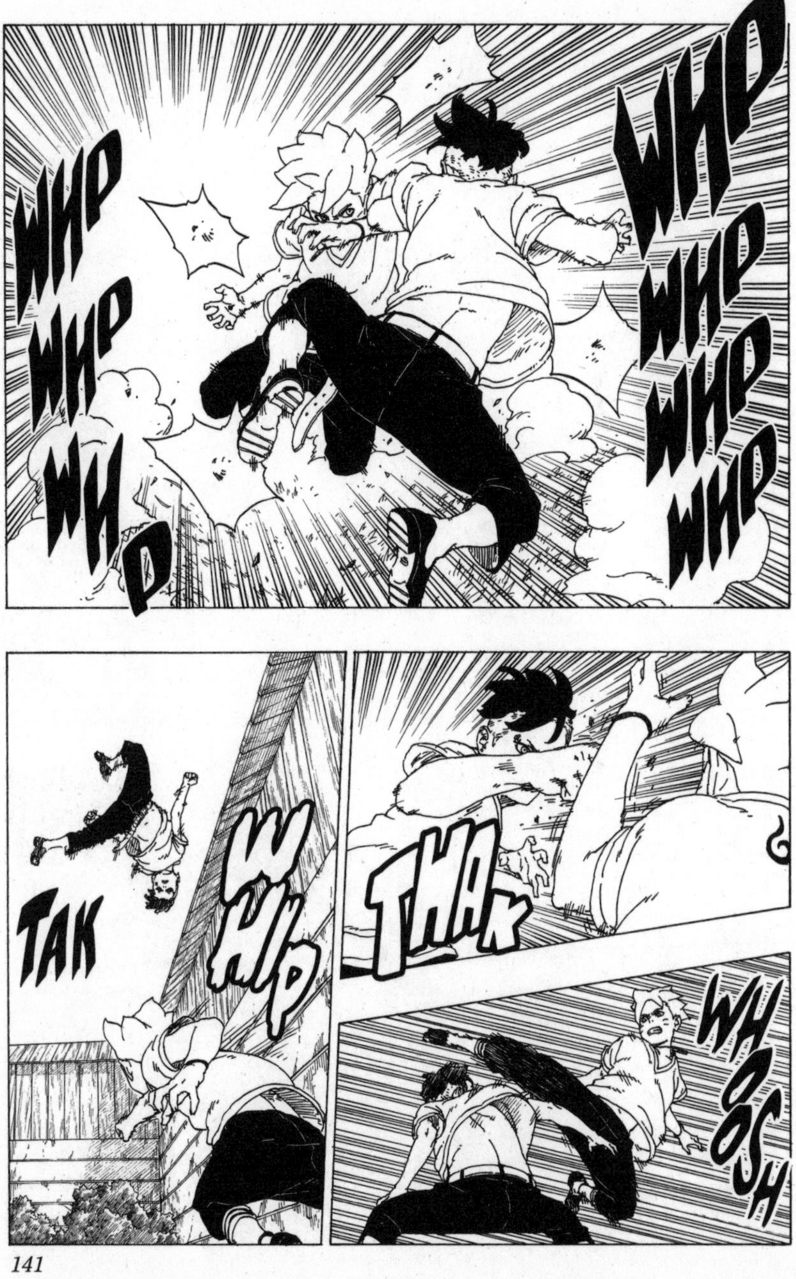
WHIP
WHIP
WHIP
WHIP
WHIP
WHIP
WHIP
THAK
WHOOSH
WHIP
TAK

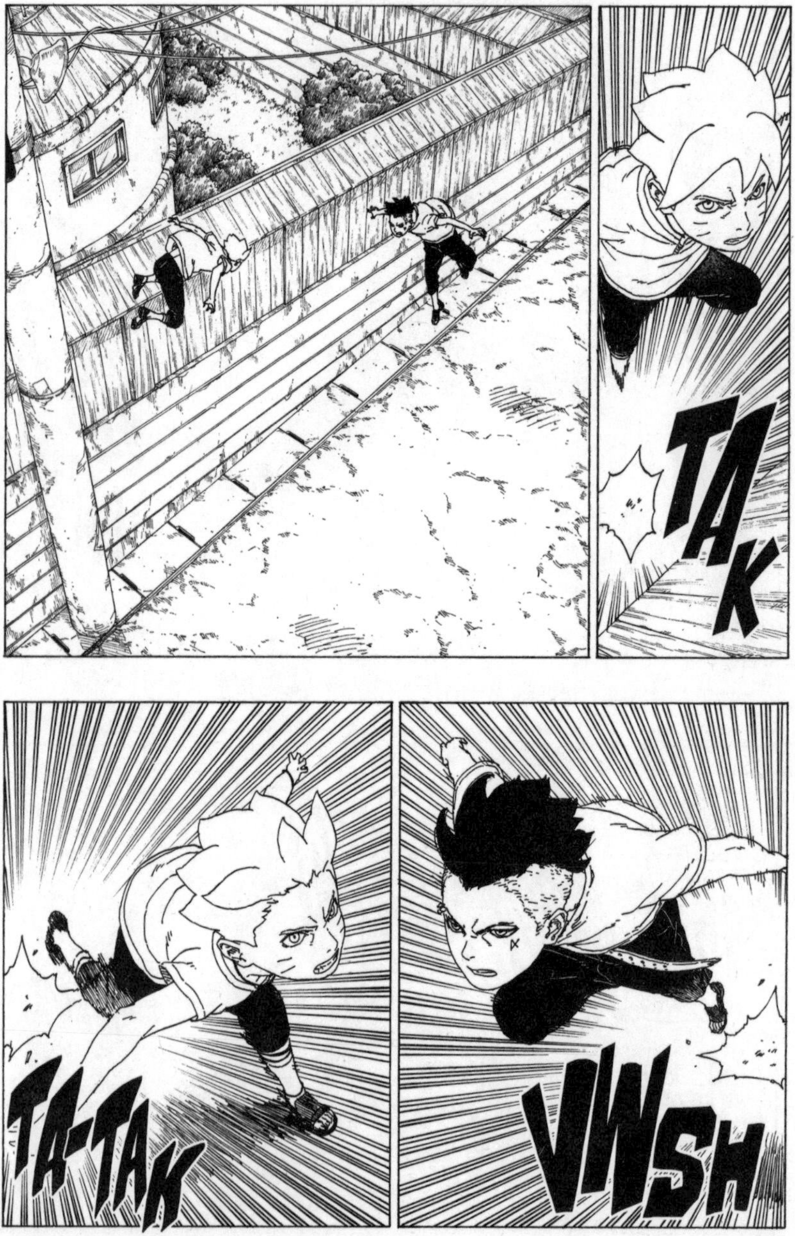
TAK
VWSH
TA-TAK

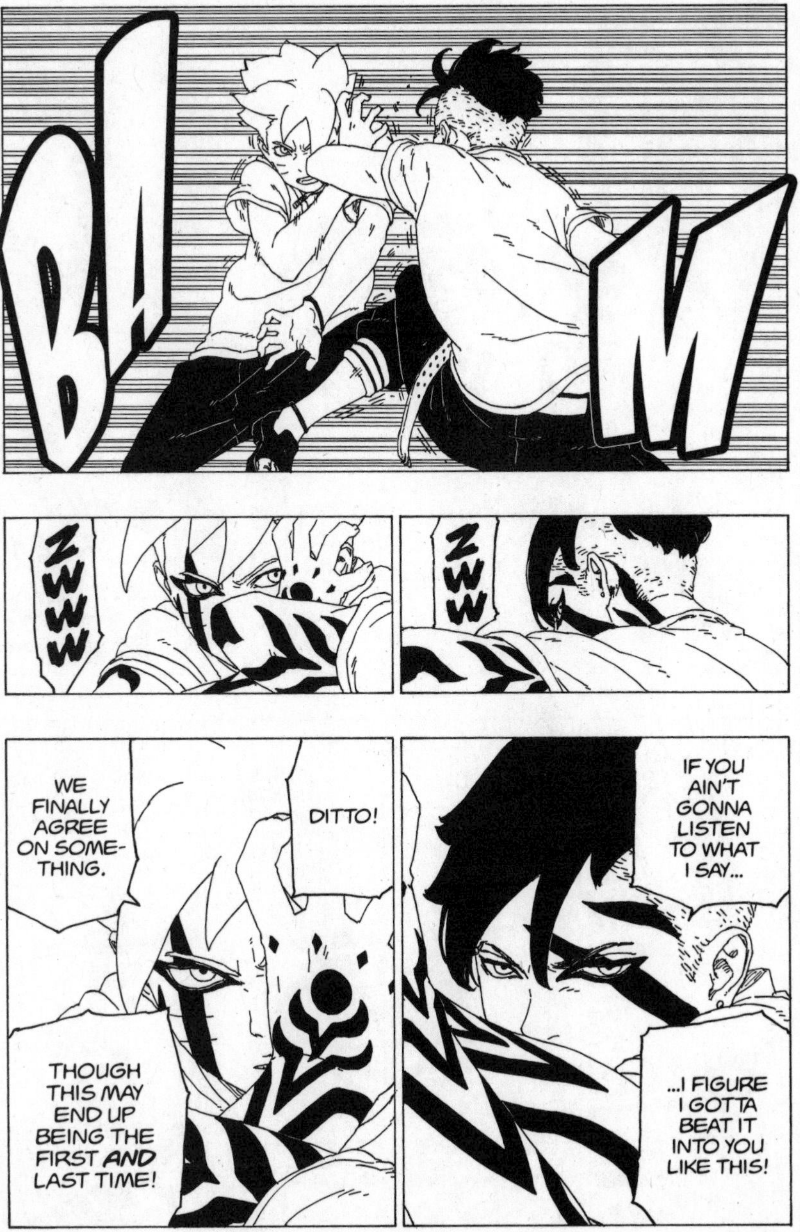
BAM
ZWW
ZWWWW
IF YOU AIN'T GONNA LISTEN TO WHAT I SAY...
...I FIGURE I GOTTA BEAT IT INTO YOU LIKE THIS!
DITTO!
WE FINALLY AGREE ON SOME-THING.
THOUGH THIS MAY END UP BEING THE FIRST ***AND*** LAST TIME!

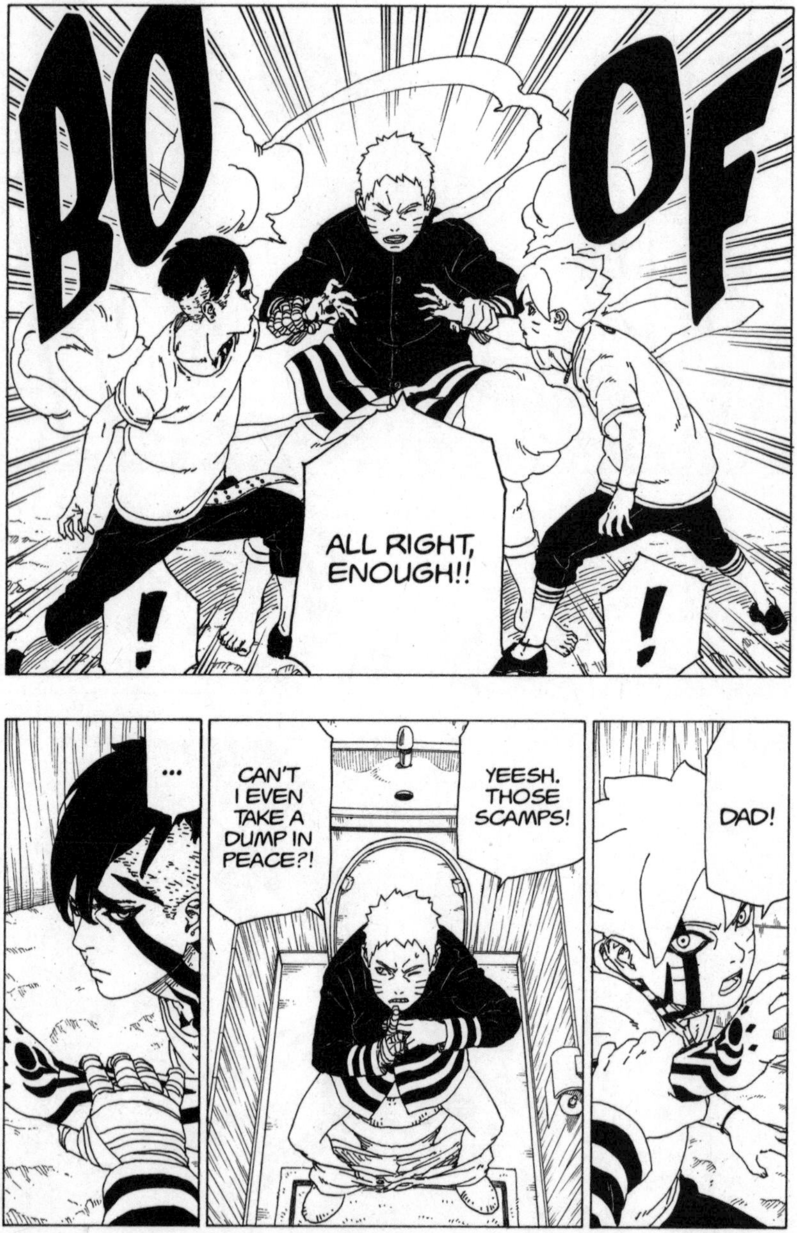
BOOF
ALL RIGHT, ENOUGH!!
!
!
DAD!
YEESH. THOSE SCAMPS!
CAN'T I EVEN TAKE A DUMP IN PEACE?!
...

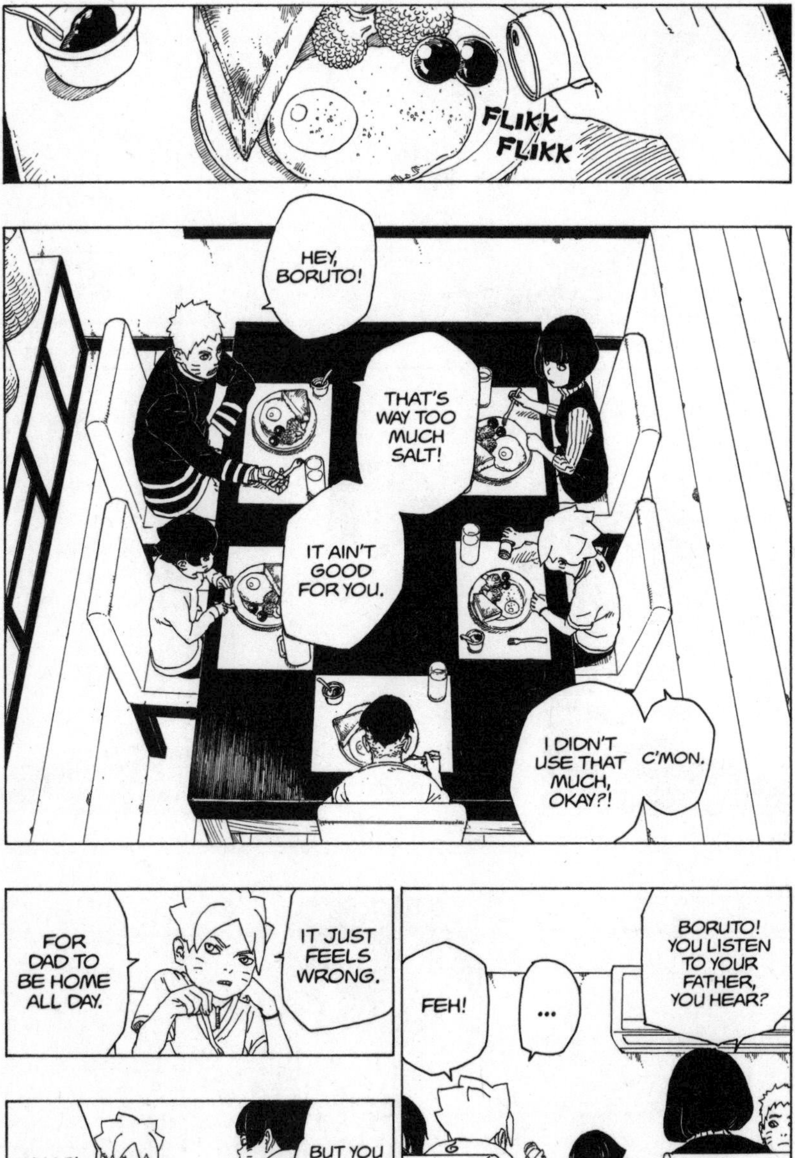
FLIKK FLIKK
HEY, BORUTO!
THAT'S WAY TOO MUCH SALT!
IT AIN'T GOOD FOR YOU.
C'MON.
I DIDN'T USE THAT MUCH, OKAY?!
IT JUST FEELS WRONG.
FOR DAD TO BE HOME ALL DAY.
BUT YOU LIKE IT!
WHA?!
BORUTO! YOU LISTEN TO YOUR FATHER, YOU HEAR?
...
FEH!

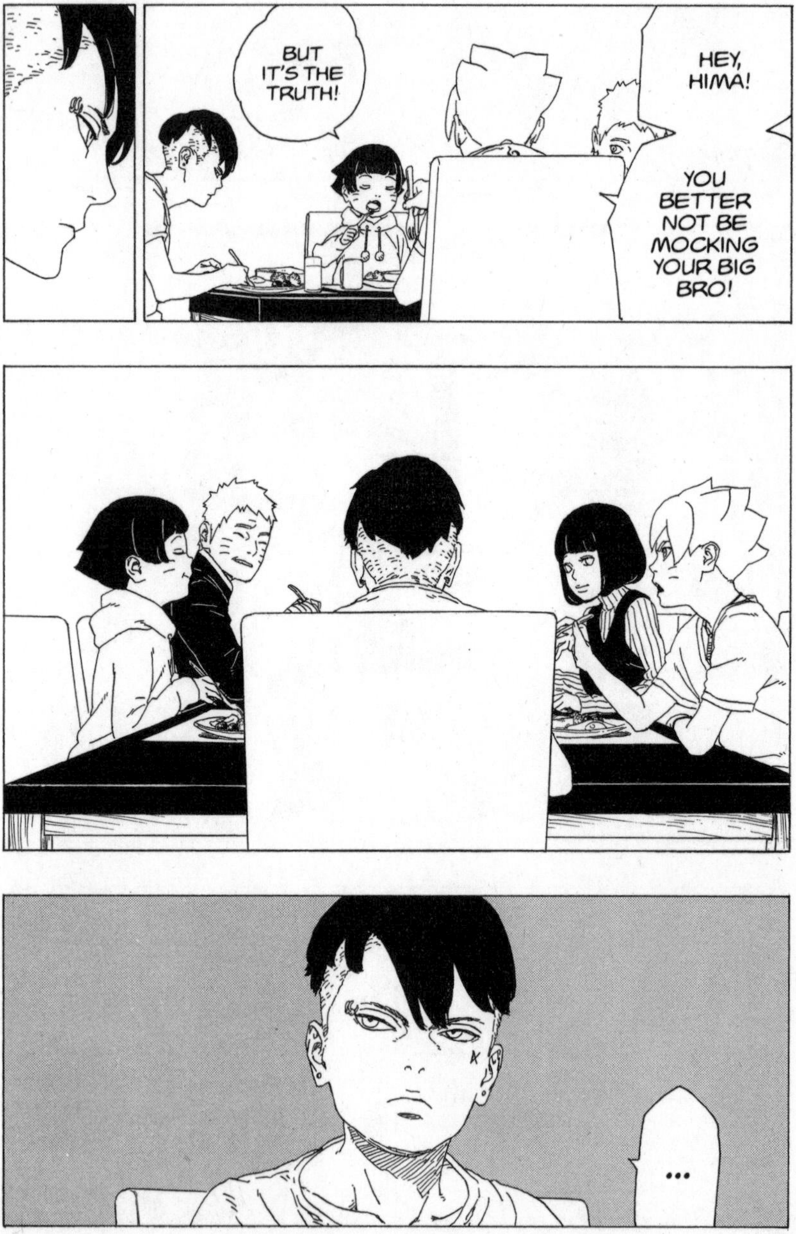
HEY, HIMA!
YOU BETTER NOT BE MOCKING YOUR BIG BRO!
BUT IT'S THE TRUTH!
...

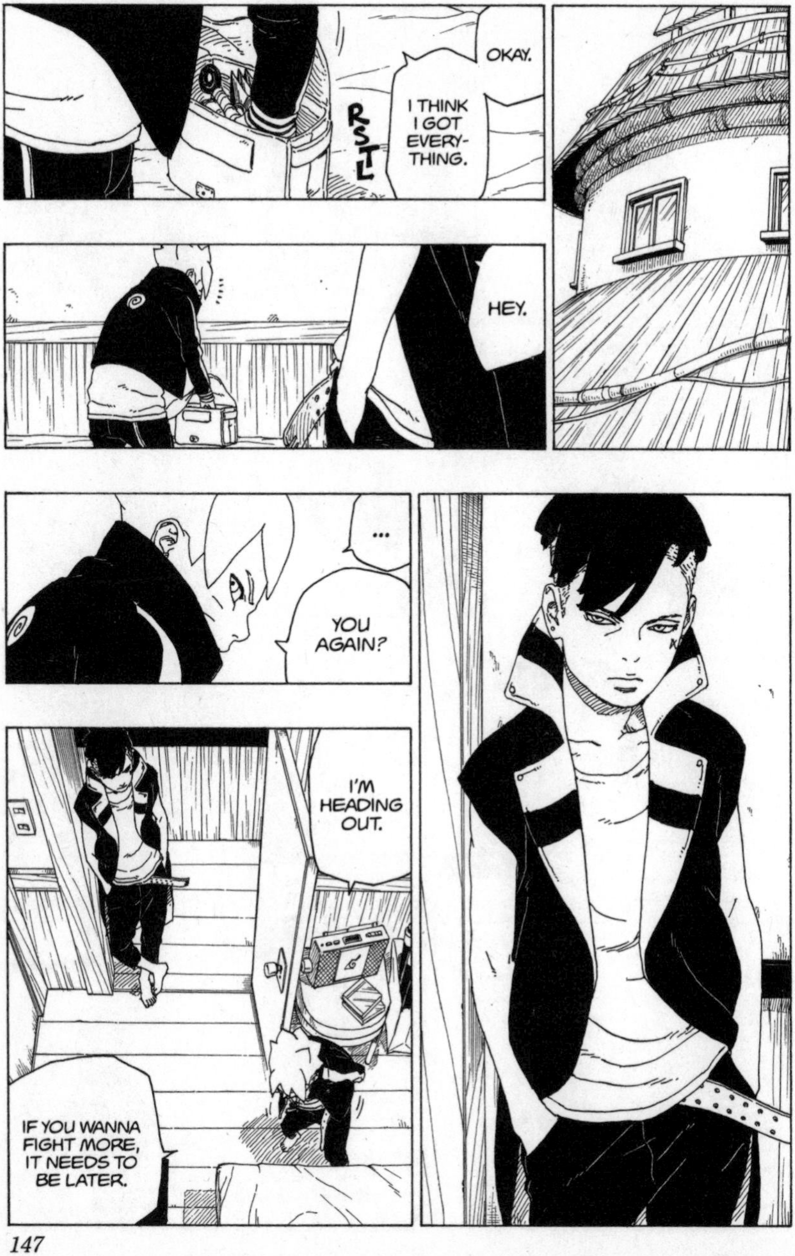
OKAY.
I THINK I GOT EVERYTHING.
RSTL
HEY.
...
YOU AGAIN?
I'M HEADING OUT.
IF YOU WANNA FIGHT MORE, IT NEEDS TO BE LATER.

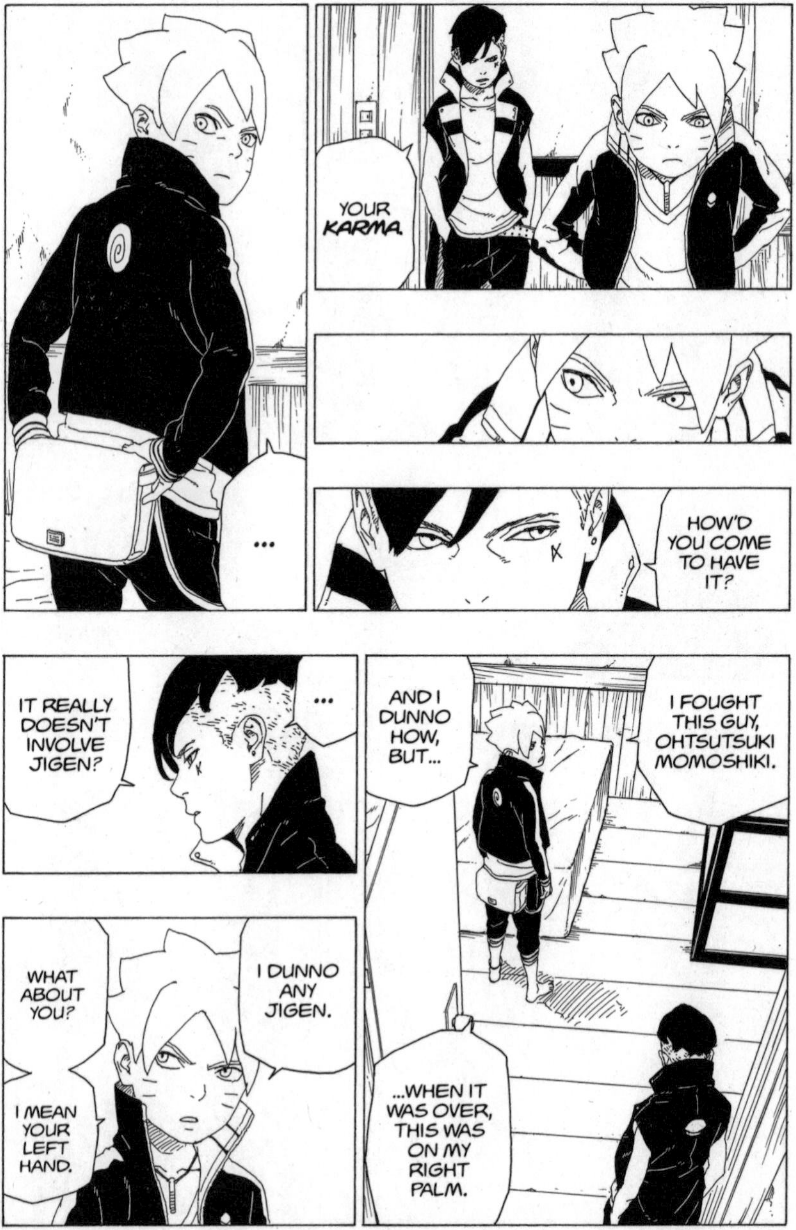
YOUR KARMA.
HOW'D YOU COME TO HAVE IT?
...
I FOUGHT THIS GUY, OHTSUTSUKI MOMOSHIKI.
AND I DUNNO HOW, BUT...
...WHEN IT WAS OVER, THIS WAS ON MY RIGHT PALM.
...
IT REALLY DOESN'T INVOLVE JIGEN?
I DUNNO ANY JIGEN.
WHAT ABOUT YOU?
I MEAN YOUR LEFT HAND.

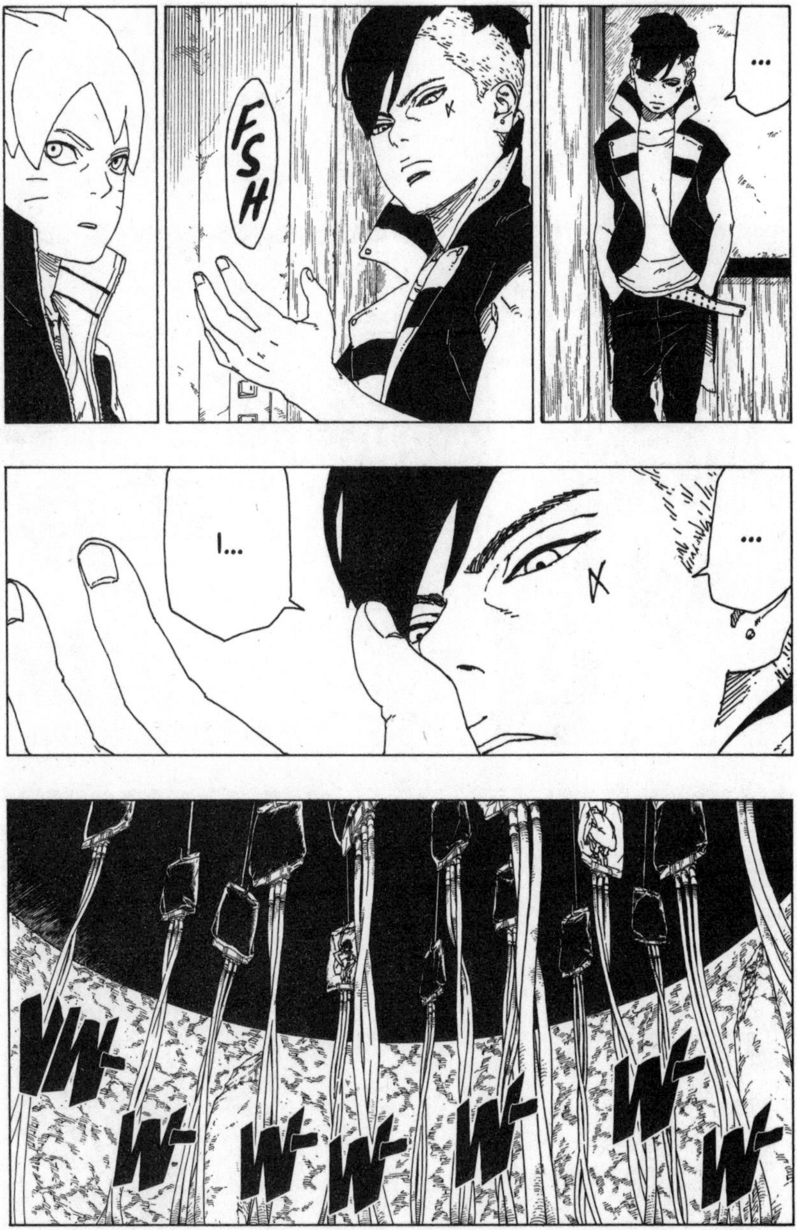
...
FSH
...
I...
W-W-W-W-W-W-W-W-

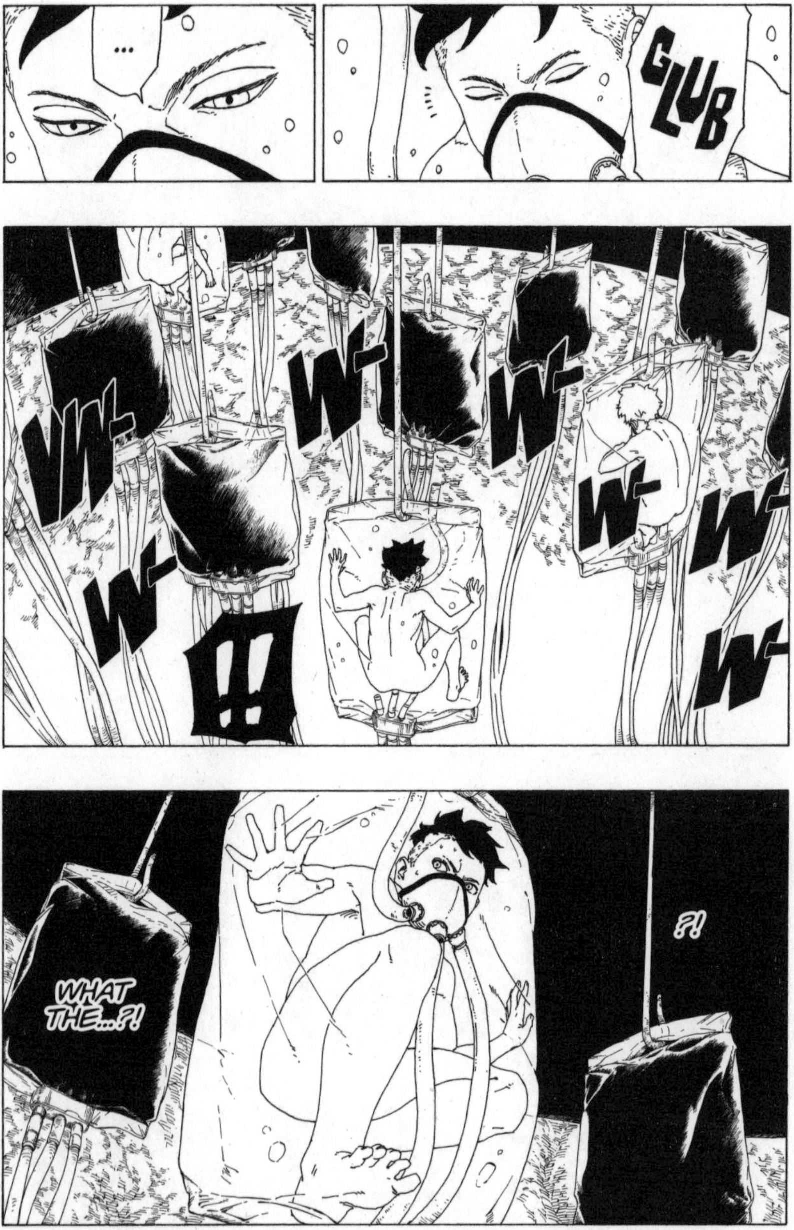
GLUB
...
W-
W-
W-
W-
W-
W-
W-
!!
?!
WHAT THE...?!

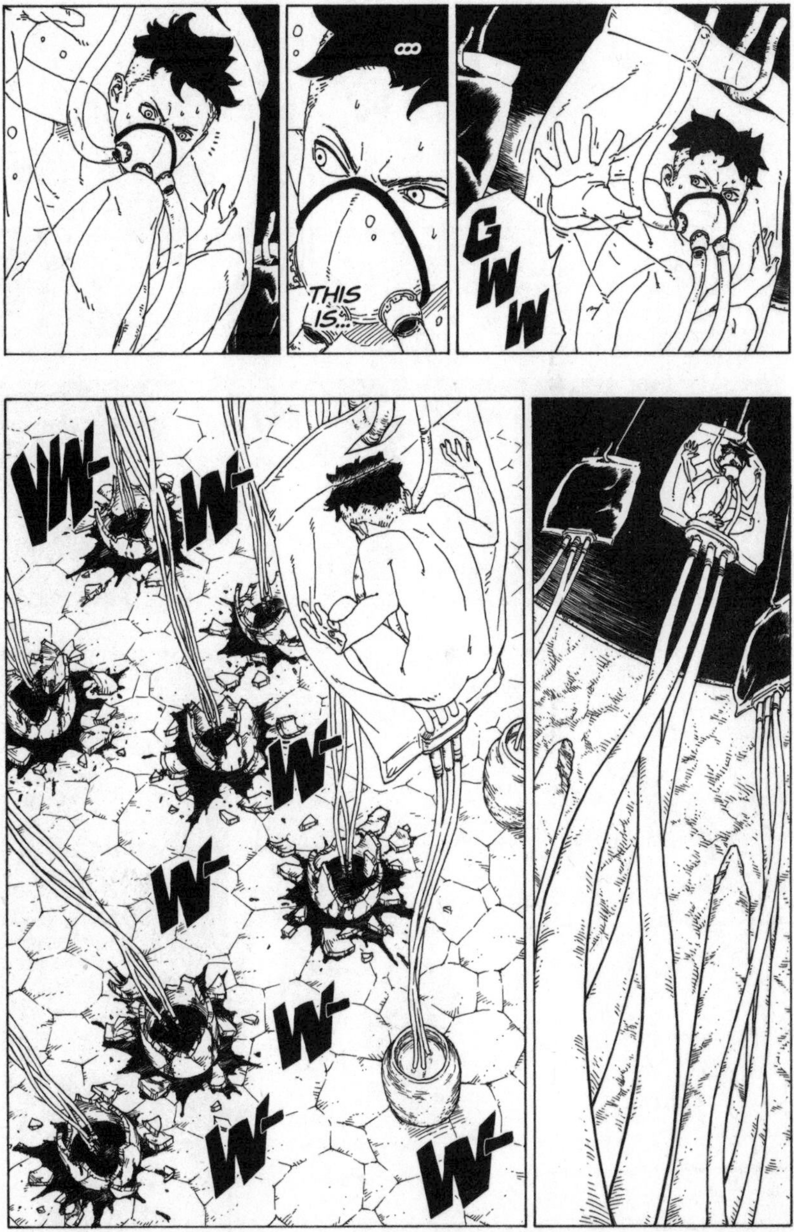
GWW
THIS IS...
VW-W-W-W-W-W-W-

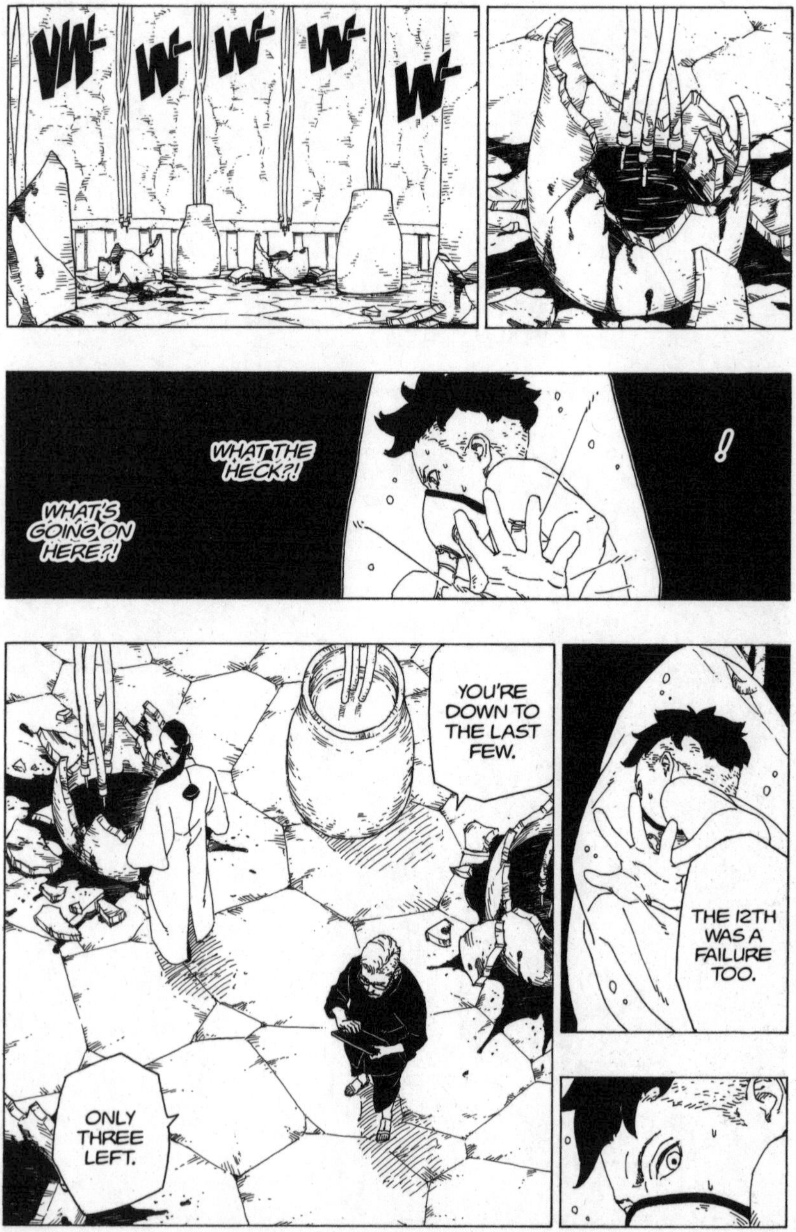
VW- W- W- W- W-
!
WHAT THE HECK?!
WHAT'S GOING ON HERE?!
THE 12TH WAS A FAILURE TOO.
YOU'RE DOWN TO THE LAST FEW.
ONLY THREE LEFT.

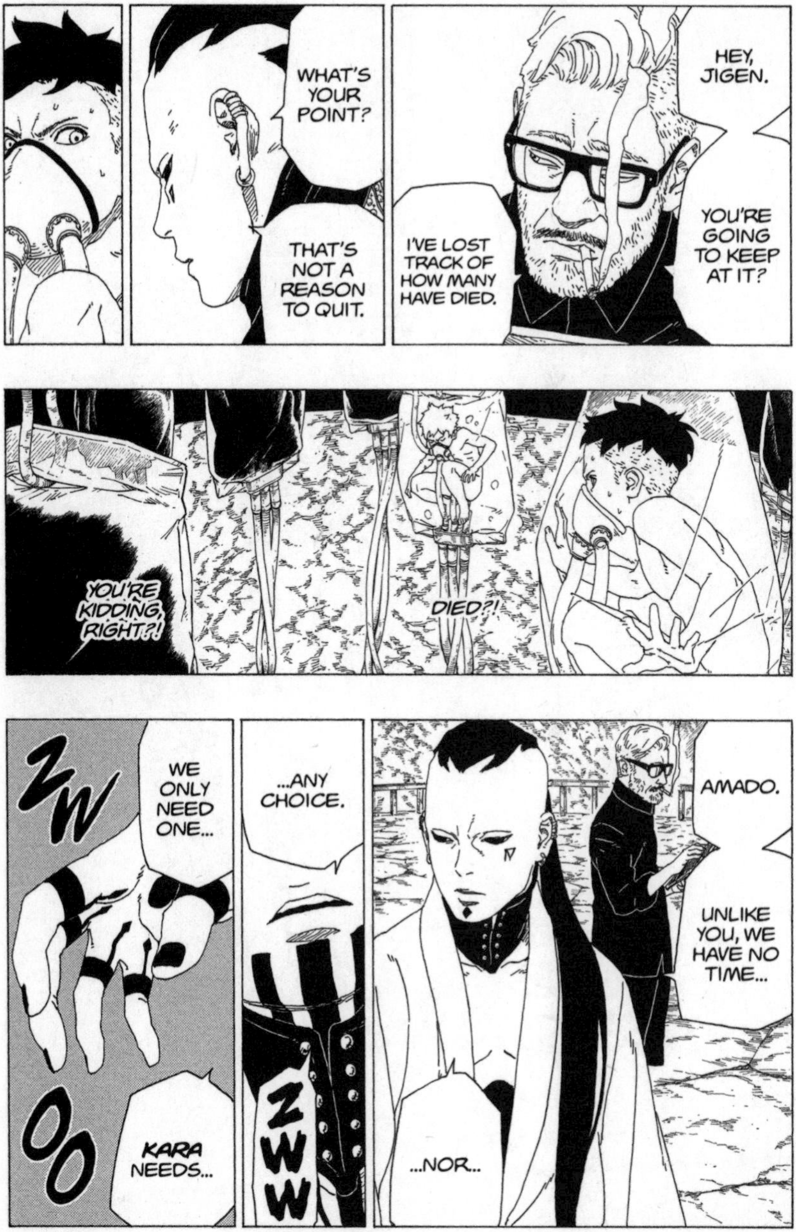
HEY, JIGEN.
YOU'RE GOING TO KEEP AT IT?
I'VE LOST TRACK OF HOW MANY HAVE DIED.
WHAT'S YOUR POINT?
THAT'S NOT A REASON TO QUIT.
DIED?!
YOU'RE KIDDING, RIGHT?!
AMADO.
UNLIKE YOU, WE HAVE NO TIME...
...NOR...
...ANY CHOICE.
ZWW
WE ONLY NEED ONE...
KARA NEEDS...
ZW
OO

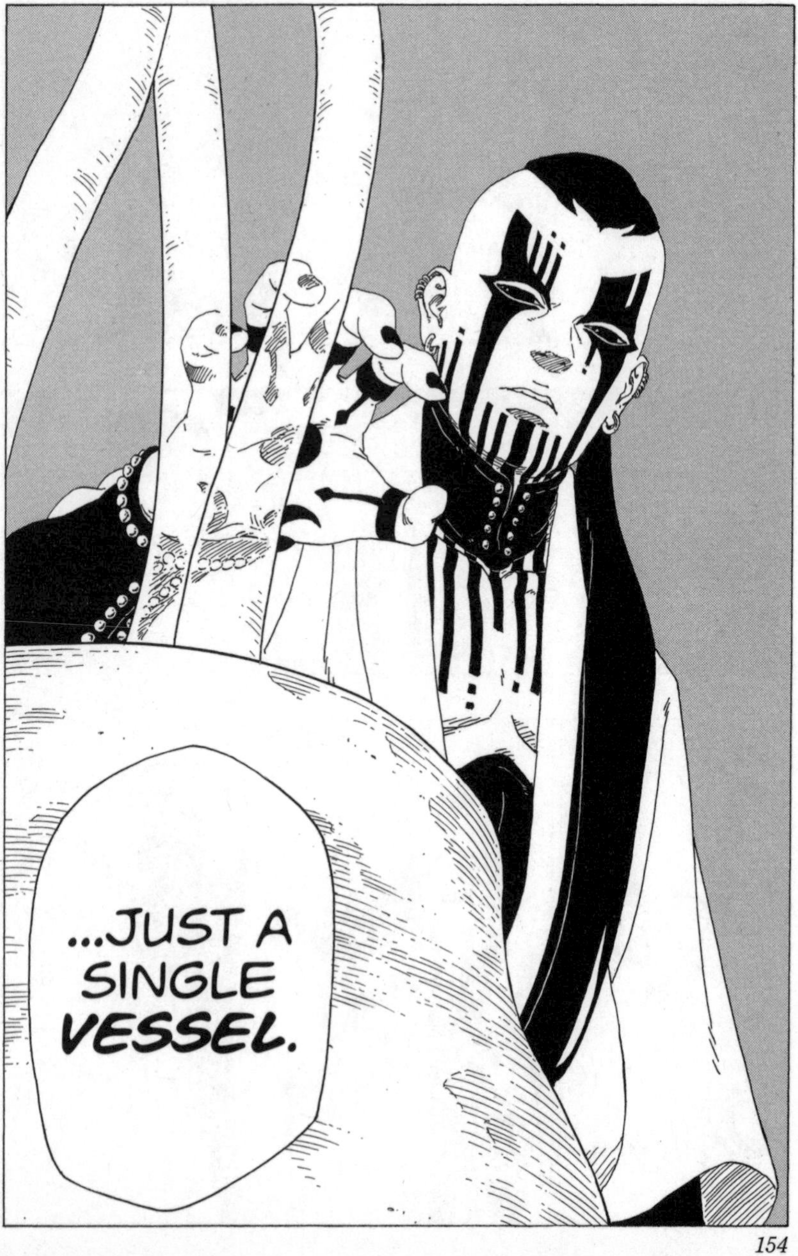
...JUST A SINGLE **VESSEL.**

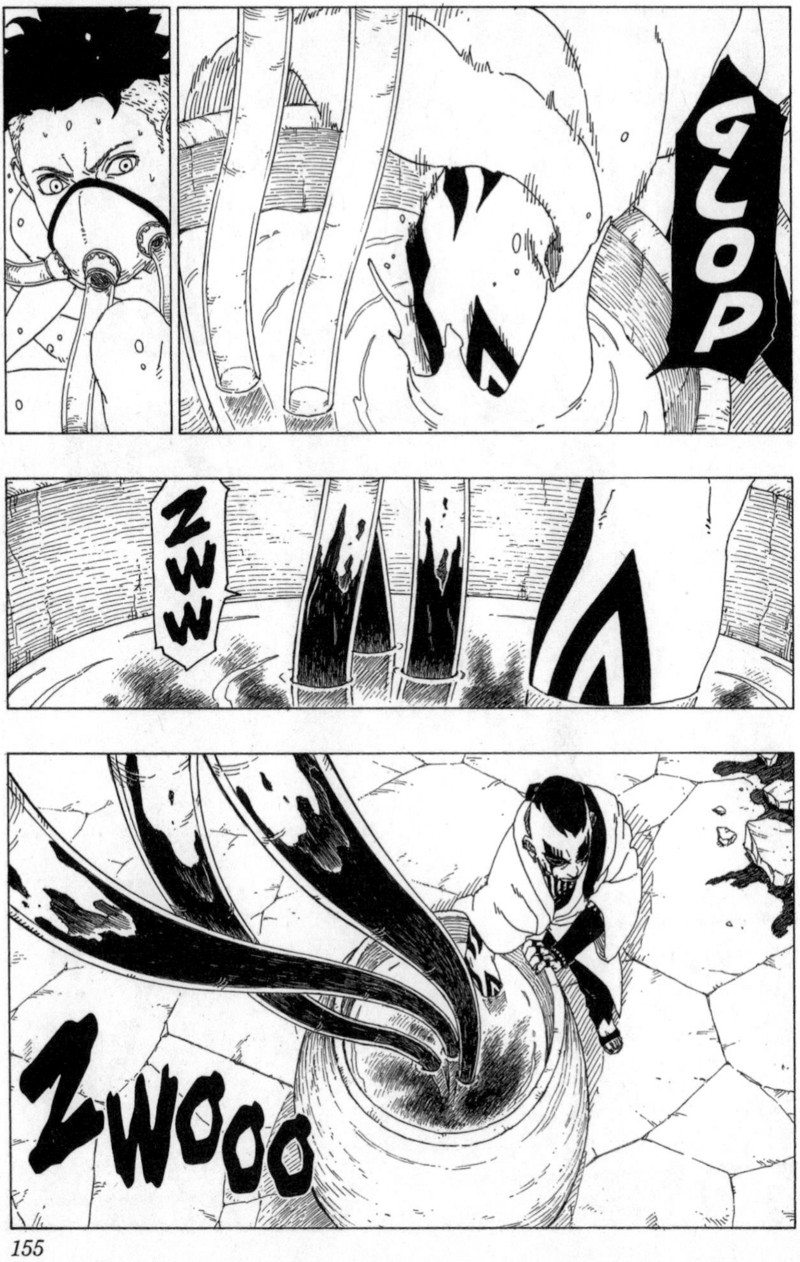
GLOP
ZWW
ZWOOO

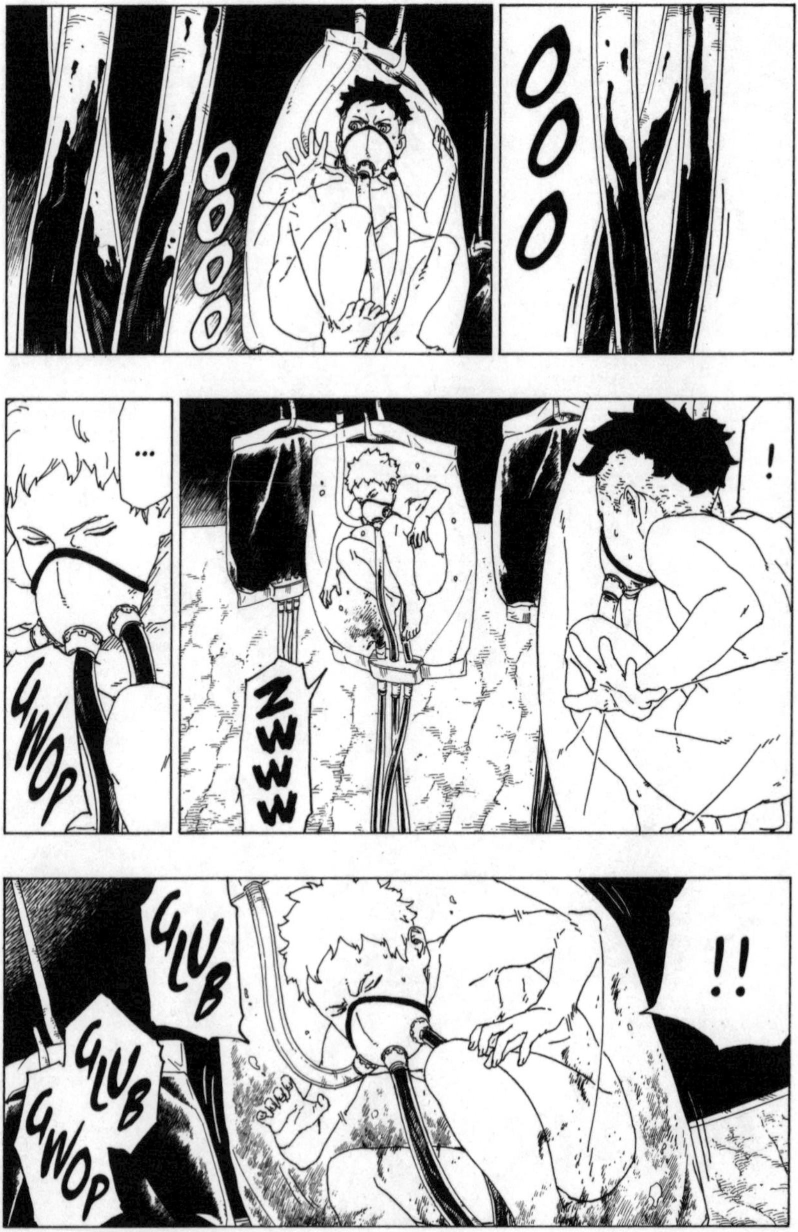
OOO
OOOO
!
ZWWW
...
GWOP
!!
GLUB
GLUB
GWOP

?!
GWOP
GLUB GLUB
NWWW
GWOP
GLUB
NWOOO

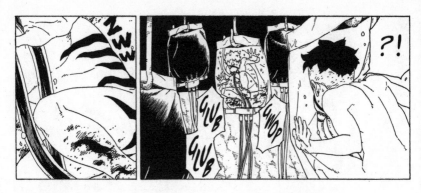

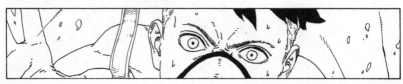

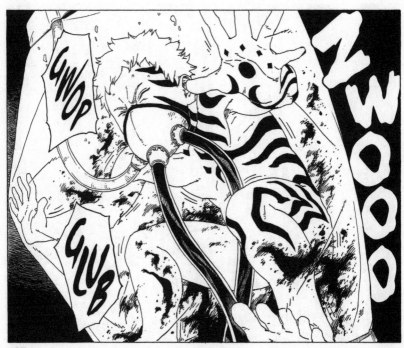

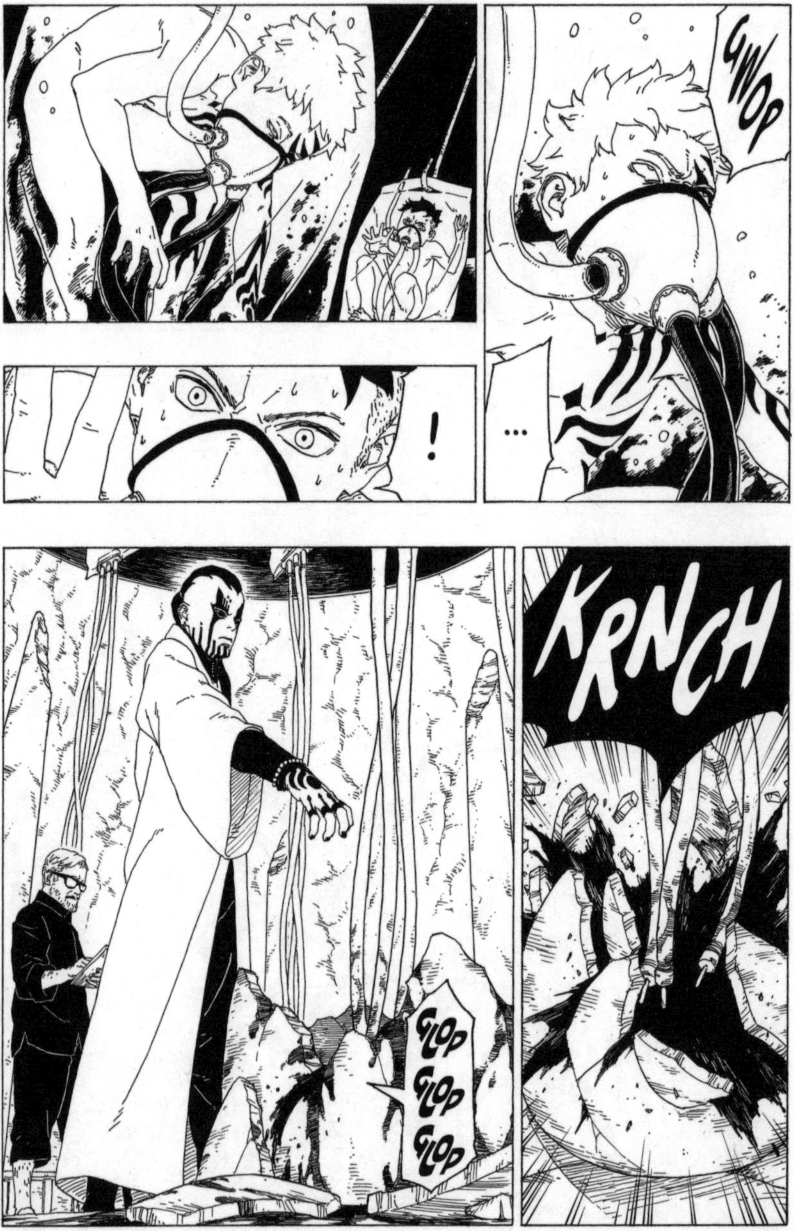
GWOP
...
!
KRNCH
GLOP GLOP GLOP

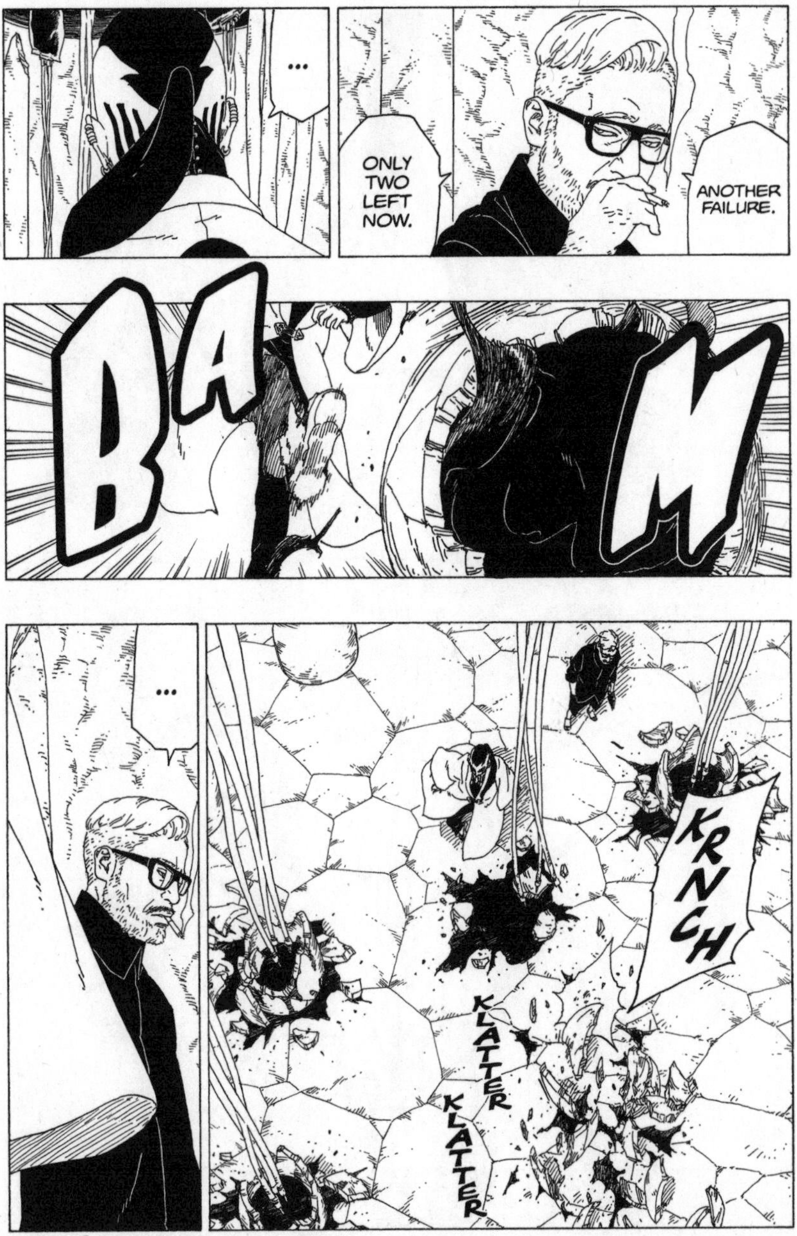
ANOTHER FAILURE.
ONLY TWO LEFT NOW.
...
BAM
KRNCH
KLATTER KLATTER
...

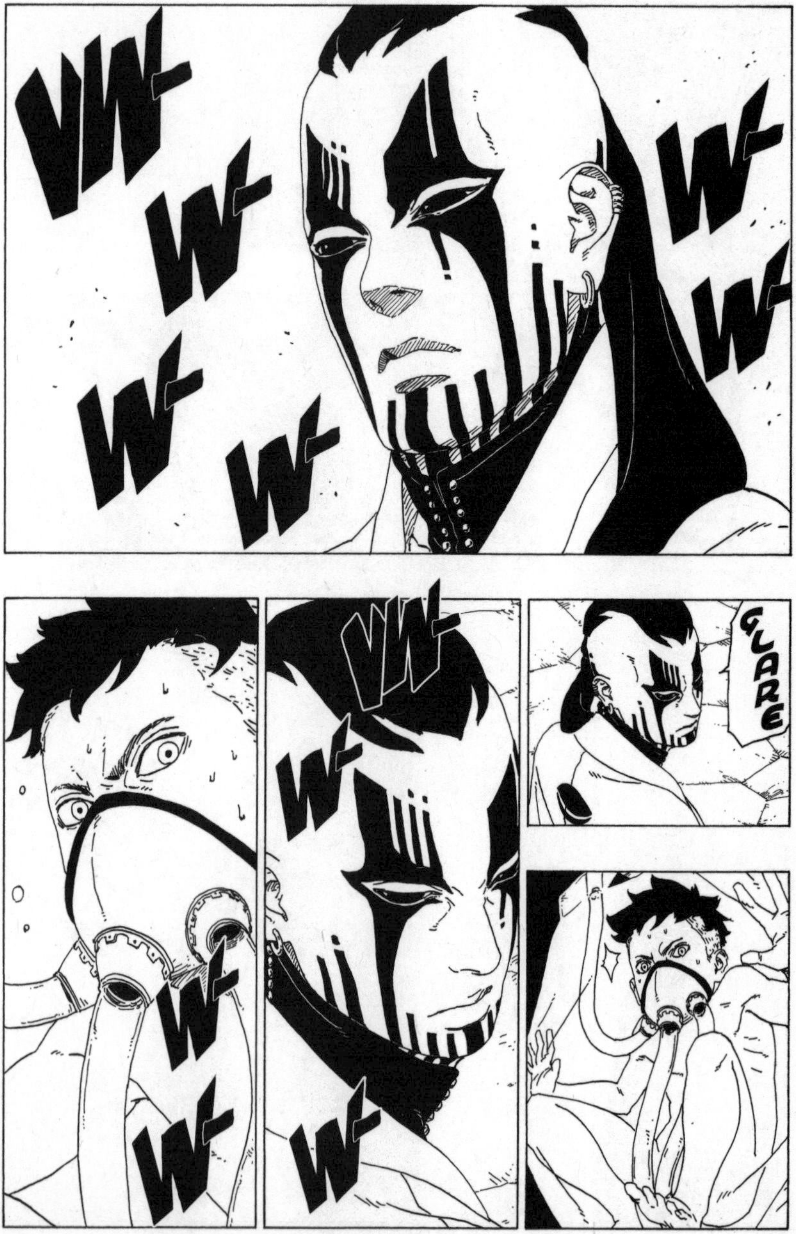
W-
W-
VW-
W-
W-
W-
GLARE
VW-
W-
W-
W-
W-

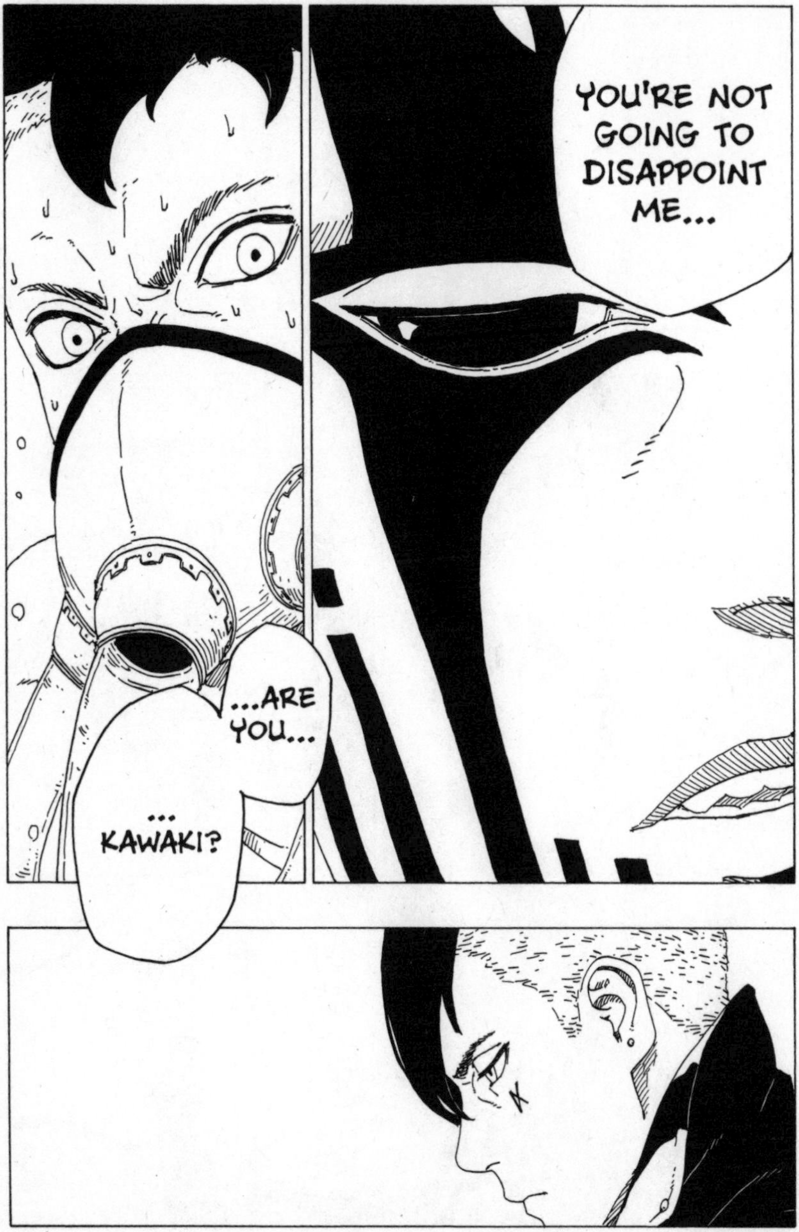
YOU'RE NOT GOING TO DISAPPOINT ME...
...ARE YOU...
...KAWAKI?

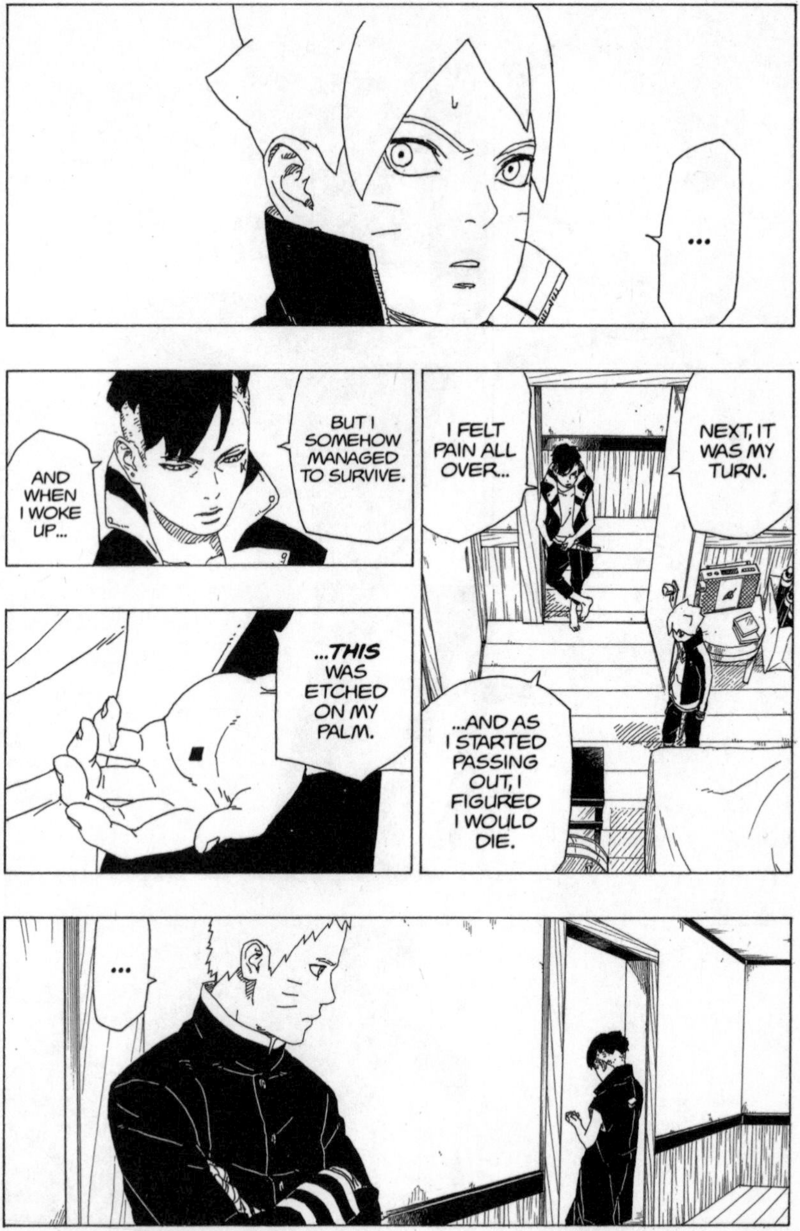
...
NEXT, IT WAS MY TURN.
I FELT PAIN ALL OVER...
...AND AS I STARTED PASSING OUT, I FIGURED I WOULD DIE.
BUT I SOMEHOW MANAGED TO SURVIVE.
AND WHEN I WOKE UP...
...THIS WAS ETCHED ON MY PALM.
...

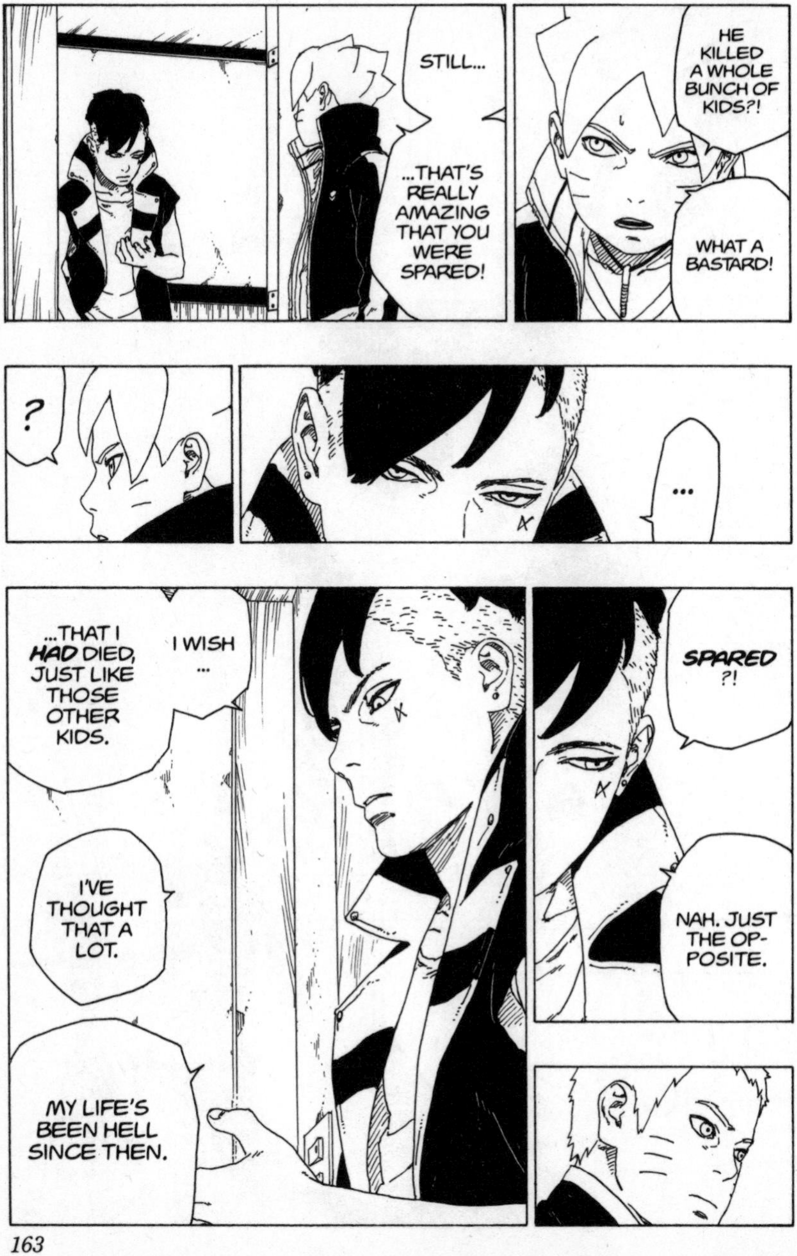
HE KILLED A WHOLE BUNCH OF KIDS?!
WHAT A BASTARD!
STILL...
...THAT'S REALLY AMAZING THAT YOU WERE SPARED!
...
?
SPARED?!
NAH. JUST THE OP-POSITE.
I WISH ...
...THAT I **HAD** DIED, JUST LIKE THOSE OTHER KIDS.
I'VE THOUGHT THAT A LOT.
MY LIFE'S BEEN HELL SINCE THEN.

...

AND THAT HELL...

...IS STILL GOING ON.

KYEE

THROB

!

UNH!

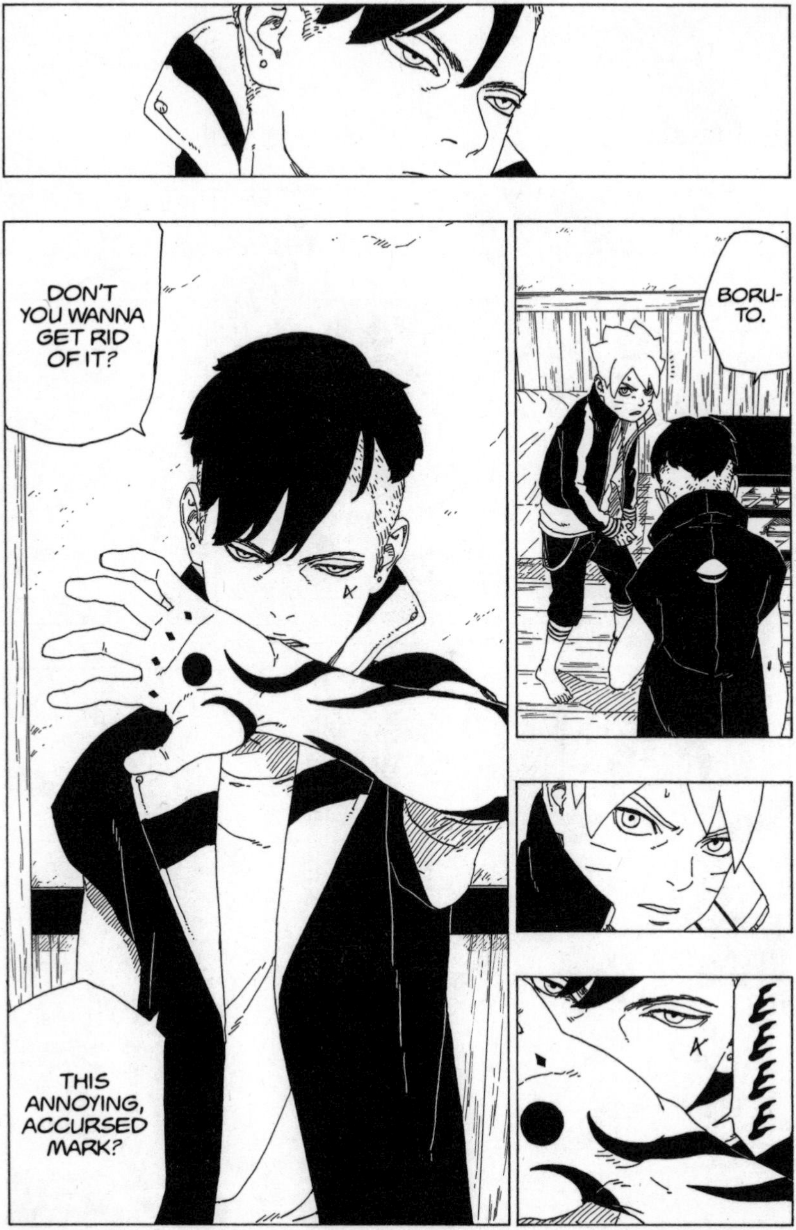
BORU-TO.
EEEEE
DON'T YOU WANNA GET RID OF IT?
THIS ANNOYING, ACCURSED MARK?

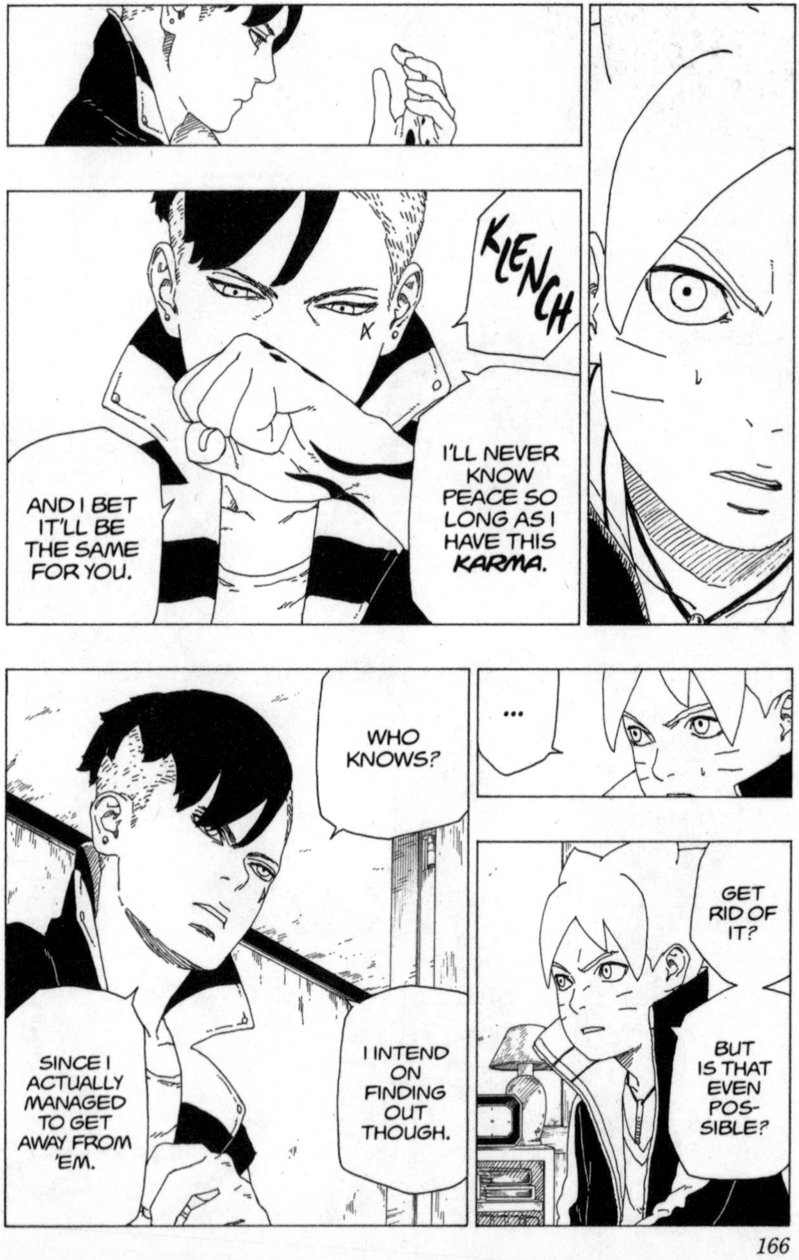
KLENCH
I'LL NEVER KNOW PEACE SO LONG AS I HAVE THIS *KARMA*.
AND I BET IT'LL BE THE SAME FOR YOU.
...
GET RID OF IT?
BUT IS THAT EVEN POS-SIBLE?
WHO KNOWS?
I INTEND ON FINDING OUT THOUGH.
SINCE I ACTUALLY MANAGED TO GET AWAY FROM 'EM.

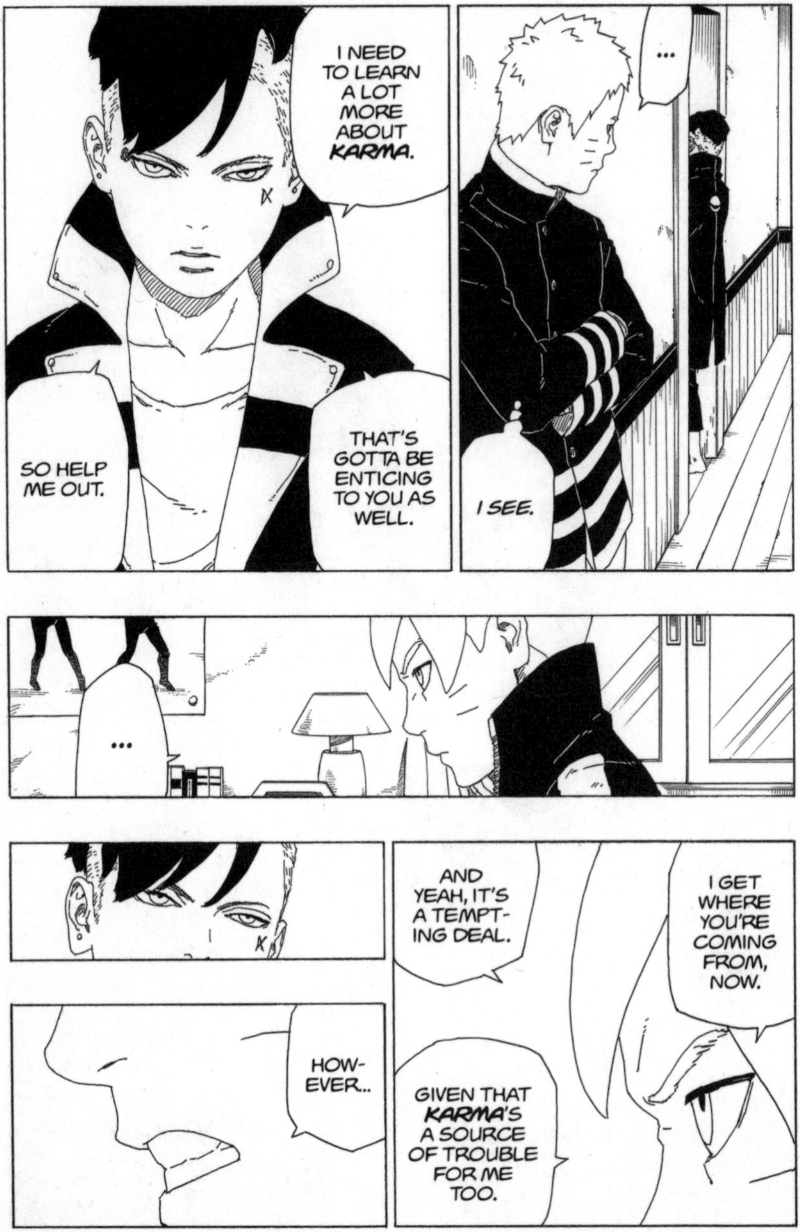
...
I SEE.
I NEED TO LEARN A LOT MORE ABOUT *KARMA*.
THAT'S GOTTA BE ENTICING TO YOU AS WELL.
SO HELP ME OUT.
...
I GET WHERE YOU'RE COMING FROM, NOW.
AND YEAH, IT'S A TEMPT-ING DEAL.
HOW-EVER...
GIVEN THAT *KARMA*'S A SOURCE OF TROUBLE FOR ME TOO.

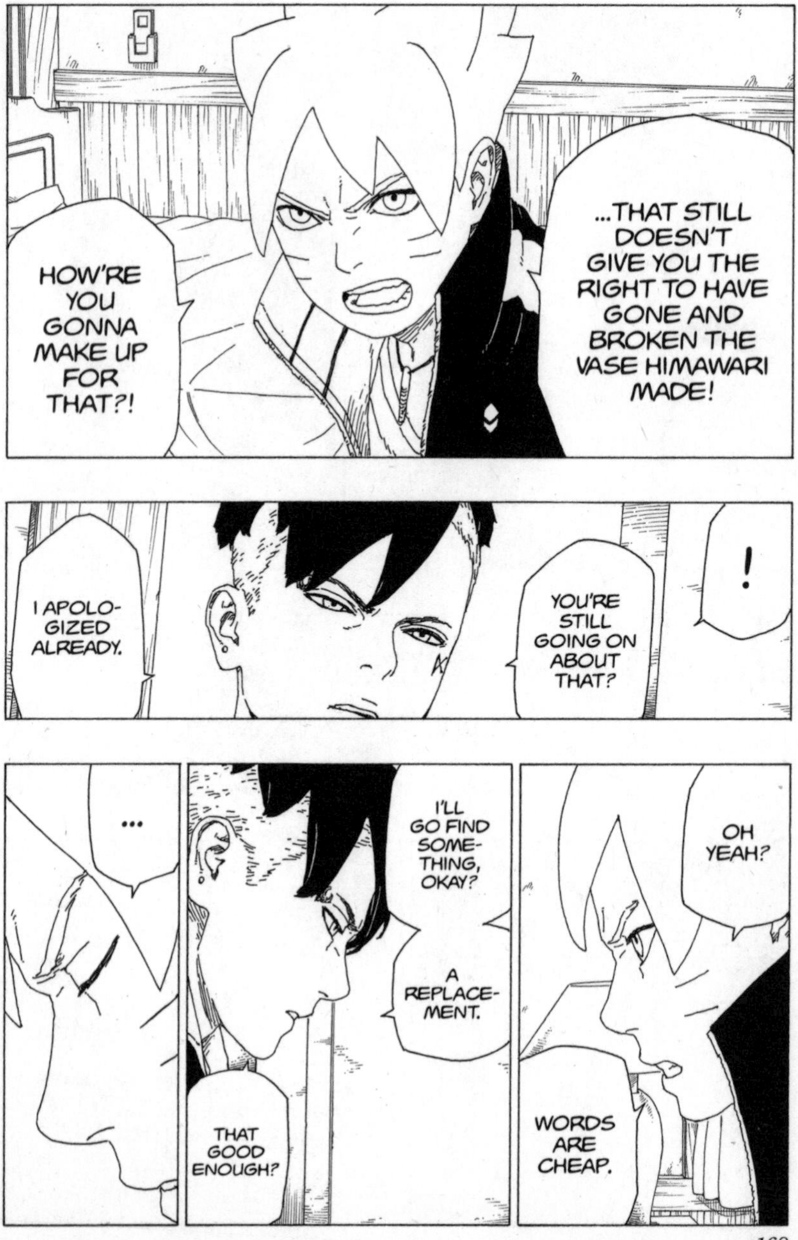
...THAT STILL DOESN'T GIVE YOU THE RIGHT TO HAVE GONE AND BROKEN THE VASE HIMAWARI MADE!
HOW'RE YOU GONNA MAKE UP FOR THAT?!
!
YOU'RE STILL GOING ON ABOUT THAT?
I APOLOGIZED ALREADY.
OH YEAH?
WORDS ARE CHEAP.
I'LL GO FIND SOMETHING, OKAY?
A REPLACEMENT.
THAT GOOD ENOUGH?
...

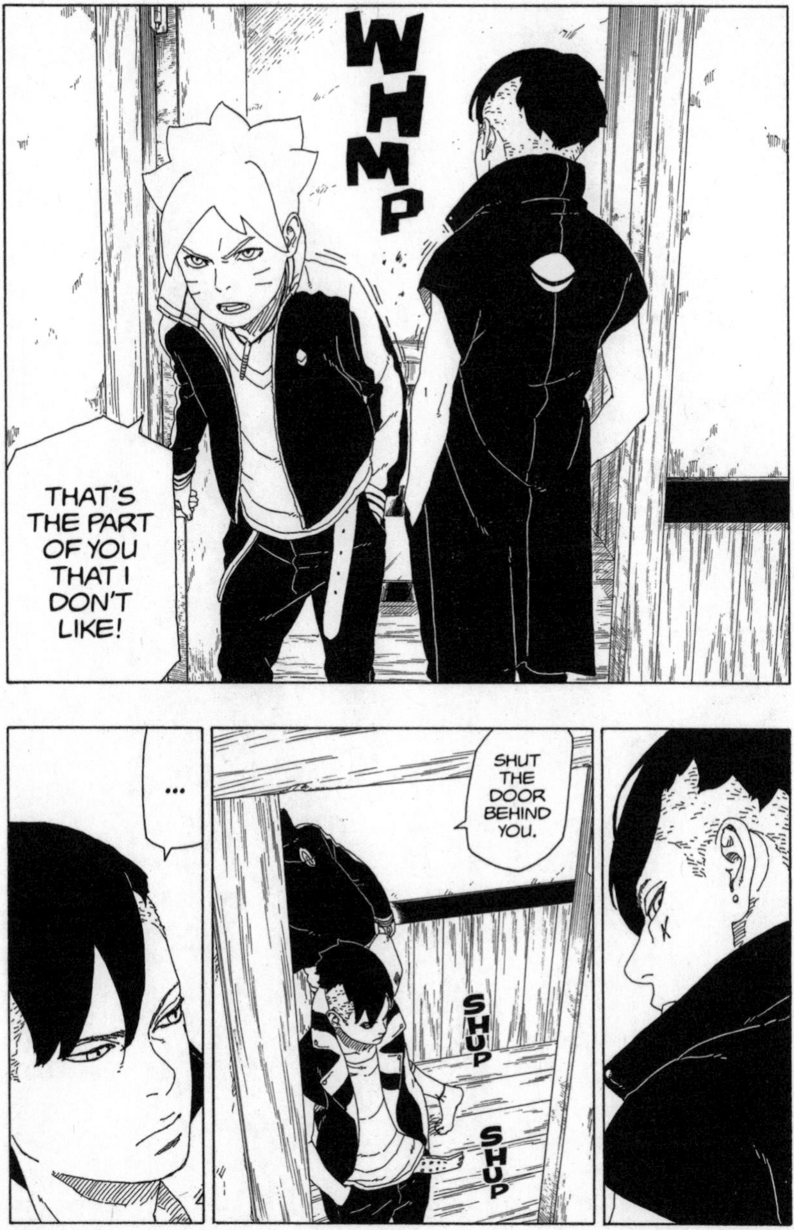
WHMP
THAT'S THE PART OF YOU THAT I DON'T LIKE!
SHUT THE DOOR BEHIND YOU.
SHUP
SHUP
...

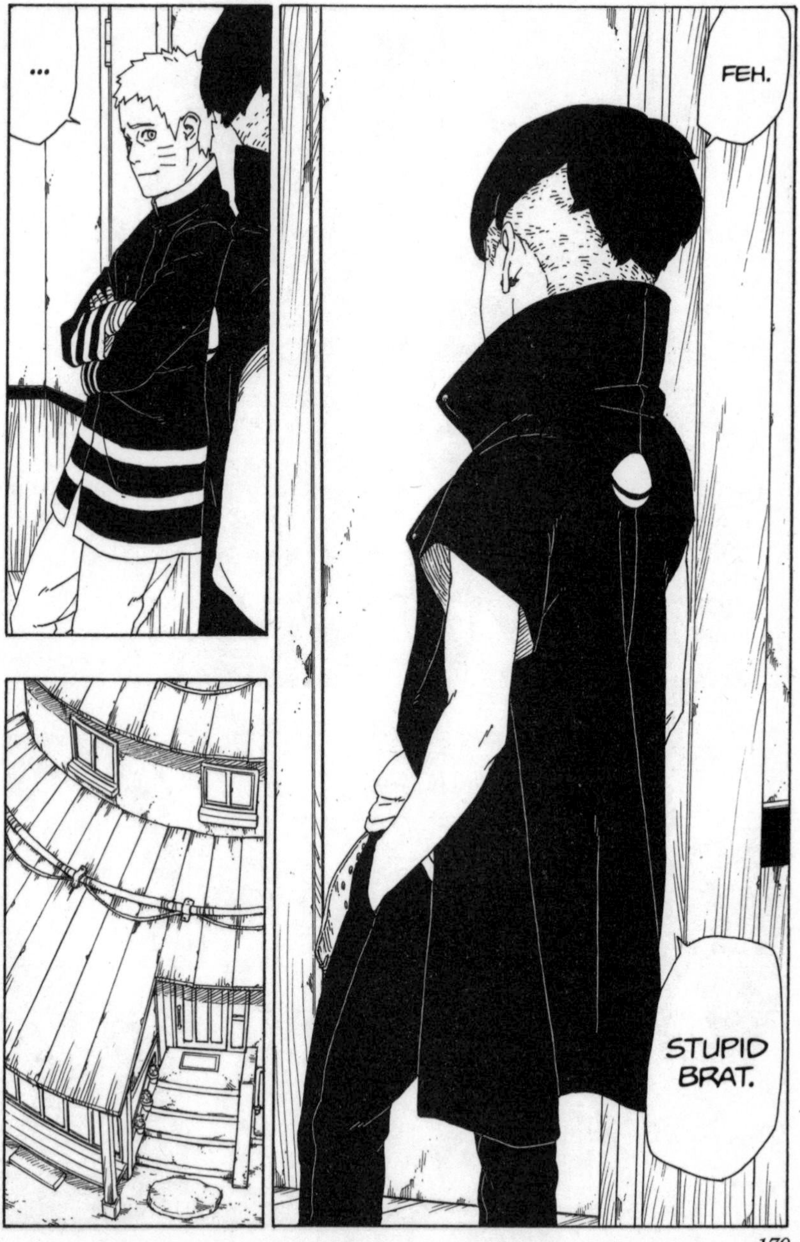
FEH.
STUPID BRAT.
...

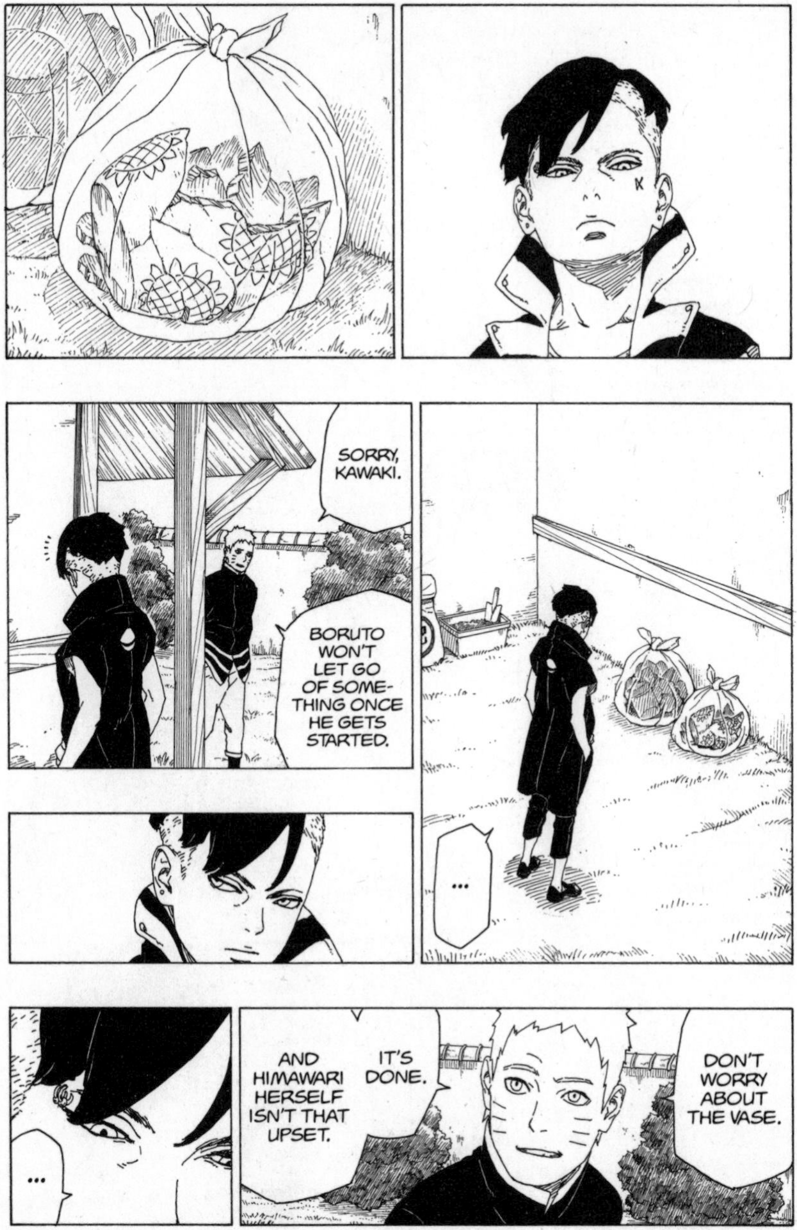
...
SORRY, KAWAKI.
BORUTO WON'T LET GO OF SOME-THING ONCE HE GETS STARTED.
DON'T WORRY ABOUT THE VASE.
IT'S DONE.
AND HIMAWARI HERSELF ISN'T THAT UPSET.
...

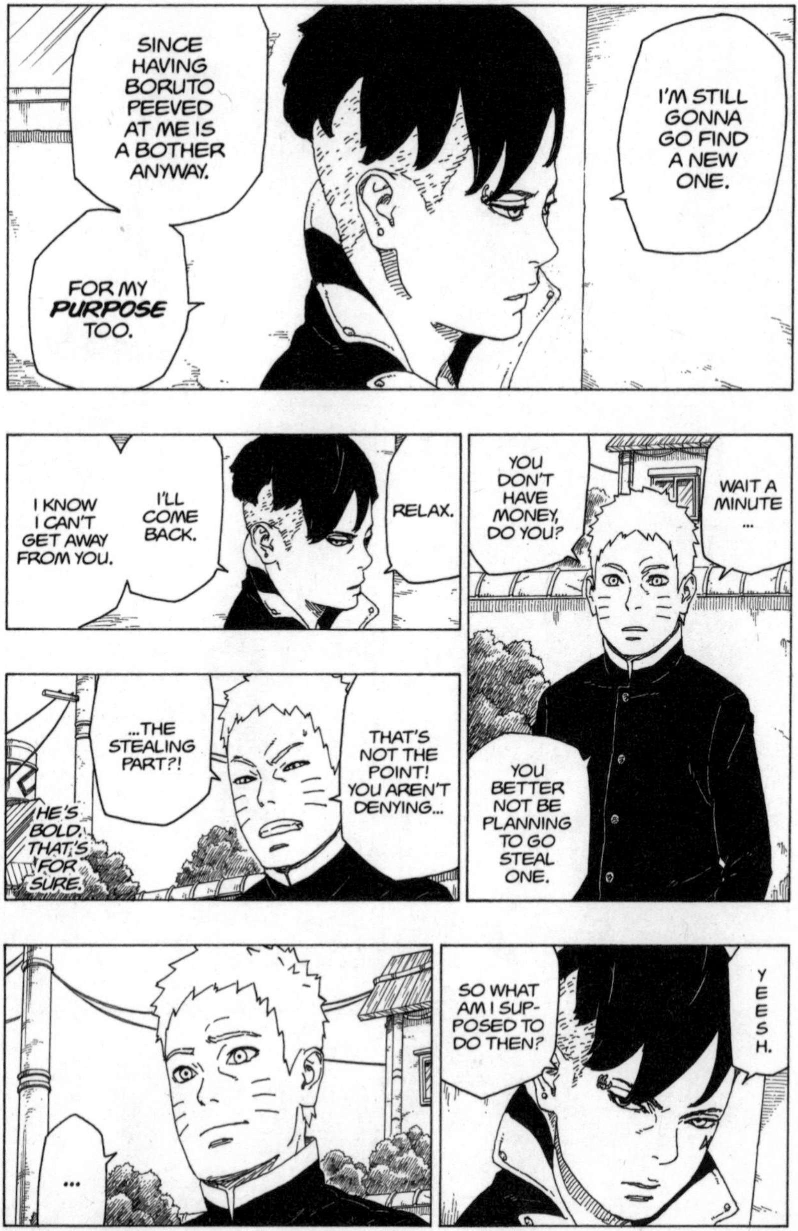
I'M STILL GONNA GO FIND A NEW ONE.
SINCE HAVING BORUTO PEEVED AT ME IS A BOTHER ANYWAY.
FOR MY PURPOSE TOO.
WAIT A MINUTE ...
YOU DON'T HAVE MONEY, DO YOU?
YOU BETTER NOT BE PLANNING TO GO STEAL ONE.
RELAX.
I'LL COME BACK.
I KNOW I CAN'T GET AWAY FROM YOU.
THAT'S NOT THE POINT! YOU AREN'T DENYING...
...THE STEALING PART?!
HE'S BOLD. THAT'S FOR SURE.
YEESH.
SO WHAT AM I SUP-POSED TO DO THEN?
...

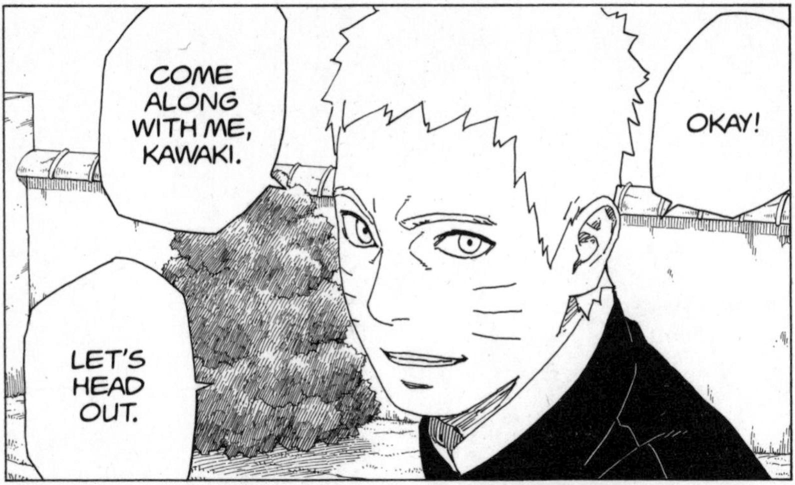
OKAY!
COME ALONG WITH ME, KAWAKI.
LET'S HEAD OUT.
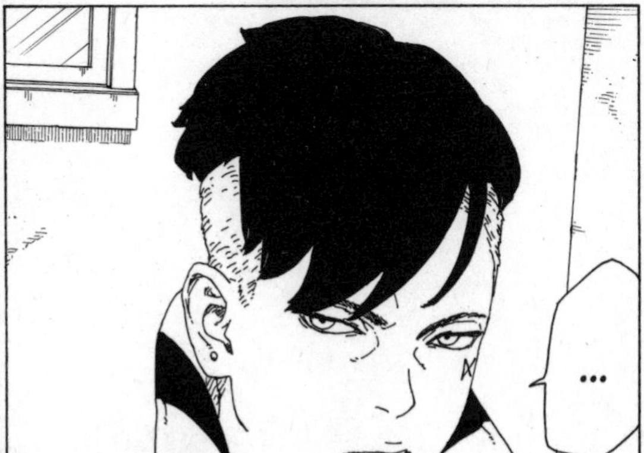
...
HUH?
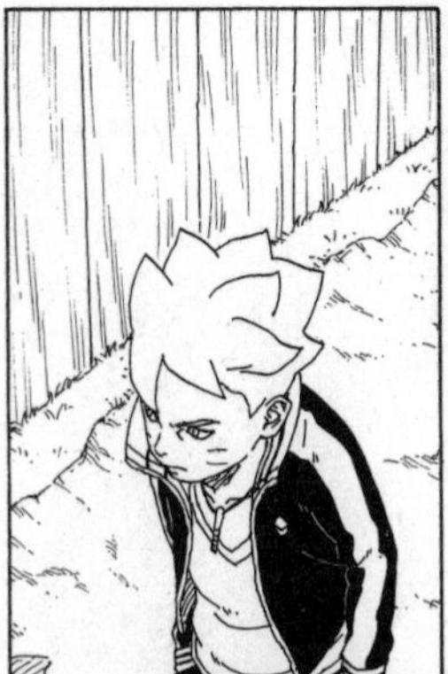

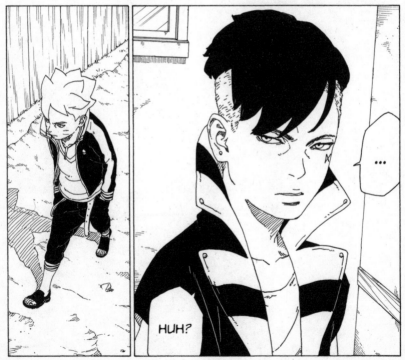

Black ✽ Clover

STORY & ART BY YUKI TABATA

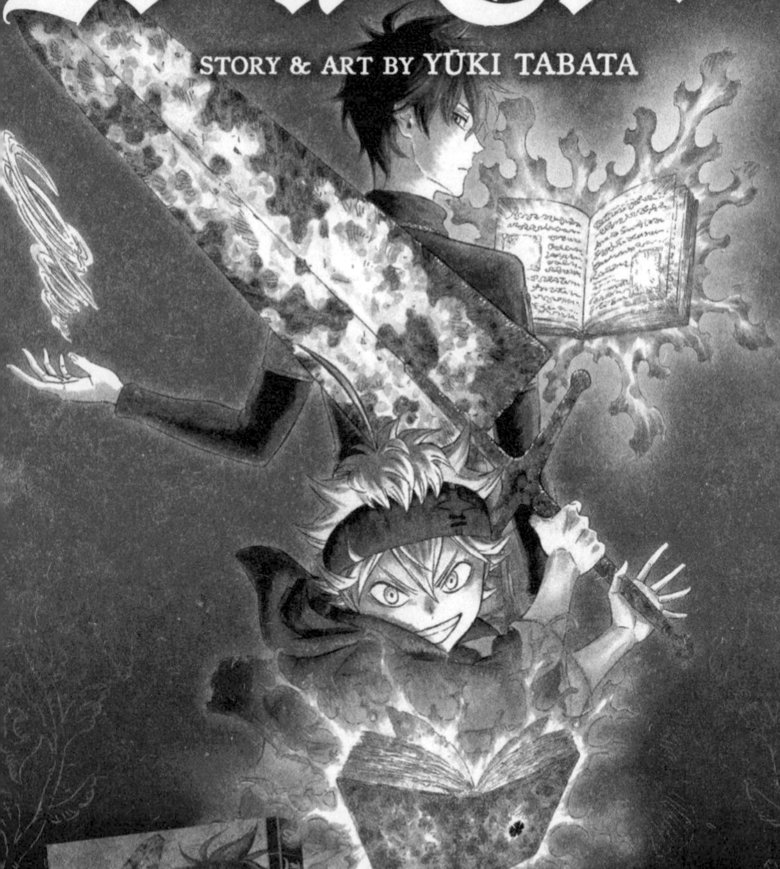

Asta is a young boy who dreams of becoming the greatest mage in the kingdom. Only one problem—he can't use any magic! Luckily for Asta, he receives the incredibly rare five-leaf clover grimoire that gives him the power of anti-magic. Can someone who can't use magic really become the Wizard King? One thing's for sure—Asta will never give up!

SHONEN JUMP

VIZ media
www.viz.com

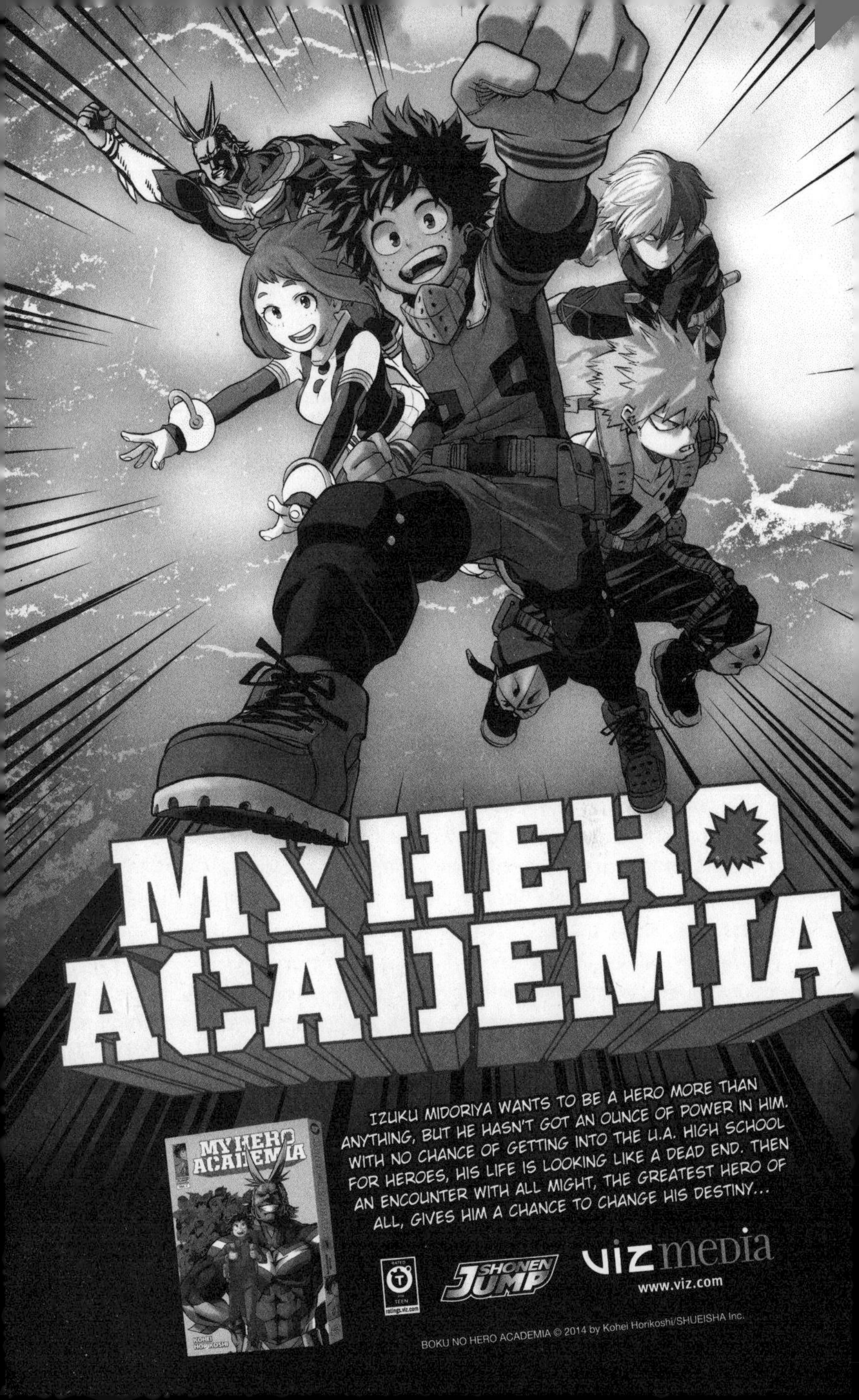
MY HERO ACADEMIA
IZUKU MIDORIYA WANTS TO BE A HERO MORE THAN ANYTHING, BUT HE HASN'T GOT AN OUNCE OF POWER IN HIM. WITH NO CHANCE OF GETTING INTO THE U.A. HIGH SCHOOL FOR HEROES, HIS LIFE IS LOOKING LIKE A DEAD END. THEN AN ENCOUNTER WITH ALL MIGHT, THE GREATEST HERO OF ALL, GIVES HIM A CHANCE TO CHANGE HIS DESTINY...
MY HERO ACADEMIA
KOHEI HORIKOSHI
RATED T TEEN
ratings.viz.com
SHONEN JUMP
VIZ media
www.viz.com
BOKU NO HERO ACADEMIA © 2014 by Kohei Horikoshi/SHUEISHA Inc.

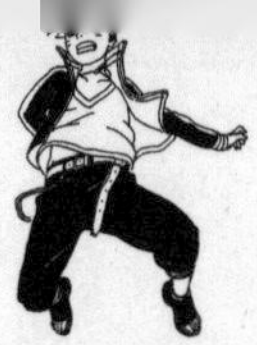

YOU'RE READING
IN THE
WRONG DIRECTION!!

W HOOPS! Guess what? You're starting at the wrong end of the comic!

...It's true! In keeping with the original Japanese format, **Boruto** is meant to be read from right to left, starting in the upper-right corner.

Unlike English, which is read from left to right, Japanese is read from right to left, meaning that action, sound effects and word-balloon order are completely reversed... something which can make readers unfamiliar with Japanese feel pretty backwards themselves. For this reason, manga or Japanese comics published in the U.S. in English have sometimes been published "flopped"—that is, printed in exact reverse order, as though seen from the other side of a mirror.

By flopping pages, U.S. publishers can avoid confusing readers, but the compromise is not without its downside. For one thing, a character in a flopped manga series who once wore in the original Japanese version a T-shirt emblazoned with "M A Y" (as in "the merry month of") now wears one which reads "Y A M"! Additionally, many manga creators in Japan are themselves unhappy with the process, as some feel the mirror-imaging of their art alters their original intentions.

We are proud to bring you **Boruto** in the original unflopped format. Turn to the other side of the book and let the ninjutsu begin...!

—Editor

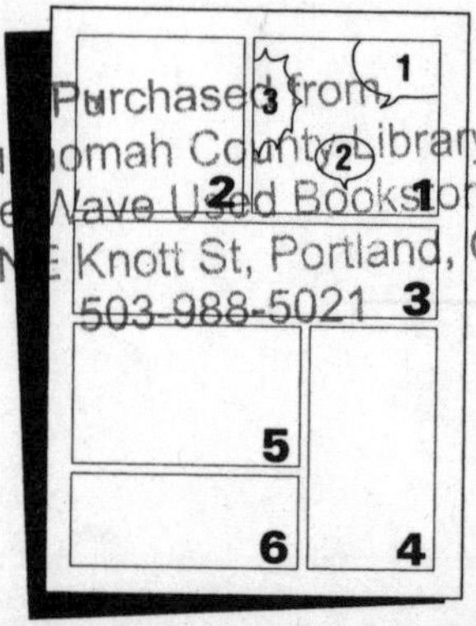
1
3
2
2
1
3
5
6
4